The Riddle of the Pyramids

Kurt Mendelssohn FRS

85 illustrations

15 in color

42 line drawings

THAMES AND HUDSON

First published in paperback in the United States in 1986 by
Thames and Hudson Inc., 500 Fifth Avenue,
New York, New York 10110

Library of Congress Catalog Card Number 27388 X

Printed and bound in the German Democratic Republic

Contents

Preface

By a curious and unforeseen twist of events, this book can be regarded as the payment of a debt of long standing. When, in the early thirties, I came to England as a refugee, I was given the facilities to continue my research work in low temperature physics. However, there were at that time no academic positions available and I had to live on grants. One of these was provided by the late Sir Robert Mond, FRS, who generously provided me with money which had been earmarked for excavations in Egypt. Sir Robert was a noted chemist whose interest in later years turned to Egyptology, a subject which has much benefited by his scholarly research and his munificence. This book is dedicated to his memory in gratitude.

Dr I. E. S. Edwards, CMG, of the British Museum, the late Professor Walter Emery and Mr Dows Dunham of the Boston Museum of Fine Arts have kindly given me much advice and many hours of their time. The staff of the Griffith Institute, and, in particular, Dr J. Malék, have been immensely helpful in guiding me through the maze of Egyptological literature. In addition, I am indebted to Professors M. D. Coe and R. F. Heizer for comments on Mexican archaeology. Last, but not least, I like to record my thanks to Mr Peter Clayton, FSA, for many clarifying discussions and for his unfailing help in the preparation of this book and in the choice of illustrations.

Cyril Band, R. Bowl and Miss J. Burrage of the Clarendon Laboratory Photographic Department have gone to great trouble in turning my colour slides into halftone illustrations, and Mr N. Ionides has kindly transformed my rough sketches into professional line diagrams.

K.M.

Introduction

This is a book about a scientific discovery. Having spent my life as a professional scientist, I have written it up just as I would have recorded any other discovery. The training of a scientist sets limitations by which the average story writer is usually not bound. Above all, the scientist has to guard against the ever present danger of approaching his subjects with preconceived theories which he then sets out to prove as being correct. Fortunately, this danger did not exist in the present case, simply because I had no theories on the subject at all. Not having any theories was not too difficult either since I did not even know the subject well enough at that time.

As so often happens in scientific enquiry it all began with a chance observation which, while interesting and stimulating in itself, did not appear to be of more than limited importance. Although I was fully aware of the great riddle presented by the pyramids, namely the question why this immense effort had been made 5000 years ago, I was not at that stage aware that my chance observation might provide the key to it; neither did it enter my mind that I might possibly contribute to its solution. However, a scientific discovery is usually not, as so many people imagine, a sudden flash of intuition by which the whole truth is revealed in one glorious instant. In ninety-nine out of a hundred cases it is a slow, and often laborious, process – very much like a detective story in which the clues have to be patiently assembled, and many false leads have to be eliminated.

Just as is the case with a detective story, the process by which the scientist obtains his final result is as intriguing to him as the result itself. Certainly, the result must remain the ultimate aim but much of the satisfaction with the achievement is vested in the way that led to it. It is for this reason that in my account of the pyramid problem I have essentially adhered to the chronological order of the various stages which ultimately led to the solution. It was a task which to me, as a scientist, was superbly exciting, and it is the joy of this excitement, more than anything else, which I should like the reader to share with me.

There is another reason for recording the events in their chronological sequence. However sure the scientist may feel that he has not slipped up somewhere in his arguments and conclusions, nobody would be so conceited as to believe that his deductions are infallible. It is therefore essential that he should present a full account of his work so that it can be checked at every stage.

The thesis put forward in this book is an extremely simple one. The pyramids of Egypt are immensely large, immensely ancient and, by general consensus, extremely useless. These fantastic man-made mountains, containing altogether more than 25 million tons of quarried limestone, and with very little space inside them, were heaped up in little more than a century. Nevertheless, however useless they appear to us, they must have been considered as extremely useful by the ancient Egyptians since they expended an almost unbelievable amount of labour in constructing them. In the course of history attempts have been made to explain the function of the pyramids as astronomical observatories, as granaries, as refuges from the Flood, as repositories of divinely inspired prophecies, or even as the work of visitors from another planet.

Archaeological evidence, however, leaves no doubt that the pyramids served as funerary monuments for the early pharaohs. Whether they were the actual burial places, as most people believe, or whether they are merely cenotaphs, will be discussed later. It is, in any case, a matter of only secondary importance to our own considerations. The fact remains that all archaeological and literary finds attest to the existence of funeral rites and of a large body of mortuary priests in connection with the pyramids. On the basis of this inescapable conclusion it had to be assumed that this early civilization had mobilized all its resources and directed its entire labour force to produce nothing better than a gigantic royal tomb. This assumption is made even more difficult by the fact that the era of large pyramids was relatively short and that, for centuries before and after, pharaohs were buried less ostentatiously, and certainly much more cheaply.

It is our thesis that the generally accepted conclusion that the large pyramids are nothing more than royal tombs may be based on a subtle logical error. While it is readily admitted that the pyramids served as royal mausolea, it does not necessarily mean that this was the only purpose of their construction. In fact, it probably was not even the main purpose. The discovery of this main purpose is the story told in this book.

No discovery ever stands on its own; it is always based on an existing body of accumulated knowledge into which it has to fit and to which it has to make an original contribution. In our case the body of existing knowledge is the field of Egyptology. For over a century professional

Egyptologists have excavated the tombs and temples of Egypt, deciphered and translated the inscriptions on the walls and in the papyri, correlated archaeological and scriptural evidence, and in this way built up a remarkably consistent picture of a civilization that died thousands of years ago. Their painstaking research and their conclusions by now fill about 20,000 volumes of books and bound periodicals. Thanks to this massive treasure house of information I have been able to study the background to my own work on the pyramids. Without this immense volume of fact, collected by Egyptologists, my own observations would have neither purpose nor meaning.

When setting out on this work I was delighted to discover that, with one somewhat bizarre exception, Egyptologists did not resent the intrusion of a stranger in their midst. Quite on the contrary, they were invariably most helpful, patiently explaining to me the relevant features of their work and guiding me through the maze of Egyptological publications. Their attitude, that of true and devoted scholars, has been to welcome and listen to the scientist in the hope that he may make some contribution to their own field. Without their appreciation of my efforts and their enthusiastic encouragement of my work, the present book would never have been written. I am grateful to them, not only for their help but for having so generously opened to me a beautiful and exciting field of study.

Clearly it is impossible to write sensibly about the pyramids or venture to make a contribution to the subject without reference to the basic work of Egyptologists. The first three chapters are therefore largely devoted to a description of the setting in which the problem had to be approached and ultimately solved – I hope correctly. Since we are exclusively concerned with the first few centuries of Egyptian history this period is the only one to which space could be devoted. Even so, this era could not be treated in depth, and we have had to restrict ourselves to those aspects which have a direct bearing on the history of the pharaonic sepulchres. Most of the facts used in these historical chapters have been extracted from the Egyptological literature, except for some of the conclusions and speculations, as well as for the references to contemporary African customs, which are my personal responsibility.

When dealing with the pyramids of Egypt it is inevitable that one's thoughts should turn also to those other large pyramids which were built in Central America. Curiously enough, the pattern of pyramid development in Mexico closely parallels that in Egypt. Here again we find a relatively short, and early, period in which giant pyramids were erected, preceded and followed by rather more modest structures. Our conclusion will tend towards similar reasons for building these immense pyramids as those which obtained in Egypt. The only differences are, firstly, that the overt purpose of the pyramid in Egypt was a tomb while in Mexico it was a human sacrifice, and secondly that the two pyramid eras are separated by two and a half thousand years. I fortunately had several occasions to study the pyramids in the Valley of Mexico and in Yucatan even before seeing an Egyptian pyramid. A chapter on the pyramids in Central America and on their relation to our general thesis has therefore been appended.

Like so many detective stories the present one starts with an exotic holiday. After having spent part of the winter 1964/65 at the University of Kumasi in Ghana, my wife and I felt that a little holiday in Cairo might ease the transition from the steaming jungle of West Africa to an English winter. We had travelled through Egypt several years earlier and, of all the treasures to be seen and sites to be visited, the pyramids had exerted on me a peculiar fascination. It was neither their size nor their great age which intrigued me but the combination of the two. Here, almost at the dawn of our civilization, men had erected a set of monuments so gigantic that nothing even faintly approaching their grandeur has ever been attempted again in our cultural orbit. I suddenly realized that here, on the desert plateau above the Nile, man had indulged in his first large-scale technological venture. Since there was no prototype effort, the organization of work must have been superb to be able to achieve this astonishing success. What was behind it all and how had the whole project been designed? I felt that I wanted to go back to Egypt and have a closer look at the pyramids.

The return trip from Africa presented as good an opportunity as any, and before I left England the Professor of Egyptology at Oxford, Jaroslav Černý, kindly gave me an introduction to the Head of the Antiquities Service in Cairo. The latter received me kindly and issued me with an impressive looking document in Arabic which I could not read and which, as I understood, counselled the custodians of ancient monuments to provide me with all the help that I might require. The custodians of the more remote pyramids usually turned out to be a couple of Bedouins with official armbands and two rifles between them.

In order to overcome the language difficulty we hired from an agency a guide, supposedly well-acquainted with the monuments in question. His name was Ali, and the qualifications set out on his visiting card might have made him eligible as Assistant Keeper of the Cairo Museum. His job was to find a reliable driver with a reliable car, but we were somewhat taken aback when Ali appeared dressed for the expedition in a black suit, white collar and pinstriped tie. He competently guided us to the Dahshur pyramids but was aghast when he realized that we were set on climbing into these edifices. He had already fallen foul of the Bedouins by brandishing our document and stressing his own importance in the enterprise. He now ordered them to take us into the pyramids. However, the Bedouins had their revenge by pointing out to Ali that he, being in charge of his important foreigners, would have to accompany them wherever it was their crazy wish to go. They kindly indicated to him a perilous looking wooden ladder leading 12 m. up into the entrance of the Bent Pyramid. Ali was fat, hot in his dark suit, and evidently subject to vertigo, but go he must! It was worse inside the pyramid, hotter and also dark, except for the light of our electric torch. Moreover, there was another, not too substantial ladder, again 12 m. high, leading to the upper chamber on which Ali got stuck, and I had to push him in order to get up myself. On the return, the Bedouins lit the way down for my wife, but when I pointed to Ali, who had remained on the top shivering with fatigue, vertigo and, probably, superstition, the Bedouins just shrugged their shoulders and went on. Finally, I succeeded in easing him down but, by mutual consent, this was the first and last trip on which we had Ali's company.

Plates 27, 28

One of my main objects was to visit the pyramid at Meidum, the only one of the great pyramids which I had not seen on my first trip. It stands rather isolated from the rest of the other great pyramids, over 50 kilometers south of Saqqara. Its impressive size is curiously enhanced by its heavily ruined state. The square shaped core rises steeply like a tower of 40 m. at an angle of over 70° out of the surrounding rubble. Flinders Petrie and Borchardt have explained the ruin as due to the action of stone robbers. In one of his publications, Petrie mentions that fellahin came with donkeys to cart away limestone. This is a question to which we shall have to return later when we discuss the true nature of the pyramid's ruined state.

Plates III, IV

My own reaction was that something, somewhere, was wrong, but I had no idea what it was. Stones have been taken from all pyramids, particularly from those near Cairo where cheap but durable building material was needed. Even so, none of the Giza pyramids have lost their basic shape while here, in the loneliness of Meidum, with no great city ever in its neighbourhood, a large pyramid had suffered incomparably worse. Something did not fit, but having no clue where the inconsistency lay, I resorted to the scientist's time-honoured method in such cases: taking data. It consisted in using my camera quite indiscriminately, recording everything I could think of in the hope that some of the shots might turn out useful – sometime in the future. There was no clear idea of when and what this future use might be. After all, I was on a holiday and knew that when I returned home I should have to deal with a host of problems, none of them having anything whatever to do with pyramids and their problems.

Then, in October 1966, a disaster occurred in the small Welsh mining village of Aberfan which shocked the world. After heavy rain a large mine-tip had started to slip, burying in the space of a few minutes a school with 116 children. I suddenly realized what it was that I had been missing out at Meidum. The time had now come to get my photographic record out of storage, and to have a very close look at it.

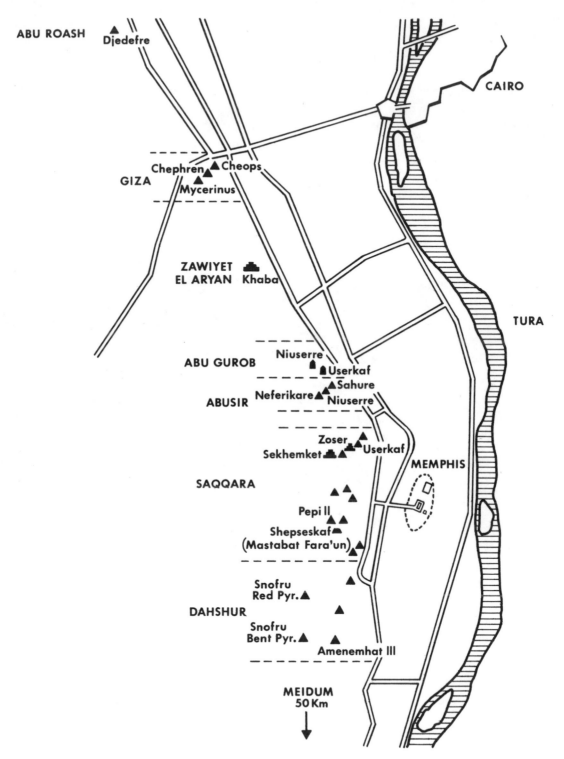

ABU ROASH
▲ Djedefre

CAIRO

GIZA
Chephren ▲ ▲ Cheops
▲
Mycerinus

ZAWIYET
EL ARYAN ▆ Khaba

TURA

ABU GUROB Niuserre
▲
▆ Userkaf
▲ Sahure
Neferikare ▲ ▲ Niuserre
ABUSIR

Zoser ▆ ▲
Sekhemket ▆ ▲ ▲ Userkaf

MEMPHIS
SAQQARA
▲ ▲
▲
Pepi II ▲ ▲
Shepseskaf ▄ ▲
(Mastabat Fara'un)

▲
Snofru
Red Pyr. ▲
DAHSHUR   ▲
Snofru
Bent Pyr. ▲ ▲
Amenemhat III

MEIDUM
50 Km
↓

Map of the pyramids. Those named are mentioned in the text.

14

1 Prelude to the Pyramids

The land of Egypt is the child of the Nile. More than 4000 miles above its mouth the White Nile rises in the swamps and lakes of equatorial Africa. After having covered half its course, it is joined by the Blue Nile in the Sudan and after another 200 miles the big stream receives its last tributary, the Atbara. In large bends the Nile then forces its way over five cataracts, the most northerly of which is at Assuan, the ancient Syene. From here onwards Egypt begins and the Nile valley becomes a narrow emerald band of vegetation through the surrounding desert until, more than 800 miles downstream, the waters fan out into the Delta.

Ten or twenty thousand years ago the increasing aridity of the Sahara forced the nomadic hunters into the Nile valley and the Delta where they developed agriculture and husbandry. The crops were wheat and barley and they tamed the sheep and a long-horned breed of cattle. The early inhabitants were segregated into tribes, each with its local god, often represented by a totem animal, such as the lion, the crocodile, the baboon, the ibis and many others. Later on, all these gods became the emblems of Egypt's provinces, or *nomes*, as they were called. In historic times there were forty-two nomes, twenty in the valley and twenty-two in the Delta. As time went on, some of the tribes formed groups and about six thousand years ago they had coalesced into two kingdoms, that of the valley, Upper Egypt, and that of the Delta, Lower Egypt. The physical and economic differences between the two kingdoms were responsible for a division which remained significant throughout the three millennia of Egyptian history. The king of Upper Egypt wore a white crown to which was affixed the head of its totem animal, the vulture. The crown of Lower Egypt was red and carried the head of the cobra. When finally the two kingdoms were united the crowns were combined, with the vulture and cobra heads side by side. Down to the final eclipse of Egyptian power, this unification was remembered on the monuments of the kings where the gods of the two kingdoms, Seth and Horus, were shown binding together the lily of Upper Egypt and the papyrus of the Delta in heraldic pose.

Fig. 1

Fig. 2

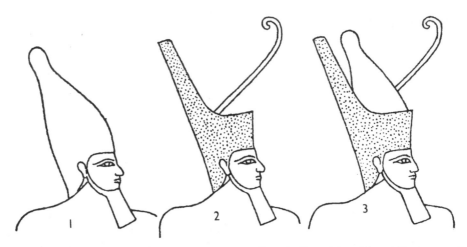

1 The white crown of Upper Egypt (1), the red crown of Lower Egypt (2) and the combined crown of the unified kingdom (3)

The oldest source for our knowledge of Egyptian history is a list of pharaohs, drawn up in chronological order, by Manetho in the third century BC. Manetho was probably a priest at the ancient sanctuary of Heliopolis and he compiled his list in Greek at the request of Ptolemy I. No manuscript of Manetho's original work has survived and we have to depend on later transcripts made in the early Christian era by Josephus, Africanus and Eusebius. After Champollion had deciphered the hieroglyphs, additional historical sources became available from inscriptions on temple walls and from papyri. These earlier sources are particularly valuable since they give the kings' names in hieroglyphic and not in the grecianized form used by Manetho. Finally, we have parts of an early stela, called the 'Palermo Stone' because the largest fragment known is kept in the museum at that city. The list on the Palermo Stone predates Manetho by over two thousand years and it was compiled when the events of the Pyramid Age were still fresh in the minds of the priests. One of the curious difficulties met by Egyptologists is the fact that every pharaoh had no fewer than five names, each of which had to be used for a particular purpose and the choice of which we do not fully comprehend. Thus it has happened again and again that events ascribed to persons of different names in fact referred to the same king.

Even greater were the difficulties encountered when trying to ascribe actual dates to the various reigns and dynasties. In early times the Egyptian empire developed essentially in isolation, not providing the historian with any contacts with other civilizations from which comparative dates could have been derived. Only a few decades ago the opinion of individual Egyptologists concerning one of the early kings

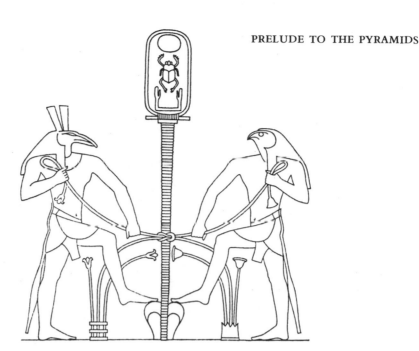

2 The gods Seth (left) and Horus (right) binding together the lily of Upper Egypt and the papyrus of Lower Egypt

often varied by several centuries. However, due to such methods as radioactive carbon-dating and, above all, by painstaking correlation of all the available data, a remarkably reliable table of 3000 years of Egyptian history has now been established.

Manetho begins his list of kings with the unification of Upper and Lower Egypt under a pharaoh whom he calls Menes, and this event is generally taken as the beginning of Egyptian history, now dated as about 3200 BC. There follows a series of no fewer than thirty dynasties, most of which seem to correspond reasonably well with the groups of pharaohs recorded by other sources. It has become customary to sub-divide this enormous list, spanning three thousand years, into a number of historical periods which are given in Table I.

The two intermediate periods, between the Old and the Middle Kingdom and between the Middle Kingdom and the New Kingdom respectively represent breaks in the even course of Egyptian history. The second break was caused by the incursion of foreign elements, the Hyksos or shepherd kings about whom we know, however, relatively little. It appears that no such invasion took place during the First Intermediate Period which terminated the Old Kingdom. Instead, it seems that after more than five centuries of strong central rule the country relapsed into regionalism, leading to upheaval and evidently civil war. The general insecurity and lawlessness of this period destroyed much vital evidence from the Old Kingdom and particularly from the pyramids which were all pillaged during this time.

Table I *Outline of Egyptian chronology*

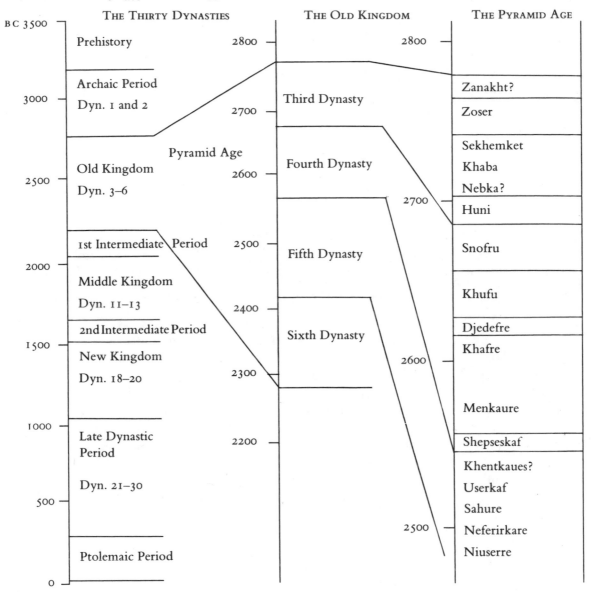

THE THIRTY DYNASTIES	THE OLD KINGDOM	THE PYRAMID AGE
BC 3500 Prehistory	2800	2800
Archaic Period Dyn. 1 and 2	Third Dynasty	Zanakht?
3000	2700	Zoser
Pyramid Age	Fourth Dynasty	Sekhemket / Khaba / Nebka?
Old Kingdom Dyn. 3–6	2600	2700 Huni
2500	Fifth Dynasty	Snofru
1st Intermediate Period	2500	Khufu
2000 Middle Kingdom Dyn. 11–13	2400	Djedefre
2nd Intermediate Period	Sixth Dynasty	Khafre
1500 New Kingdom Dyn. 18–20	2300	2600
		Menkaure
1000 Late Dynastic Period	2200	Shepseskaf
Dyn. 21–30		Khentkaues? / Userkaf / Sahure
500		2500 Neferirkare
Ptolemaic Period		Niuserre
0		

The table shows that pyramid building was a very early feature of
Egyptian history and that the 'Pyramid Age' proper did not last very long.
In fact, the five largest pyramids were all built in the space of only one
century. It is true that pyramids continued to be built for another thousand
years but they became much smaller and soon also much shoddier. Mud
Plate 44   brick was substituted for limestone and shapeless grey mounds of
crumbled brick are all that is left of them today. On the other hand, the
early impressive stone structures of the true Pyramid Age have, with one

18

exception, survived in essentially the same form in which they were erected 5000 years ago. The exception, the ruined pyramid of Meidum, will furnish the basis of our considerations.

Before we turn to the Pyramid Age itself, however, an account must be given of the preceding centuries which set the stage for the magnificent achievements of the Old Kingdom. When at the beginning of the Third Dynasty the first pyramid was built for King Zoser, the Step Pyramid at Saqqara, pharaohs had worn the double crown of Upper *Plate II; Fig. 10* and Lower Egypt for about four hundred years. Manetho's assertion that, about 3000 years before his time, the two lands were unified by a king called Menes, is borne out by the earlier hieroglyphic king lists. Archaeological finds, particularly a number of palettes for eye make-up, depict what are evidently historical scenes. One of these palettes, which probably served magic or ceremonial purposes and which is contemporary with the time of unification, shows a victorious king with the crown of *Fig. 3* Upper Egypt smiting the enemy and on the other side the same king wearing the crown of Lower Egypt. His name is given as Narmer. He, or possibly his successor Hor-aha, may correspond to Manetho's Menes. As mentioned earlier, the multiple names used by the pharaohs make identification often hazardous.

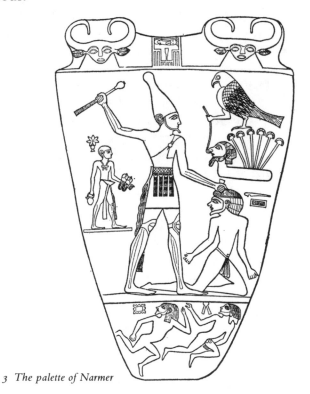

3 *The palette of Narmer*

Earlier archaeological finds show that well before the time of unification various closely related cultures flourished in the Nile Valley for a long time. Then, about a century before Narmer a sudden change seems to have come over the country. The burial customs took a different form, the tombs showed monumental architecture and, above all, hieroglyphic writing made its appearance. It is significant that the first written records already show a script which had passed the stage of mere pictograms and in which the characters had already assumed sound values. In other words the earliest known Egyptian hieroglyphs definitely represent a syllabic language. Thus there must have existed an earlier phase in which the pictures of a bird, a lizard or a lotus, were combined into words having a similar sound, a step which the Chinese civilization never took.

The sudden appearance of this well-developed form of writing indicates that it was most likely imported into Egypt from elsewhere, and most Egyptologists are inclined to think that at about 3400 BC a large-scale invasion of Egypt took place. Where the invaders came from is not known. Burial customs and certain architectural features are similar to the earliest Mesopotamian civilization but striking differences make it unlikely that this was the origin of the invaders. It seems more probable that the rulers of Egypt and of Mesopotamia had a common ancestry from which they derived similar traits. Who these ancestors could have been remains an open question and only a vague indication is provided by certain aspects of their beliefs which, as we shall see, are of a definitely African character.

The invading dynastic race which was to usher in the pharaonic civilization of Egypt called themselves the followers of Horus. Horus was a sky god whose totem animal was the falcon. The falcon appears on the Narmer palette, where it is shown holding an enemy captive, and

Fig. 6

it surmounts the name of the pharaoh on the memorial stelae which were erected at the tombs of the early kings. Horus also enters the name of the king himself as, for instance, in Hor-aha, and the falcon god is retained as the pharaoh's title well into the Pyramid Age. Horus was thus closely connected with the divine kingship of the pharaoh and he stood high above the totem animals of the local tribes which represented the gods of the individual provinces. His only serious rival seems to have been the god Seth of Ombos whose totem was a composite four-legged creature with an ant-eater's snout, large ears, cut off at the top, and a raised tail. Seth was possibly the god of the indigenous population whose stronghold appears to have been Upper Egypt, whereas Horus was originally connected with the Delta. It was perhaps through the Delta that the invaders first entered Egypt, conquering from there Seth's country in the Nile valley. Although these events date back to Egypt's prehistoric period, the

Fig. 2

juxtaposition of Seth and Horus as representing Upper and Lower Egypt is retained in representations throughout Egyptian history.

The enmity between Seth and Horus is expressed in a different form in the Osiris legend which probably stems from archaic times but reached its general religious importance only much later. The myth relates how the good King Osiris was treacherously murdered by his evil brother, Seth, who hacked his body to pieces and scattered them throughout the land. They were collected and buried by his wife, Isis, and Seth was defeated by Horus, the son of Osiris and Isis. The origin of this legend may have its roots in the struggle of the conquering dynastic race, the followers of Horus, with the original population of Seth's worshippers. Its significance for our considerations lies in the identification of Osiris with the dead pharaoh, the recovery of his corpse and the continuation of his existence in a new form after death. The inviolate preservation of the body in a strong and well protected 'eternal house' thus became one of the foremost tasks of Egyptian civilization.

It is, in fact, from the tombs that practically all our knowledge of life in ancient Egypt is derived. In the cities of the dead at the edge of the desert above the Nile valley, the dry, hot air from the Sahara has helped to preserve the dead and their possessions. It has also covered the graves with dunes of blown sand, concealing their entrances and guarding their rest until it was disturbed by the spade of the modern excavator. Unfortunately thousands of years before the curious arrived, the greedy had done their work only too well. Almost everywhere they had stripped the dead of their wealth, broken and scattered what seemed valueless, exposing the bodies and other contents of the tombs to disintegration. The further one goes back in history, the more time and opportunity did the tomb robbers have to wreak destruction. When we reach the Pyramid Age there are few objects left from that remote time of the first flowering of human society. Even the stones of the monuments were stolen to be turned into city walls and mosques, and only the pyramids themselves, whose immense bulk and strength withstood all onslaughts, remained to furnish us with the story of their time – provided we know how to read it.

In the development of man, death has been a fairly late discovery. The animal does not recognize death. A mother monkey will carry her baby around in the usual manner even after it has died, until its body has completely disintegrated. Less than a century ago the aborigines of central Australia had not yet accepted the inevitability of natural death. When one of their number died from illness or old age, they were sure that he had been killed by magic, and magic was invoked to discover the murderer. Once he was found, the deceased was avenged by either violence or again by magic. Even to this day man has not quite made his peace with the discovery of death. Many, if not most, of us still cling to the hope of a hereafter in one form or another in which we can continue as individual and recognizable personalities for ever.

The ancient Egyptians were rather closer to the disconcerting discovery of death than we are today. Their belief in a life after death was even firmer and also more concrete. In due course they developed a complicated ritual to assure eternal life for each man and woman, but in early times the individual seems to have put his own trust for survival after death in the continued existence of the divine king. The pharaoh's tomb, its grandeur and splendour, as well as the ritual and sacrifices attending it, therefore became the concern of everyone. The arrival of the dynastic race in Egypt was heralded by the construction of large and impressive tombs for their kings.

The eternal life which awaited the Egyptian after his death was very much the same existence as he had known before. He would work in the fields or, if he were rich, he would supervise this work, count his cattle and poultry, sit with beautiful girls at banquets, being entertained by still more beautiful girls. They would offer drink, play music and dance along on the walls of the tomb which also show us his garden and the ponds where he could hunt ducks or spear fish. The pictures on the walls of their tombs tell us more about the life of the Egyptian people than what we know about the Greeks, the Romans or even about the Middle Ages.

Plates 1–4
Fig. 4

Unlike the battle scenes or the solemn processions on the temple walls, the pictures in the tombs were, of course, not meant to be seen. They were shut in with the dead owner as a magical device to provide him with all the comforts which he had known in his lifetime. They were to supplement the offerings which priests, paid for their services, had to place before the dummy door of his sepulchre. The furniture, the ointments and the gaming boards which were put into his grave all served the same purpose; to make sure that in the eternal life he had all that he had enjoyed in this one. In other words, the Egyptians believed that they could take it with them.

Plate IX

Around the early tombs of the kings the archaeologists found the graves of retainers and women who had gone with the king when he died. The skeletons showed that they were young women and there can be little doubt that they had been put to death at the pharaoh's funeral. Like the women in the death pits of Mesopotamia, these harem ladies showed no signs of violence and it may be assumed that they went to their deaths voluntarily, as the retainers and household officials may have done.

4 *The happy afterlife. Relief showing musicians and dancers in the mastaba of the Vizier Mereruka at Saqqara*

Human sacrifice, if it can be called such, at the death of the divine king is an age-old custom which in Africa has persisted almost to this day. Less than a century ago, a hundred men and women would accompany the king of the Ashanti on his journey from this world into the next. As soon as the king had died the queen mother, the most important person in the state, would send messengers to a number of harem women to tell them that the time had come for them to go with their husband. The ladies would, first of all, take leave of their relatives. Then, decked in white robes and adorned with all their jewellery, they attended a solemn banquet at which they would freely partake of palm wine and rum until they were unconscious. When this stage had been reached, women executioners entered and strangled the widows with leather thongs. Court officials and other dignitaries also would choose a voluntary death, but the same was evidently not true for servants or slaves who had to be dispatched forcibly. This fear of sacrificial death has remained deeply ingrained and when in 1970 King Prempeh II of the Ashanti died, none of our servants at the university could be induced to go out after nightfall. The streets of Kumasi, the Ashanti capital, were deserted and finally the local newspaper had to announce in a banner headline: 'No deaths reported in Ashanti in connection with the funeral of the Asantehene'.

These facts are mentioned because in this and other aspects, to be referred to later, a curious similarity exists between the habits and customs of the Akan tribes of today with those of Ancient Egypt. The Ashanti migrated into West Africa only a few centuries ago. Until then they had lived in the Sudan, the only place in which the traditions of ancient Egypt had been preserved intact until about fifteen hundred years ago. When in 660 BC the pharaoh Tanuatamun had to flee before the invading Assyrians, he turned south to the Egyptian Sudan, whence his forefathers had come. His successors continued the migration and eventually established their capital at Meroë, above the mouth of the Atbara. There they re-created a pharaonic court with Egyptian customs, which went as far

Plate 45

as the building of small pyramids for their burials, until they were dispersed by the Abyssinians. Their heritage, a mixture of Egyptian tradition and African customs, including human sacrifice, has lived on, almost to the present day, in the tribal life of the Sudan. A village society in virtual isolation tends to keep its cultural pattern largely unchanged in its basic character for a very long time. A village cemetery, recently excavated, showed an unbroken series of funeral gifts from Egyptian amulets to modern Manchester trash. It is, of course, dangerous to rely too much on this similarity between African customs which have been retained to this day and a civilization that flourished thousands of years ago. On the other hand it is equally unrealistic to disregard completely the undoubtedly existing parallels. If nothing else, we can look upon some of the customs and beliefs which have survived in Africa as a possible pointer to the thoughts and motives of the people of Ancient Egypt which have been lost to us. When later in this chapter we return to this similarity it will always be with the proviso that much of it must remain conjecture.

The custom of human sacrifice seems to have been abolished in Egypt in early dynastic times. When the Pyramid Age is reached, no traces of it were left. Even the ritual killing of the divine king when he had lost his virility had by then been replaced by a ceremonial renewal of his powers in the Sed festival which soon assumed the character of a regnal jubilee. Courtiers and relatives continued to be accorded the privilege of being laid to rest close to the pharaoh's sepulchre and their tombs stand in neat long rows by the sides of the pyramids at Giza. However, they no longer had to accompany the god immediately and instead occupied their eternal houses in their own good time.

Plates 32, 35

Since we will be mainly concerned with the design, construction and function of the pyramids, the royal tombs of the first two dynasties which precede them are of particular interest. Menes, to seal the act of unification of the two lands, is credited with having founded the capital of his new realm. He chose the place at which Upper and Lower Egypt meet, at the apex of the Delta where the long narrow Nile valley fans out into the fertile plain of accumulated silt. He is said to have diverted the course of the river in order to gain space for the new city which he called White Walls, indicating that originally the capital was also a fortress. To us the city is known by its Greek name of Memphis. It remained the seat of the pharaonic government, with short interruptions, for one and a half millennia. In the early Middle Ages, four thousand years after its foundation, Memphis was still a magnificent city but from then onward its importance declined at the expense of the Arab town of Cairo, 20 miles to the north.

Today almost nothing is left of Memphis; only the area of the great temple of Ptah, the local god of Memphis, can still be traced. The palaces and houses, built of mud brick and wood, have crumbled long since and have sunk into the muddy agricultural soil. At the western part of the ancient Memphis area, and close to the rim of the desert, stands the Arab village of Saqqara. Above it, on the desert plateau, overlooking the Nile valley, stretches for several miles the ancient necropolis – one of the most important archaeological sites in Egypt. It is dominated by the Step Pyramid which for a long time was regarded as the oldest pharaonic tomb.

Plate II; Fig. 10

In 1912 J. E. Quibell, who had twenty years earlier made some important discoveries about the pre-dynastic 'Scorpion' king in Upper Egypt, shifted his activities to Saqqara. Digging in the northern sector of the necropolis, he established the existence of some large archaic tombs. Unfortunately, the work was interrupted by the First World War and interest in it was not revived immediately afterwards. Finally, in the early thirties, when G. A. Reisner of Harvard was engaged in compiling his monumental work on the development of the Egyptian tomb, he suggested to the Egyptian Antiquities Department that digging in the area should be resumed. The work was undertaken by Cecil Firth, who was then Chief Inspector of Antiquities, but it was again interrupted by Firth's untimely death. In 1936 the excavations were entrusted to Walter Emery who, except for the interval of the Second World War, kept up the exploration of the Saqqara necropolis until his death in 1971. Emery's important discoveries during this long period of work have vastly increased our knowledge of life and conditions in Egypt just before the Pyramid Age.

Following the lead provided by the work of Quibell and Firth, Emery turned his attention to the large structures first noted by them. His careful and extensive excavations yielded what appeared to be the tombs of the successors of Menes, the first kings to rule in the new capital. Each tomb consists of a superstructure of mud brick, surmounting a pit excavated in the rock beneath, which evidently held the burial chamber and storage space for tomb furniture and offerings. Most of the Saqqara tombs, as indeed others in Upper Egypt, were destroyed by fire, probably already in the Early Dynastic period. Moreover they all appear to have been robbed in antiquity and, in fact, no actual burial has been found in any of them. Hence the determination of ownership relies entirely on such evidence as jar sealings or wooden and ivory tags, originally attached to funeral equipment, which bear the king's name. Unfortunately, sometimes a pharaoh's name may not only appear in his own tomb but also in that of his predecessor which he may have finished after the latter's death. In addition, the name of some nobleman, such as the king's vizier, is occasionally found and then the question arises whether the excavated tomb is indeed that of the pharaoh himself or had belonged to some high dignitary. While in most cases the evidence is sufficiently strong to assign a tomb to a particular king, it has to be admitted that a slight element of uncertainty is always present.

However this may be, the pattern of tomb construction and its development has clearly been established by Emery's excavations. When the sand had been removed it turned out that in spite of their extreme age and the fragility of mud brick, the superstructures of most tombs had remained intact up to the height of several feet. In fact, the protection afforded by the blown sand was so complete that even the vivid colours in which the walls had been painted are well preserved. The pattern of these decorations represents ornamental matting used as hangings to embellish the bare walls, and this indicates that the tombs were replicas of the royal palaces of Memphis which themselves have long since vanished without a trace. The idea that the palace of the dead king was designed on much the same lines as the one which he had inhabited during his lifetime is supported by the structure of the buildings which is essentially that of a dwelling–place. Emery found that their outer walls show the same recessed panelling which recurs in the enclosure walls of the step pyramids. This type of construction was possibly modelled on ancient fortresses and the fact that the same recessed panelling is also found in Mesopotamia suggests that the basic pattern originated in very early times.

Fig. 5

While Emery's work left no doubt about the lay-out of the tombs and has provided us with detailed ground plans, it cannot tell us anything about the original height of these buildings. The thicknesses of the walls show that they may have risen to more than three metres and it is generally assumed that they were covered with a shallow curved roof. This reconstruction is based on the shape of early sarcophagi which also seem to have been miniature models of the palace. At the narrow ends the curved roof most probably ended in upright retaining walls. The Saqqara tombs are of considerable size. They are on average 50 to 60 metres long and half as wide. They generally stand on a low podium which sometimes carried rows of sculptured life-size bulls' heads to which natural horns had been affixed.

Plate 6

The inside of the structures, like a real palace, is divided by walls into a large number of rooms. However, there are no doors between them, because the spirit of the departed should presumably be able to pass through a wall without hindrance. The central rooms obviously constituted the burial place while the outer chambers contained the tomb furniture and provisions. Emery found in them huge quantities of stone jars and basins as well as ceramic pots and vases. In the later tombs the burial chamber and some special storage rooms were located below the

5 Plan and section of a typical tomb of the first two dynasties, showing the central mound (1) and the subterranean tomb chamber (2) (after Edwards)

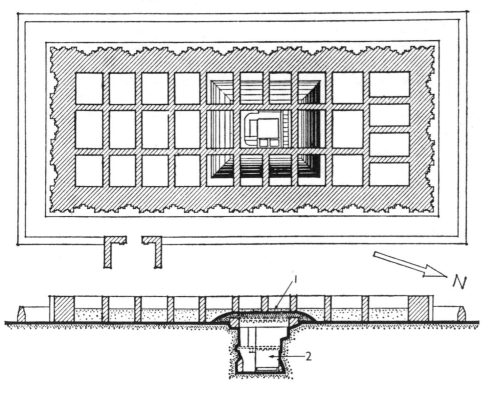

floor level and roofed over with timber. Gradually these subterranean apartments were located in a still deeper pit and concern about tomb robbers is evident in the provision of a huge stone slab which could be lowered into the access passage as a portcullis. The whole funeral palace was surrounded by an enclosure wall and in front of the tomb itself stood two stone stelae, giving the name and titles of the king.

In addition the tombs contained a feature so inconspicuous that it was at first overlooked, but it was of the greatest importance for the coming Pyramid Age. Within the superstructure, and exactly above the underground burial chamber, was a small mound of earth, sometimes protected by stone slabs. This mound is clearly a relic of the little heap of sand which marked the pre-dynastic graves. It is likely that the Egyptians in their extreme conservatism retained this mound as the central and most important feature of the burial. In the later funeral palaces this mound was further protected by a stepped structure and it is possible that these steps symbolized the means by which the dead king was to ascend to heaven. There is reason to believe that this central grave mound was developed under the Third Dynasty into the step pyramid as a gigantic stairway for the deceased pharaoh.

At the northern end of the tomb of Hor-aha, the first king after unification, are some dummy buildings, representing either his estate or a court for celebrating his jubilee festival, and an oblong pit. This pit has the shape of a boat and there can be no doubt that it contained the barge which the pharaoh used for his voyage into the next world. A number of such boat pits have been found near the Giza pyramids, including an enormous one which was discovered only in 1954 and contained a ship 43 metres in length.

Plate 35

If our account of the pharaonic burial places of the first two dynasties could end here, it would provide a straightforward prelude to the following Pyramid Age. Unfortunately, this is not so since at least one other set of royal sepulchres of the same kings whose tombs Emery found at Saqqara have been discovered three hundred miles to the south in Upper Egypt. In 1896 the Director of the Antiquities Service, J. de Morgan, discovered at Nagadah close to Luxor a tomb that was equal in size and construction to those excavated later by Emery at Saqqara. At first it was thought to belong to Hor-aha but more detailed investigation showed that the owner was Hor-aha's mother, Queen Nithotep. One year later Amélineau found a number of large tombs at Abydos but unfortunately he was mainly interested in digging for collector's items and in the course of his operations destroyed much of the evidence which could have led to a reconstruction of the superstructures. Flinders Petrie took over these excavations at the beginning of this century and he was able to show that the tombs belonged to the kings of the first two dynasties. At first it was believed that the structures were much smaller than those at Saqqara but recent exploration has shown that at Abydos funeral palaces of equal size existed.

Petrie's work left little doubt that the Abydos tombs could be ascribed to the early kings, and some Egyptologists are of the opinion that the same cannot be said of the Saqqara tombs. Their main argument is that these pharaohs cannot have been buried in two places and that the claim of the Abydos tombs is better established. Others are of the opinion that both the Abydos and the Saqqara tombs are royal funerary monuments but that only one set were true burials while the other merely served as cenotaphs. There is, indeed, much to be said for this explanation. Memphis had become the capital and the residence of the pharaohs of the two kingdoms and it would be only natural that their tombs should be in the Saqqara necropolis, overlooking the city. In fact, the Saqqara funeral palaces are strung along the edge of the desert plateau where they could be seen from the valley. On the other hand, the rulers of the united Egypt had come from the south and their ancestors were presumably buried at the sacred burial ground of Osiris at Abydos. There were thus compelling reasons for the pharaohs of the first two dynasties to be remembered by tombs at this city.

It is often maintained that these two tombs which most of the early kings owned represented their position as rulers of Upper and Lower Egypt respectively. Some Egyptologists, including Emery, have even suggested that each of these pharaohs had probably not only two but three funeral palaces – the tomb at Abydos for Upper Egypt and another tomb at Buto in Lower Egypt, in addition to the one at Saqqara. Buto was the ancient capital of the Delta but hardly any of the ancient structures there survive, having long ago been engulfed in the silt of the Nile inundations, leaving only three large mounds of later periods. The tomb at Saqqara would then have been the main sepulchre, most likely containing the body of the king. However that may be, it is important for our own considerations to realize that there seem to have existed tombs with all the trappings of funeral monuments but containing no actual burial. Who or what was buried in these multiple tombs must remain a matter for conjecture.

Although in the four centuries spanned by the first two dynasties there reigned a series of pharaohs, each wearing the double crown of Upper and Lower Egypt, the period hardly represents an aspect of steady consolidation. Stresses and contradictions of different origin became so interwoven that today it is almost impossible to separate them. First of all, the unification was clearly based on the conquest of the north by the south, and on the Narmer palette the king is shown inspecting the beheaded corpses of his (northern) enemies while the Horus falcon is bringing in as captives the tribes of the Delta. On another early representation, a macehead, we see the lapwing folk of Lower Egypt, hanged by their necks on ropes dangling from the totem standards of the southern nomes. However, both the victors and vanquished were ruled by the 'followers of Horus', that is, by members of the dynastic race. A different type of confrontation which goes back to the time before unification existed between the invading followers of Horus and the indigenous population worshipping the god Seth of Ombos. Here, a much older regional conflict must have existed between Horus in the Delta and Seth in Upper Egypt.

Fig. 6

This second conflict, possibly owing to its religious implications, appears to have been the more deep-seated one. It evidently flared up towards the middle of the Second Dynasty, under a king named Sekhemib. This pharaoh either forsook or was forced to forsake his god Horus, changing his own name to Peribsen and replacing the falcon surmounting his name by the Seth animal. A sign of the disorders during his reign is the burning of most of the earlier tombs and this may have been a revenge which the indigenous population took upon the invaders. No record has yet been found of what happened in the next three reigns but the fourth king after Peribsen, Kha-sekhem, again places the falcon above his name. Nevertheless, the civil war must have continued into his reign, as is shown by two statues of him which have survived. They show Kha-

Plate 5

sekhem seated in his jubilee robes while the base is surrounded by a series of dead or dying figures and bears the inscription: 'Northern enemies 47,209'. Although the rebellion was evidently quelled, in the end compromise rather than conquest seems to have been the solution for the two kingdoms. The name of the next pharaoh, the last of the Second Dynasty, Kha-sekhemui, carries the meaning 'The two gods are at peace in him.' The name, moreover, is surmounted by the Horus as well as by the Seth animal.

With Kha-sekhemui the final unification of the two kingdoms appears to have been achieved and this is signified by his marriage to the princess Nemathap of Lower Egypt. It seems that a similar marriage had marked the beginning of the unification four centuries earlier when the conquering Narmer married a northern princess, Nithotep, who was honoured after her death by the enormous tomb found by de Morgan at Nagadah in Upper Egypt.

The marriages contracted by the princesses Nithotep and Nemathap were, however, of much greater significance than the political unions entered upon by the European monarchs of the sixteenth and seventeenth

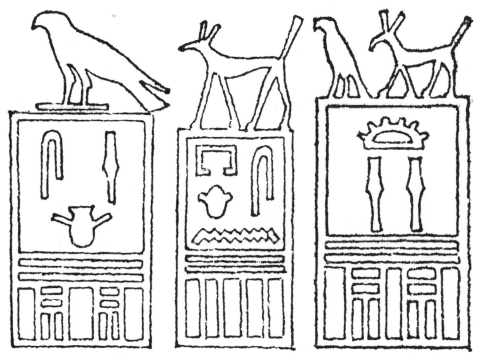

6 The serekh *of the Pharaoh Sekhemib* (left) *who later changed his Horus name to the Seth name* Peribsen (centre) *and the* serekh *of Kha-sekhemui* (right), *combining both gods*

centuries. Egyptian society was matrilineal, which means that inheritance, including that of the throne, always went through the female line. A prince could never become pharaoh by being his father's son; he had to be his wife's husband. In the royal harem there was always a 'great queen', the woman who by virtue of her descent had the power to confer kingship. When Tutankhamun died, it was his young widow, Ankhesenamun, the daughter of Akhenaten and his great queen Nefertiti, who held in her person the fate of the Empire. By a curious chance the diplomatic correspondence of her court has come down to us. She wrote to the king of the Hittites: 'My husband is dead and I have no son. Send me one of your sons and he will be my husband and lord of the land of Egypt'. It was, in fact, by his marriage to this 'daughter of the god' that Tutankhamun earlier had become pharaoh.

Matrilineal succession and inheritance were the reasons for the great number of consanguine marriages in the Egyptian royal house. In order to gain the throne, the son of the pharaoh usually had to marry his own sister because only she could pass on the valid succession. If for no other reason, prudence required that no potential great queen, who on the matrimonial couch would be able to confer the crown, should be left unmarried, lest she became the prey of a political adventurer. In addition to brother-sister unions, pharaohs sometimes married their daughters: for instance, Amenhotep III who married his own daughter, Sitamun, by his wife Tiye, because Sitamun was next in line of great queens. It has also been suggested that Ankhesenamun, before marrying Tutankhamun, had become her father's widow and that there had been a daughter of his incestuous union called Ankhesenpaaten Tashery.

The concept of matrilineal descent, which became so important for the Egyptian monarchy, is an extremely ancient one and long antedates the idea of a, to us obvious, connection between father and son. It clearly stems from an age in which the mechanism of paternity was unknown or imperfectly understood. After all, the relation between frequent intercourse and occasional birth, complicated, as it is, by a long gestation period, can hardly have been an obvious one to primitive man. An Australian aboriginal woman would date conception from the first movement of the foetus, and the totem of the place where she felt it was then thought to have entered the mother. This very plausible idea leaves no room for the father and the nearest male relative will be the child's maternal uncle since he and the mother can be traced to the same woman – the maternal grandmother.

To the Egyptians the role of the father was, of course, well known but the ancient matrilineal structure of society, whose real origin may have been long forgotten, was conservatively retained. This has happened in other parts of the world, too, and it is interesting that the Akan tribes of Africa, to whom reference has already been made, have retained the rule of matrilineal inheritance to this day. Since in Ashanti brother-sister marriages are not permitted, the king can never be the son of his predecessor. He is usually the son of the previous king's sister. This, of course, explains the exalted position of the queen mother, to whom, just as in Egypt, custody of the crown reverts at the death of the king.

Our description of the effort, time and expense which the Egyptians lavished on their tombs leaves no doubt that they were much preoccupied with life after death. We have said nothing so far about how they expected to survive in eternity and the simple reason is that we do not know it with any degree of certainty. The Egyptian language contains a number of words relating to characteristics of a person which are not part of his body, such as his name and his shadow, and spiritual significance was allotted to both. The two most important attributes often referred to, but unfortunately not as easily comprehended as name or shadow, were the *ka* and the *ba*, neither of which has as yet been fully understood. The *ba* is usually believed to be the 'soul' which is released from the body at death but does not completely leave, hovering about it as a human-headed bird. Therefore, with not much to go on, reference to similar beliefs among the Akan tribes might, at least, provide some hints.

Like the Egyptians, the Ashanti differentiate between a number of spiritual attributes to the body. Two of these, the *kra* and the *sunsum* are transmitted from the father, one at conception and the other at birth, both leaving the body after death. The *kra* is the quality of animated life while the *sunsum* is more connected with the personal character of the individual. It sometimes leaves the person's body during his sleep to travel in his dreams. These attributes may possibly correspond to the Egyptian *ba*, sometimes represented as a bird beside the inanimate body.

In contrast with these transient attributes, the Ashanti *abusua*, or blood soul, has permanence and was, in fact, in existence before the individual was born; it also continues to exist after his death. Its existence is eternal but it is incarnated into the living body of the child by its mother; and it is definitely connected with the mother's clan. The *abusua* therefore appears to have certain qualities associated with the Egyptian *ka* and this parallelism is supported by a curious similarity. In order to promote fertility the Ashanti bind on to the back of the woman an Akua-ba doll. This figure, which is quite different from ordinary African sculpture, consists of a severely stylized cylindrical body, stumps of arms and a round disc-shaped head. Its form is thus identical with the ancient *ankh*, the hieroglyph for 'life'. If we accept this parallelism, we would expect the ancient Egyptian *ka* to be closely connected with the concept of matrilineal descent and to be the carrier of its ancestry through the mother. It also might be associated with the idea of reincarnation in the female blood line to which so far little attention has been given. Moreover, the Ashanti explain the desirability of cousin-cousin marriage in the royal house as the need to preserve purity of the blood and to 'keep the great names'.

It cannot be emphasized too strongly, as has been stated before, that considerations of this kind should be regarded as merely conjectural. No firm conclusions must be based on such ideas which cannot serve any other purpose except to provide an indication of the possible meaning of the *ka*. If further work should establish the connection of the *ka* with matrilineal descent, it would certainly show why the great queen was regarded as the true and only custodian of the Egyptian kingship. It is significant that in the registers of the Palermo Stone not only the names of the pharaohs are given but also the names of their mothers. How far the Egyptians went in emphasizing maternal descent is shown by Emery's very last discovery. In 1851 Mariette had discovered the Serapeum at Saqqara, the immense subterranean tomb holding the sarcophagi of the sacred Apis bulls. Emery, 120 years later, found nearby a similar tomb, holding the remains of the equally sacred mothers of these animals.

7 A twentieth century 'Akua-ba' fertility doll of the West African Ashanti tribe, showing great similarity with the Egyptian hieroglyph 'ankh', meaning 'life'

2 The Pyramid Age

The Princess Nemathap was evidently a daughter of the Delta and not a member of the southern royal family whose blood ran through the Second Dynasty. By her marriage to Kha-Sekhemui she must have supplanted the southern heiress but there is no doubt that she became the great queen. Her official seal bore the title 'king-bearing mother' and she was venerated as the acknowledged founder of the Third Dynasty. The king whom she bore was styled by Manetho as Zoser and he was generally referred to by this name in later times. Contemporary monuments list him under his Horus name 'Neterkhet', a fact which confused scholars for a considerable time.

Plate 46

It is not quite certain that Zoser was indeed the first pharaoh of the Third Dynasty, since some sources give priority to a 'Horus Zanakht' who may have been Zoser's elder brother. If so, he evidently died early, leaving no monuments at Saqqara. It certainly was under Zoser's reign that the great architectural achievements of the Third Dynasty were ushered in, giving evidence of a new unity of purpose in Egypt which was conspicuously lacking under his predecessors. Through the union of Kha-Sekhemui and Nemathap and with the conciliation of the gods Horus and Seth, the country was suddenly released from the ravages of civil war and became free to turn its creative power to peaceful activities.

One last reminder of the past disorders was found only in recent years. When exploring the foundations of the Step Pyramid, the archaeologists broke into a 33-metre deep shaft which had been left undisturbed since Zoser's time. It ended in a long gallery filled with the fragments of about 35,000 jars and dishes made of alabaster and hard stone, of which 8000 have since been restored. On these, seals of all pharaohs of the two preceding dynasties were found, with the notable exception of those of the heretic Peribsen. The fragments may have been rescued from the royal tombs that were sacked and burnt by the rebels, to be piously reburied. The entrance to the shaft was covered up by an enlargement of Zoser's tomb, which set the Step Pyramid like a gigantic seal upon the buried unhappy past.

Fig. 9

Although very little is known about Zoser's life, he became one of the most famous pharaohs in the history of Egypt. This fame is based on the magnificent funeral complex at Saqqara and, above all, on the grandiose Step Pyramid which forms its centre. Nothing even faintly approaching these monuments in size and splendour had ever been created by man and, when beholding it, we cannot but realize that, almost 5000 years ago, the human race had suddenly moved into a new age. The most astonishing feature of this development was the lack of any preparatory phase; it seems that within one generation Egypt had stepped from a semi-tribal state into a highly organized society, capable of an astounding communal effort.

Plate II; Fig. 10

Even more surprising is the realization that the immense technological advance required for pyramid building was not due to a technical revolution. The methods of using stone as a building material and the metal and stone tools employed had been well-known in the Second Dynasty. What was new in Zoser's time was the degree to which all these activities were suddenly escalated. Pyramid-building was a milestone in the history of man because it was his first true application of large-scale technology. Like all later technological efforts, down to our day, pyramid construction relied on tools and methods which were already well-known but the potentialities of which had not as yet been recognized. The keys to the problem were manpower and organization. The first was provided by a pacified and united country while for the second a unique human genius was required. His name, which the Egyptians cherished and later venerated for more than 3000 years, was Imhotep.

Although Imhotep eventually became a legendary figure, whom the Greeks worshipped under the name of Asklepios, his greatness was fully recognized in his own lifetime. In the ceremonial court of the Step Pyramid stood the pedestal of a statue which has vanished and which bears, after the name of Imhotep, the citation: 'Chancellor of the King of Lower Egypt, First after the King of Upper Egypt, Administrator of the great Palace, Hereditary Nobleman, High Priest of Heliopolis, Builder, Sculptor and Maker of Vases in Chief'. Imhotep certainly was not a royal prince. A later inscription states that his father, Ka-nefer, was Director of Works of Upper and Lower Egypt, providing us with the interesting information that, even in ancient Egypt, technology was administered by a professional meritocracy. Imhotep is said to have come from Upper Egypt but he will probably have been buried, not far from Zoser, at Saqqara. Archaeologists have been searching for his tomb for a long time, but so far in vain. A few years ago hopes were raised high when Emery found a gallery with the mummies of birds and animals sacred to Imhotep, and one felt that the great architect's tomb could not be far away. Then the work was interrupted by Emery's death and Imhotep's tomb remains one of the many secrets still held by the desert sand at Saqqara.

In the memory of the Egyptian people Imhotep lived on as a mathematician, a physician and the inventor of building in stone. This last statement is essentially true, although stone had been occasionally employed in the tombs of the first two dynasties, mainly for portcullises and for some flooring. This shows that methods for quarrying and working stone had been developed some time earlier. However, the degree to which stone was quarried, transported and dressed for a royal tomb of the Second Dynasty bears no relation to the effort required for Zoser's funeral monument. In the first case it amounted to a few tons of limestone,

Fig. 10

whereas the Step Pyramid complex contains at least one million tons. It is almost impossible to conceive how this increase of production could have been achieved in just one generation. Whereas the labour force required to construct one, or even two, mud brick tombs for each pharaoh would have been readily available, this can certainly not be said of the immense number of men required to build a pyramid. In fact, the size, organization and, above all, the economic aspects of the employment of this gigantic army of workers is one of the crucial problems for understanding the meaning of pyramid building, to which we shall return in a later chapter. However, before we can discuss these problems, we first must give a description of the pyramids themselves.

Here we will have to consider two aspects: first the pyramid structures and secondly the tomb chambers and passages which they contain. As will become apparent later, these two features may not be as intimately connected as has generally been assumed, and they may, in fact, have served

Fig. 8

very different purposes. However, no two of the pyramids and their internal systems are identical and, for simplicity's sake, we will give for each pyramid a complete description of external and internal features, in the historical order in which they were built.

Zoser's Step Pyramid at Saqqara, although vastly different in size and conception still retains a few vestiges of the royal tombs of the two preceding dynasties. The tomb chamber is a subterranean structure, sunk at the bottom of a square shaft of 7 m. diameter and 28 m. deep. This chamber consisted of two separate parts arranged one on top of the other and constructed of pink granite. Access to the lower cavity is by a circular

8 *Sections of the seven large pyramids of the Old Kingdom, drawn to the same scale. A Zoser's Step Pyramid at Saqqara, showing the successive building phases (cf. fig. 9 and p. 38). B The ruined pyramid of Meidum with Petrie's reconstruction of its three building phases (cf. fig. 16 and p. 80). C and D The 'Bent' (southern) Pyramid of Dahshur. E The 'Red' (northern) Pyramid of Dahshur. F Khufu's pyramid at Giza, showing Borchardt's conjectured internal buttress walls (cf. p. 122). G Khafre's pyramid at Giza. H Menkaure's pyramid at Giza.*

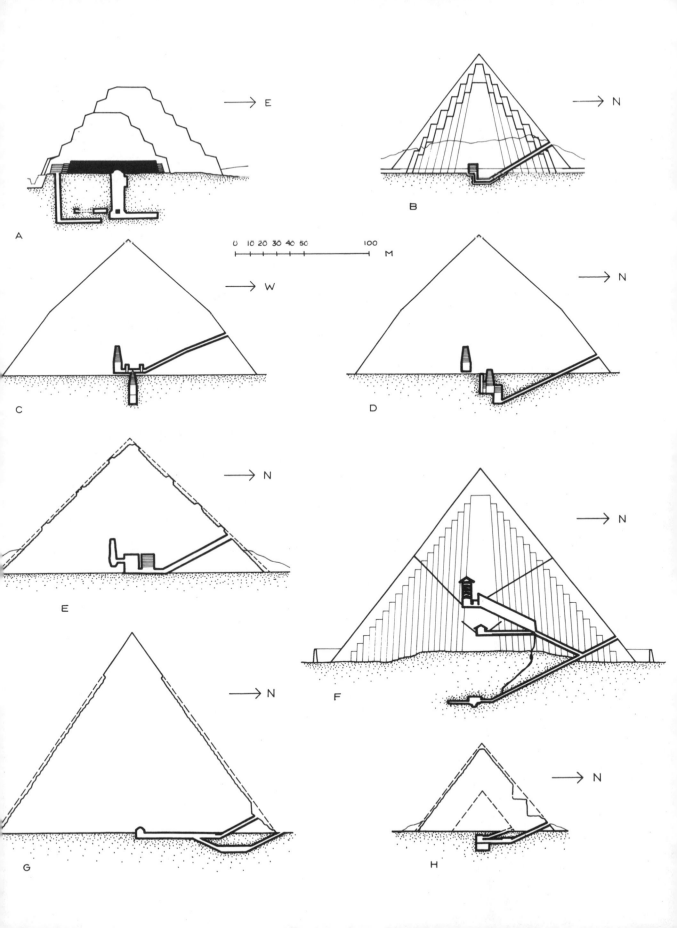

A

→ E

B

→ N

0 10 20 30 40 50   100
                    M

C

→ W

D

→ N

E

→ N

F

→ N

G

→ N

H

→ N

Plate 8

hole of less than 1 m. diameter in its ceiling. This hole was closed by a granite plug which is shaped like a bottle stopper and which weighs three tons. The cavity itself is about 3 m. long, 1.7 m. wide and of the same height. It was evidently robbed in antiquity but may have contained the body of the king; a mummified human foot was found in it. Nothing is left today of the upper chamber in which the plug was stored. Above its roof the shaft was originally filled with rubble. This rubble, together with the roof of the upper chamber, was removed, possibly during the Twenty-sixth Dynasty in the sixth century BC. Access to the tomb chamber was through a sloping passage which had been tunnelled through the rock north of the shaft. Outward from the bottom of the shaft radiate a maze of passages and galleries which originally may have contained funeral equipment and tomb furniture. Some of the galleries have remained unfinished while the walls of others were covered with blue tiles and sculptures in low relief. A few of the latter show Zoser evidently performing ritualistic acts.

The top of the shaft, after it had been filled with rubble, was originally covered by a solid stone structure, 63 m. square and 8 m. high, which possibly had a slightly curved roof. This type of superstructure is similar to the brick buildings covering the tombs of nobles of this period. They are usually called 'mastabas', a term used by the Arabs for the bench in front of their houses. Zoser's mastaba, the first sizable stone structure

Fig. 10

ever erected, stood in the centre of a large, oblong court, 545×277 m., with its long axis oriented roughly in a north-south direction. This court

Plate 9

Plate 6

was surrounded by a wall of dressed limestone 10.5 m. high with recessed panelling, similar to the façades of the funeral palaces in the preceding dynasties. Thus there exists a certain similarity to the layout of the earlier royal tombs, with Zoser's mastaba taking the place of the ancient burial mound, and the enclosure being possibly a reminder of the panelled tomb walls.

The central feature of the pyramid complex, the mastaba, underwent

Fig. 9

no less than five alterations, each extending the original plan, and culminating eventually in the pyramid of six steps as we see it today. These changes of design are revealed to us by the incursion of stone robbers

Plate 7

who have laid bare some of the inner structure, particularly at the corners and at the lowest step. For a time, the first mastaba must have been considered as the final form of the monument since its walls of fine Tura limestone were carefully dressed and planed. The first alteration consisted of an increase of its size in all directions by 3 m., and this was followed by an extension, on the east side only, of $8\frac{1}{2}$ m. Previously, eleven shafts of 33 m. depth had been sunk into the rock, each ending in a long horizontal gallery at its bottom. These galleries which extended into the rock

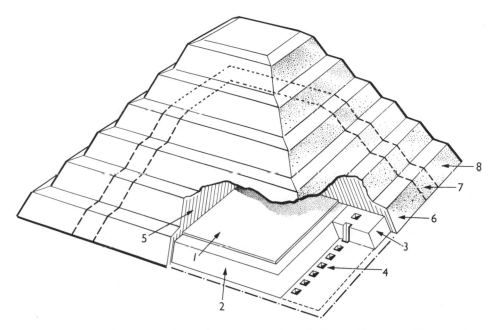

9 *Isometric section of Zoser's Step Pyramid at Saqqara. It shows the three building stages of the original mastaba (1,2,3), the shafts leading to the subsidiary tombs (4) and the internal buttress walls (5) of the superimposed pyramid structure. The initial pyramid with four steps (6) was first extended to the north and west (7) and then further enlarged and raised to a height of six steps (8)*

underneath the pyramid were probably the tombs of Zoser's relatives, but most, if not all, of them had been entered by thieves in antiquity. In one of the galleries two alabaster sarcophagi were found, one of which contained the mummy of a child; the other was empty. It was in one of these deep subterranean galleries that the large quantity of stone vessels from the earlier dynasties were found. The extension of the mastaba to the east covered the mouths of these shafts and this extension may have been intended as a mastaba marking these subsidiary graves. After the shafts had thus become inaccessible a narrow stairway and connecting subterranean passages were cut leading to the tombs, but it is not clear whether this was done in Zoser's time or by later intruders.

However, before the stones of the new extension could be dressed, a further change was instituted. The elongated mastaba was first extended in all directions by another 3 m. and then an entirely novel type of structure was erected on the new foundation. It was a pyramid made up of four steps and reaching to a height of about 40 m. This was a most imposing edifice, looking out above the enclosure wall and towering over the whole of Memphis. However, more was still to come. The next move was to enlarge the pyramid of four steps towards the north and west until it covered an area of 125 × 110 m. This enlargement was merely an intermediate building phase, preparatory for the final achievement of a pyramid of six steps, rising to a height of 60 m. By transforming the pyramid of four steps into one of six steps, the quantity of stone used was raised from 200,000 tons to 850,000 tons. In fact, after the first minor alterations, each of Imhotep's projects became more ambitious than the last one. It seems that, as the work progressed, far from exhausting his resources, he was able to command an ever increasing labour force. Zoser's Step Pyramid looks as if six mastabas, each smaller than the lower one, had been piled up on top of each other, and this is the manner in which it is usually described. While admittedly the aspect of the Step Pyramid conveys just this impression, its construction is based on a completely different architectural principle. Whereas the original mastaba

Fig. 20

was made up of horizontal courses of masonry, the Step Pyramid consists of an accretion of steep buttress walls which slope inwards at an angle of about 75°. The height of these buttress walls successively decreases towards the outside of the pyramid, giving the whole structure its step-like appearance. This basic design, which was evidently repeated in every later pyramid, was first noted by Perring who investigated the Step Pyramid in 1837. Climbing it, he discovered this pattern of construction, but in his and all later drawings the obvious conclusion was not drawn that the inner core of the edifice, too, had to be built up in the same manner. The stabilizing effect of this design will be discussed in greater detail later, and it bears testimony to Imhotep's genius in erecting a tall and, at the same time, safe building.

Fig. 10
Plate II

The surrounding court contains a number of large buildings which, however, are all solid dummies, probably replicas of the palaces which the pharaoh had inhabited in his lifetime. They clearly follow the practice established, as we have seen, much earlier by Hor-aha. Other structures in the enclosure appear to be the replica of a ceremonial court, used by the king for celebrating his jubilee, the Heb-sed festival. Adjoining the pyramid at its northern side is a mortuary temple, now much ruined, in

Plate 10

the *serdab* of which was found the famous limestone statue of Zoser. The king is shown seated in a shroud-like garment which leaves only the hands and feet free and which may have been the apparel worn for his ritual death at the Heb-sed ceremony. However, the most mysterious

Plate 9

feature is a large mastaba at the southern end of the enclosure. It covers a second tomb at the bottom of a shaft sunk into the rock to a depth of over 30 m. In design, including the access by a sloping tunnel, it is very similar to the tomb underneath the pyramid. Here, too, galleries were

Plate 46

attached to the tomb chamber and they also contained reliefs showing Zoser, and walls covered with blue tiles. Although this southern tomb had also been entered in ancient times, the robbers had done less damage

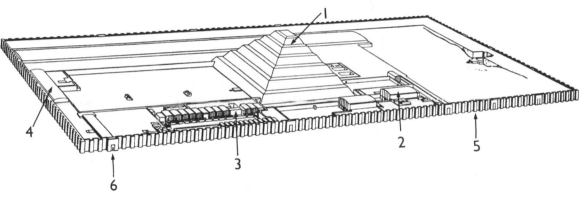

10 *The Pyramid Complex of Zoser at Saqqara. The Step Pyramid (1) stands in the centre, with the dummy buildings of the palace (2) and the Heb-sed Court (3) on the east side. The southern tomb (4) adjoins the temenos wall (5) whose gates, except for one (6), are also dummies*

than in the main shaft. In particular, the room above the burial chamber was found intact and it also contained a large granite plug with which the entrance to the tomb underneath could be stopped-up. This tomb, again a chamber of rose granite and empty, provided a surprise, It is only 1.6 m. long and could not have accommodated an outstretched human body which, moreover, would have had to be introduced through a channel width of 80 cm by 40 cm. What, if anything, was buried in this chamber is a matter of conjecture, but it may possibly have contained the king's viscera.

All the buildings of the pyramid complex are constructed of local limestone, quarried nearby. The outer covering, however, consists of fine white limestone from Tura on the opposite bank of the Nile. The casing blocks of limestone not only had to be planed but also fitted very carefully, an impressive task considering that the surface to be treated in this manner amounted to about 70,000 square metres. Much of this ancient glory has been restored in the last few decades by C. M. Firth, J. E. Quibell and, above all, by J.-P. Lauer who, on behalf of the Egyptian Department of Antiquities have investigated and reconstructed much of the Step Pyramid complex of Zoser.

It has been known for many years, mainly through aerial photography, that another walled enclosure, similar in size to Zoser's, lay buried under the sand close to the Step Pyramid. In 1951 the Antiquities Service entrusted their Curator at Saqqara, Zakaria Ghoneim, with the excavation of this area. His work not only established the existence of an enclosure wall of the panelled pattern but also the remains of a step pyramid in its centre. Not only stone robbers but also later builders of the Pyramid Age seem to have made heavy inroads into these structures. On the other hand, Egyptologists have tended to overestimate the damage that has been done to massive monuments by depredations of this kind. A simple numerical estimate shows that it is quite impossible to steal a whole pyramid in order to re-use its stones. For a pyramid such as that discovered by Ghoneim, it would mean the removal of more than half a million tons of stone. Unless another big structure for which these stones could have been used is found nearby, theft becomes an unconvincing explanation, and it is more likely that the pyramid was never finished.

Fig. 11

This is certainly true in the present case. When the pyramid site was cleared of sand, a structure, 120 m. square but only 7 m. high, was discovered. It seems, in fact, unlikely that the pyramid was ever raised to a very much greater height. On the other hand, the unfinished state of the building allows much insight into its design and method of construction. There is no sign of a central mastaba and the whole building was laid out

Plate 12

from the beginning as a step pyramid with concentric buttress walls, similar to the later phases of Zoser's monument. The fact that even in this early state of erection all the buttress walls are present, shows that pyramids were built up from the outset by gradually raising the level of the whole structure at the same time and not by a successive accretion of buttress walls. In other words, during construction the site must always have presented the aspect of a truncated pyramid with a level top. The excavators also found large building ramps leading to the working area. The size of its foundation suggests that a pyramid of probably seven steps, rising to a height of roughly 70 m., was intended. The substructure differs from that of Zoser's by the absence of a shaft. Instead, the tomb chamber, which lies about 30 m. deep under the centre of the pyramid, is carved out of the rock. Access is by a sloping tunnel with the entrance north of the pyramid.

From jar sealings found in the substructure, Ghoneim determined the name of the pharaoh as Sekhemket, who was evidently Zoser's successor and may be identical with a king called Zoser-teti to whom the Abydos hieroglyphic king-list allots a reign of six years. There was no sign of a portcullis block which was meant to be lowered into the tunnel by a vertical shaft but Ghoneim found the tunnel blocked with ancient masonry which appeared undisturbed. When this was removed,

Plate 11

the roughly worked tomb chamber was found to contain a sarcophagus of unusual design. It consists of a single hollow block of alabaster, which instead of a lid has an opening at one end. This aperture was closed with a sliding door, also of alabaster, and sealed with cement that was unbroken. The excitement was great when in May 1954 this trap door was raised, only to give way to disappointment, since the sarcophagus turned out to be completely empty.

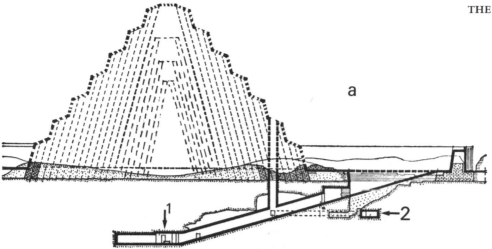

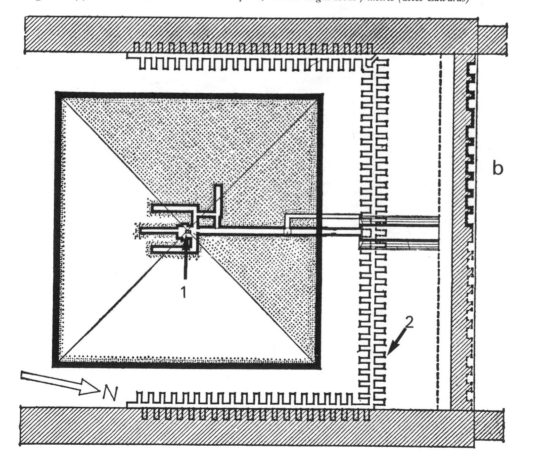

11 Section (a) and plan (b) of the unfinished pyramid of Sekhemket at Saqqara. The broken lines in (a) indicate the probable design of the planned structure. The tomb chamber (1), containing the sealed but empty alabaster sarcophagus (pl. 11), was excavated from the living rock, as were also the large magazines (2). The base was about 120 metres square, and the height about 7 metres (after Edwards)

Fig. 11

From the tomb chamber led a number of passages, also unfinished and empty, but a small quantity of gold jewellery was found in the entrance passage. Halfway along the sloping tunnel, a passage leads to a long U-shaped gallery into which open 132 small storerooms. Some of these contained stone vases.

Fig. 12

A third step pyramid was found in 1840 by Lepsius 20 miles further north at Zawiyet el Aryan. The site was first excavated in 1900 by Barsanti for the Antiquities Department and again ten years later by Reisner on behalf of the Boston Museum of Fine Arts. This pyramid, the construction of which was evidently abandoned at an early stage, resembles in almost every respect that of Sekhemket. However, it is smaller, measuring only 83 m. square. The builders had excavated in the rock the entrance passage, storerooms and tomb chamber, but the latter contained no sarcophagus. Evidence from surrounding mastaba tombs suggests that the pyramid belonged to a king named Khaba in the Abydos list, who succeeded Sekhemket and who also occupied the throne for only six years.

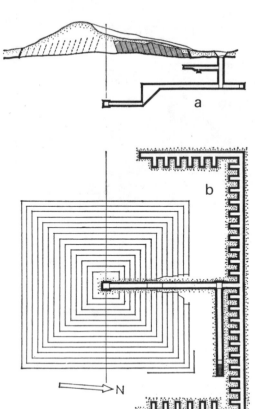

12 Section (a) and plan (b) of the unfinished pyramid of Khaba at Zawiyet el Aryan. The underground tomb chamber was found empty. The base is approximately 83 metres square (after Edwards)

Not much attention has been paid to the location of the individual pyramids. The pyramids of Zoser and his successor, Sekhemket, at Saqqara need no explanation; they were erected in the immediate vicinity of the capital Memphis and adorned its western skyline. The same can hardly be said of Khaba's monument which is 20 miles north, and certainly not of the site of the next pyramid, at Meidum, almost 40 miles upstream from Memphis. It is generally assumed that each pyramid was built in the neighbourhood of the pharaoh's palace so that he could supervise and watch with pleasure the growth of his eternal house. This may, indeed, be so. On the other hand, it should be remembered that at the building site of any large pyramid there was a permanent labour force of five to ten thousand stone masons and a seasonal one of 50,000 or more unskilled workers whose normal metabolism must have posed sanitary problems. It is, in fact, interesting that no further large pyramids were built at Memphis but that they were all erected well away from the capital.

Map

The next pyramid, at Meidum, is larger than Zoser's pyramid and it now presents the aspect of an immense square tower, rising out of huge mounds of rubble. It is the only pyramid which is heavily ruined and Flinders Petrie, who first investigated it, ascribed the devastation to stone robbers. It is this pyramid which provides the clue to the whole problem to be discussed later in this book. Here we will merely state that it underwent three consecutive building stages which were brilliantly analysed by the German Egyptologist Borchardt. The first stage was a step pyramid, similar to Zoser's, of probably seven steps, rising to a height of about 60 m. Over this was then superimposed a second step pyramid, with possibly eight tiers, which may have brought it to 80 m. in height. Each of these stages must, for a time, have been intended as final since their external walls consist of dressed and planed Tura lime-stone. In a third building phase the whole structure was covered with a smooth mantle which was meant to transform the edifice into the first true pyramid. Excavation of the rubble at the foot of the building has revealed the lower part of this mantle which is still in existence. It has an angle of elevation of $52°$ which recurs in almost all later pyramids.

Plates III, IV, VI

Fig. 16

In several important respects, the Meidum pyramid differs from its predecessors. The tomb chamber is not located at the bottom of a shaft but at the base of the pyramid itself and access to it is by a low and narrow passage passing through the body of the pyramid at an angle of $28°$ pointing, like a telescope, to the celestial pole. It is significant that this feature was already embodied in the first building phase and well before the shape of the monument was turned into a true pyramid. The small tomb chamber has a corbelled roof to withstand the pressure of the

Fig. 18

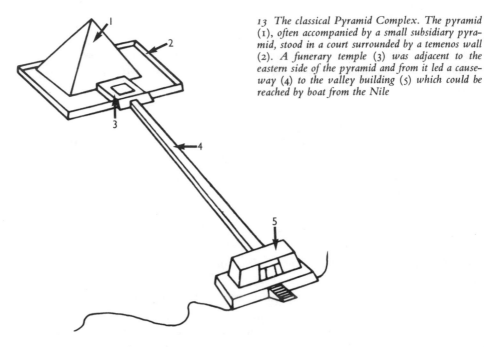

13 *The classical Pyramid Complex. The pyramid (1), often accompanied by a small subsidiary pyramid, stood in a court surrounded by a temenos wall (2). A funerary temple (3) was adjacent to the eastern side of the pyramid and from it led a causeway (4) to the valley building (5) which could be reached by boat from the Nile*

Plate 20

Fig. 13

Plate 24

superincumbent weight. It contained no sarcophagus. The surrounding wall, too, differs from the previous pattern, being much smaller and not enclosing any courts. Within it, and close to the main building, stands a now much ruined, small subsidiary pyramid. Attached to the east side of the pyramid is a small mortuary temple and from it a long causeway leads to the Nile. At its lower end stood a valley building which has now sunk into the silt. It permitted access to the pyramid complex by boat, at least during the inundation season. This pattern of an entrance passage directed towards the pole, a small enclosure and a mortuary temple with causeway to the river, was repeated in all the subsequent great pyramids. They also share with the Meidum structure a very accurate alignment according to the cardinal points.

The drastic change of the monument's shape and the equally novel conception underlying the layout and character of the whole pyramid complex indicate some profound alteration in the beliefs concerning the pharaoh's afterlife. To what extent these changes reflect some new religious and political role played by the king we can only guess at. Dr I. E. S. Edwards of the British Museum, one of the greatest authorities on the Egyptian pyramids, has suggested that the shape of the monuments may be connected with the striking spectacle produced by the rays of the sun when, after one of the rare rainstorms it breaks through the clouds, forming a huge celestial pyramid. Indeed, this phenomenon may be the origin of the *ben–ben*, the sacred conical pillar venerated in the Sun Temple at Heliopolis. The change also seems to have coincided with the ascendency of the priests of Heliopolis as a major political force in Egypt. Their domination over the power of the pharaoh had certainly become fully established in the Fifth Dynasty. Already in the Fourth Dynasty the dead king was regarded as the companion of the sun god whom he accompanied on his daily journey across the sky. Equally, the pharaoh's connection with the never setting circumpolar stars was emphasized by the direction of the entrance passage which linked them with his tomb chamber.

No other great pyramid was ever built at Meidum and the next two stone pyramids are at Dahshur, several miles south of Saqqara. It is now known that the southern one was built first. Covering an area of 190 m. square, it is a good deal larger than either the pyramids of Zoser or the one at Meidum, and it presents a curious aspect. The lower part rises at an elevation of about 54°, but when the building had reached a third of its intended height, the angle was lowered to $43\frac{1}{2}°$. This rhomboidal shape, which has earned the monument the name of the 'Bent Pyramid', reduces the originally envisaged height of about 135 m. to only 101 m. In more than one respect, the shape of the Bent Pyramid forms an essential part of our quest for the purpose of pyramid-building and we must therefore leave its explanation for the time being.

Plate V

Plate 26

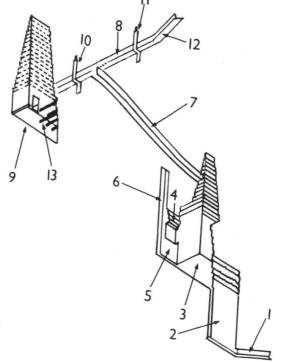

14 *Isometric section, showing the chambers and passages of the Bent Pyramid. From the polar entrance passage (not shown) a horizontal corridor (1) leads to a narrow and high entrance hall (2) which connects directly with the lower chamber (3). Two passages (4 and 5) lead to a blind vertical shaft (6). From the upper part of the lower chamber a curved and rising passage (7) leads to a horizontal corridor (8) which opens at one end into the upper chamber (9). The other end of this corridor, which is interrupted by two portcullises (10 and 11), turns into the western entrance passage (12). The upper chamber, whose roof like that of the entrance hall (2) has remained unfinished, contains a number of horizontal cedarwood beams (13), which are also shown in pl. 25. See also Fig. 8.*

Fig. 14

Much of the Bent Pyramid's interior was already described by Perring, but a great deal of further work has been done in recent years by Ahmed Fakhry. His investigations on behalf of the Antiquities Service have yielded a number of valuable new discoveries. An entrance passage, pointing to the pole star, leads to two internal chambers with corbel roofs, connected by a curious system of corridors and portcullises which suggests that either of the chambers could be closed forever while the other still remained unoccupied. Moreover, in addition to the polar passage which leads into the lower chamber, a second one connects the upper chamber with an aperture high up in the western face of the pyramid. No explanation has ever been offered for this unique feature but one may wonder whether it is not similar to the two tombs of Zoser; one under the pyramid with a north-pointing entrance, while that in the south mastaba points westward. No sarcophagus was found in either chamber of the Bent Pyramid but the upper one contains five horizontal cedarwood beams which are still in good condition. The bulk of the pyramid is an impressive advance on the earlier ones; three and a half million tons of stone, compared with one million at Saqqara and one and a half million at Meidum.

Plate 25

Like the Meidum pyramid, the Bent Pyramid has a small mortuary temple at its eastern face. A causeway leads to the valley building which has been excavated by Fakhry and which he found adorned with relief friezes of great beauty. They are of women offering-bearers representing the various nomes.

Plate 30

The next pyramid that was built stands less than a mile north of the Bent Pyramid. Its height is roughly the same as the latter but it was erected entirely at an angle of $43\frac{1}{2}°$, the same as the upper part of the Bent Pyramid. This means, of course, that the area it covers, 220 m. square, and its mass somewhat exceed that of the Bent Pyramid. It is the earliest monument which has been preserved in a complete pyramidical form, but owing to the low angle of elevation it looks rather squat and less impressive than its better-known successors at Giza. Its rather gentle slope made it more accessible to stone robbers and almost all the limestone casing has disappeared, giving it a deeper colour than its southern neighbour, which has earned it the name of the 'Red Pyramid'. It has been given less attention by archaeologists than any other pyramid, and any subsidiary buildings which may exist, and its causeway, lie still buried under the desert sand.

On the other hand its interior structure is well-known, having first been described by Perring. Later Flinders Petrie gave up his intention of exploring it when, crawling into the entrance passage, he found signs of a wild animal's lair inside, and wisely withdrew. However, it was eventually entered again and cleared by Fakhry in 1947. The entrance passage, again pointing to the celestial pole, leads to three successive chambers, the third and largest of which is 9½ m. long and just over 4 m. wide. All three chambers have corbelled roofs, that of the largest having a height of 15 m. As in the lower chamber of the Bent Pyramid the roofing blocks are carefully dressed and planed.

Plate 29

The reason why we have not given the kings' names to the last three pyramids is that their ownership has been much in doubt in the past, and even at present it is far from clear. The Abydos list ends the Third Dynasty with a pharaoh named Huni, of whom nothing is known except that he is supposed to have been on the throne for twenty-four years – a good deal longer than his predecessors Sekhemket or Khaba. The following pharaoh, Snofru, is listed as the founder of the next, the Fourth, Dynasty. Under this new dynasty, which also comprises such well-known names as Cheops, Chephren and Mycerinus, all the great stone pyramids were built. With its eventual decline also comes the end of the Pyramid Age proper. In view of the fact that the succession had always to go through a woman, the family history of the Fourth, or any other, Egyptian dynasty is, by our own patrilineal standards, a somewhat tangled affair. It is further complicated through the aspirations of sons by secondary queens and concubines to secure the crown for themselves. Reisner and Smith, as well as others, have gone to some lengths in trying to establish a genealogical table for this period. After more than 4000 years it is, of course, impossible to ferret out all the secrets of large and complex royal harems, particularly as the same girls' names may appear in successive generations. In spite of all these uncertainties we think it justified to present a chart of the Fourth Dynasty, since it may help the reader to understand the relation in which the pyramid–builders stood to each other.

Plate 47

Table 2

Huni may have been the builder of the Meidum pyramid, or at least of its earlier stepped form. However, his name has not been found anywhere in it. On the other hand, later *graffiti* in the Meidum pyramid's mortuary temple ascribe it clearly to Snofru. Moreover, a number of Snofru's courtiers were buried at Meidum. An inscription found near the Red Pyramid mentions 'the two pyramids of Snofru' and it was at first assumed that the other Snofru pyramid must be that at Meidum. More recent work at the Bent Pyramid has, however, shown that this one, too, definitely belonged to Snofru. We are therefore left with what Sir Alan Gardiner called the 'unpalatable conclusion that Snofru did possess three pyramids'. All the Fourth Dynasty pyramids are distinguished by a polar entrance passage, and if we want to invoke Huni as the builder of the early phase at Meidum, we are faced with the additional difficulty that this feature was already embodied in the first stepped structure. Whichever way we look at the problem we cannot get away from the fact that for this period there exist more large pyramids than pharaohs who could have been buried in them.

The start of a new dynasty was, as can be seen from the genealogical table, evidently due to the fact that Snofru was not the son of Huni's great queen. However, he clearly legitimized his claim to the throne by marrying the great queen's daughter, Hetepheres. On her tomb furniture, which was discovered by Reisner, she is described as 'daughter of the god' and 'mother of the king'. This king was Khufu, who is better known today by Herodotus' Grecianized appellation of Cheops. Khufu's right to the throne was clearly established by his marriage to his sister, Merytyetes, who was the vehicle of the royal blood and who carried the succession. He built the largest of all pyramids at Giza, 20 miles north of Memphis.

Plate IX

Plate 48

Plate 49

Plates XI, 32

The most striking feature of Khufu's monument, when compared with its predecessor, the Red Pyramid of Dahshur, is a return to an elevation of 52°. It also covers an even greater area of 230 m. square and comprises roughly $6\frac{1}{2}$ million tons of limestone. Rising to a height of almost 150 m. it impresses by its towering simplicity, and has always been regarded as the foremost of the Seven Wonders of the World. We will not, at this stage, estimate the work required in building it nor deal with the method of construction, which will have to be discussed later. However, we must mention here two interesting peculiarities, one concerned with the geometrical shape of the monument and the other with the unique disposition of its internal features.

A pyramid with an angle of elevation of 52° – 51°52′ to be precise – has the unique geometrical property that its height stands in the same ratio to its circumference as the radius to the circumference of a circle. This ratio is $1/2\pi$, where π is a transcendental number 3.141 . . . Khufu's pyramid is the most carefully built of all and accurate measurement of its foundation has shown that this ratio is correctly represented to better than one part in a thousand. This certainly is far too accurate to be dismissed as a coincidence, and a great number of theories, often involving divine inspiration, have been based on this astonishing numerical fact. A relatively simple solution, to which we shall return in the next chapter, provides something of an anticlimax and relieves us of the necessity to regard the great pyramid as an immense monument in stone, representing the revelation of a basic mathematical truth.

Fig. 8

It appears that the arrangement of passages and tomb chambers of Khufu's pyramid underwent three successive changes. The usual polar entrance passage in the north face of the building first runs through the masonry and then continues into the rock beneath the pyramid. Under the

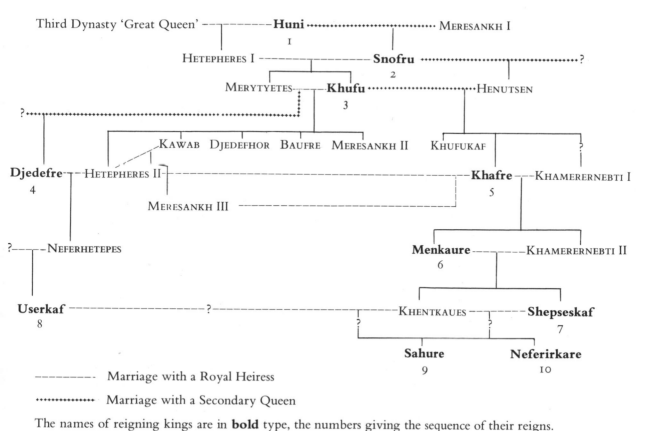

Third Dynasty 'Great Queen' -- -- -- -- -- **Huni** ·············· MERESANKH I
                                        I

HETEPHERES I -- -- -- -- -- -- **Snofru** ················· ?
                                      2

MERYTYETES -- -- **Khufu** ············· HENUTSEN
                          3

KAWAB DJEDEFHOR BAUFRE MERESANKH II   KHUFUKAF   ?

Djedefre -- HETEPHERES II -- -- -- -- -- -- -- -- **Khafre** -- KHAMERERNEBTI I
    4   5

MERESANKH III -- -- -- -- -- -- -- --

? -- -- NEFERHETEPES   **Menkaure** -- -- -- KHAMERERNEBTI II
                                            6

Userkaf -- -- -- -- -- -- -- ? -- -- -- -- -- -- KHENTKAUES -- -- **Shepseskaf**
    8   ?   ?   7

                                        Sahure   **Neferirkare**
                                           9   10

-- -- -- -- -- Marriage with a Royal Heiress

············· Marriage with a Secondary Queen

The names of reigning kings are in **bold** type, the numbers giving the sequence of their reigns.

Table 2 *Tentative genealogical table of the Fourth Dynasty*

apex, the passage ends in a chamber hewn out of the rock, whose irregular
shape and rough finish show that it was abandoned before completion.
Instead, the original descending passage was interrupted about 20 m.
from the entrance and a corridor ascending at the same angle was driven
through the existing masonry of the pyramid. After about 40 m. the
ascending corridor levels off into a horizontal passage, leading to a second
tomb chamber, again under the apex, and about 30 m. above the base of
the building. This room, without any justification called the 'Queen's
chamber', also gives the impression of being unfinished and was possibly
never used. Then the ascending passage was continued beyond the
levelling-off point, but in a much enlarged form. It now turns into an
ascending gallery of polished limestone, 47 m. long and nearly 9 m. high.
Its walls are slightly corbelled and each of the roofing slabs is held
separately by notches in the walls. This impressive high passage, usually
called the Grand Gallery, was for a long time believed to have served

Fig. 27

ritualistic purposes until it was discovered by Flinders Petrie that its real object was to serve as a store for a series of large limestone blocks. These blocks, when the tomb chamber was to be sealed, were let down into the ascending passage where, in fact, three of them are still in position.

The tomb chamber at the upper end of the Grand Gallery was further protected by three portcullises which were removed by intruders. The room itself, nowadays known as the 'King's chamber', is a room of 10.5 m. by 5.3 m.; it is 5.8 m. high and completely lined with granite. It contains an unadorned, lidless, rectangular sarcophagus which must have been placed in position while the pyramid was still building since it is too large to pass through the entrance passage. The roof of the King's chamber is made of flat granite slabs and protected from the superincumbent weight of masonry by five relieving spaces. When the tomb chamber was first entered is not known since the roof slab in the descending passage, which concealed the ascending one, only fell when the Caliph Ma'mun's men tunnelled into the pyramid in the ninth century A D. The contemporary Arabic account is, unfortunately, too fanciful to provide useful information.

Khufu's pyramid is surrounded by neat rows of mastabas and three small pyramids in which his relatives and high officials were buried. It is mainly from these burials that Reisner reconstructed the family history of the Fourth Dynasty. Also around the pyramid are located a number of boat pits which had all been robbed. Great excitement was therefore caused when in 1954 clearance of the sand at the south side of the pyramid led to the discovery of a row of 41 large limestone slabs, each almost five metres long. When they were lifted they disclosed the dismantled parts of the large ship, already mentioned in the last chapter. Preservation and reconstruction of the vessel, which had one or two cabins, is still in progress.

The next pyramid on the Giza plateau is that of Khafre, whom Herodotus calls Chephren. However, Khafre was not Khufu's immediate successor. Possibly dissension broke out in the royal family after Khufu's death; his true successor should have been his eldest son, Kawab, who, for this purpose, had already been married to the royal heiress Hetepheres II. Since Kawab was only buried in a mastaba, we may assume that his death preceded that of his father, and a prince named Djedefre ascended the throne. Djedefre was the son of Khufu by a secondary queen, and was married to a woman called Kenteten-ka, who was perhaps Queen Henutsen's daughter. Djedefre must certainly be considered an usurper since at Khufu's death a number of the latter's sons by the royal spouse Merytyetes were still alive. Nevertheless, Djedefre attempted to legalize his kingship by marrying Kawab's widow, Hetepheres II, because she was the woman in that generation who carried the succession.

Plate 37

Plates XI, 32, 35

Plate 52

Plate 50

Plate 55

Whether or not the true royal princes, Djedefhor and Baufre, died, as has sometimes been suggested, a violent death is not certain. In any case, Djedefre was evidently loyal to his father since his name was found on one of the roof slabs of Khufu's boat pit. It may, however, be significant that Djedefre shunned the Giza necropolis and instead began building a pyramid five miles further north at Abu Roash. He chose a curiously desolate spot on a steep rock, more than 150 m. above the Nile valley. To overcome the difficulty of access an immense building ramp, a mile long, and in places rising to 12 m. above the surrounding terrain, was constructed. Whether the pyramid itself was ever finished is not known since it has been used extensively as a quarry down to modern times. Its ground plan indicates a relatively modest size of 97 m. square, smaller even than Zoser's Step Pyramid. The present superstructure is only 12 m. high and the construction of the tomb chamber at the bottom of a wide shaft seems to be the return of a pattern used in the Third Dynasty. Altogether, the site suggests some form of break with the traditions of the Fourth Dynasty. If such a break took place it was of short duration. Djedefre ruled for only eight years and the crown then passed on to another of Khufu's sons: Khafre.

In the choice of his pyramid site and in the magnificence of his monument, Khafre closely followed Khufu's example, which strengthens the impression that Djedefre's tenure of the throne was regarded as an unfortunate interlude. Khafre was probably the son of Khufu's secondary queen, Henutsen, and was married to his sister, Khamerernebti I. However, his legitimate succession was ensured when he later married not only the widow of Khufu's original crown prince, Kawab, and of Djedefre, the heiress Hetepheres II, but also her daughter. This lady, Meresankh III, *Plate 50* as well as her mother, were now the first in line to confer the crown of Egypt on their husband.

Khafre's pyramid at Giza stands close to Khufu's and in size is almost its twin. Its height of 140 m. is almost the same and it appears, in fact, to *Plates XI, 32* surpass it by virtue of having been erected on slightly higher ground. Moreover, while Khufu's pyramid has been completely stripped of its casing of white Tura limestone, this has remained intact at the upper part of Khafre's monument. The pyramid measures 216 m. square, which means that its angle of elevation is slightly steeper, $52°20'$, and it therefore does not share with the great pyramid the accurate representation of the ratio $1/2\pi$. As at Djedefre's pyramid, the lowest layer of casing blocks consists of granite.

Altogether Khafre's pyramid is not quite so carefully constructed, as is apparent from the variation in size of its building blocks. On the other hand, its mortuary temple at the east face is more impressive and the

Plate 38

Plate 52

Plate I

Fig. 8

Plate 40

Plate 39

valley building at the bottom of the causeway is the most magnificent structure that has come down to us from the Old Kingdom. It is a very massive building of large limestone blocks, completely faced inside and out with polished red granite. The central hall is T-shaped and its roof is supported by sixteen unadorned square granite pillars. It has an alabaster floor. Mariette, who excavated the valley building in 1853, found in it the exquisite diorite statue of the pharaoh, now one of the greatest treasures of the Cairo Museum. Another, immense, portrait of Khafre is the head of the Sphinx which, even today, after having served as a target for Turkish artillery practice, clearly bears the pharaoh's features. The representation of a lion's body with a human head seems to have been an established type even earlier, and Khafre's architects made use of a knoll of rock for the same purpose on a gigantic scale.

Compared with Khufu's pyramid, the internal structure of Khafre's is of extreme simplicity. There is again a polar entrance passage which eventually leads to a simple tomb chamber at the base of the structure and under its apex. The only complication is provided by a second entrance, emerging a little further north under the pavement outside the pyramid, but soon joining the main corridor. When Belzoni entered the tomb chamber in 1818 he found a beautiful granite sarcophagus set into the floor, with the broken lid lying beside it. It clearly had been rifled in ancient times and contained no body. The roof of the tomb chamber consists of gabled limestone blocks, similar to the construction employed in the Queen's chamber and entrance passage of Khufu's pyramid.

Since the existence of upper corridors and chambers in Khufu's pyramid was only discovered by the accidental fall of a ceiling block in the entrance passage, a similar pattern could be suspected in Khafre's monument. It was a question to which there seemed to be no answer, except by extensive and destructive tunnelling. However, the problem was solved in a most ingenious manner by taking an X-ray picture of the building. The scheme was undertaken at the initiative and under the direction of Professor Luis Alvarez, a Nobel Laureate of the University of California, in 1970, using cosmic rays. This radiation, whose origin is unknown, impinges upon the earth at equal strength from all directions of outer space. It is the most penetrating radiation ever discovered and it can pass through the huge mass of limestone of a pyramid, although in doing so its intensity is diminished. Just as the absorption of ordinary X-rays by different types of body tissues will provide us with information on our bones and internal organs, the cosmic rays, recorded in the central tomb chamber of a pyramid will furnish a shadow picture of the body of the building. Any hidden chamber, being a void in the masonry, must then show up as a 'negative' shadow. The actual experiment and its evaluation is a very complex operation, requiring a large team of workers and highly sophisticated equipment. However, the result turned out to be negative, showing conclusively that no upper chamber exists in the Khafre pyramid.

The third great pyramid on the Giza plateau is that of Menkaure, whom Herodotus called Mycerinus, and who was the son of Khafre. Compared with the gigantic twins of Khufu and Khafre the monument is a miserable runt. With a base of 108 m. square and a height of 70 m., it contains less than one-tenth of the limestone built into each of the two great pyramids. Moreover, it marks the end of the true Pyramid Age. The one remaining pharaoh of the Fourth Dynasty built a quite different type of tomb at Saqqara and the pyramids of the next dynasty are small and very shoddy in comparison with the immense monuments erected by the kings of the Fourth Dynasty.

Plate XII

Apart from its much smaller size Menkaure's pyramid does not differ in essential design from its predecessors. The angle of elevation is the same and there is also an entrance passage pointing at the celestial north pole. The three tomb chambers are excavated in the rock under the apex of the pyramid. A blind passage from the uppermost one has been generally interpreted as indicating a change in the building plan. When in 1837 Colonel Howard Vyse entered the second chamber he found a basalt sarcophagus, a wooden coffin lid and a mummy. The latter two are now in the British Museum. The sarcophagus is unfortunately not available for examination since it now rests at the bottom of the Mediterranean. Drawings made before it was shipped show an outer design similar to an archaic palace façade, and it is assumed to have held the body of Menkaure. The coffin lid bearing Menkaure's name, however, is of the Late Period and the mummy radio-carbon dated to the early Christian era.

Fig. 8

Plate 41

The sixteen lowest courses of the casing of the pyramid are of pink granite but some of these blocks have remained undressed, indicating that the building was finished in haste. Such casing blocks of the higher courses, which were not taken away by stone robbers, show that the top was covered with Tura limestone. The hurried completion of the whole complex is also apparent in the large mortuary and valley temples, constructed of enormous limestone blocks, which were finished with the use of crude bricks and other inferior materials. An inscription found by Reisner in the mortuary temple, and another one recently discovered near the pyramid entrance, leave no doubt that the monument as a whole was completed by Menkaure's son, Shepseskaf.

Plates XII, 36

Reisner assumed that Menkaure was the son of Khamerernebti I who then, in order to assure her son's succession, must have been a sister of Khafre. On the other hand his mother may have been the twice-widowed

Hetepheres II, or even her daughter Mersankh III, both being of the royal blood. While speculation on this question depends on the relative ages of the pharaoh and these two queens, we know for certain that Hetepheres II outlived Menkaure.

Plates 53, 54

Menkaure was married to his sister Khamerernebti II and the magnificent double statue discovered by Reisner in the valley temple leaves no doubt as to the close facial resemblance of the royal couple. The figure of the queen is famous for the masterly treatment of the female form, and the position of her right arm, encircling the waist of her husband, is usually regarded as a gesture of wifely affection. However, it is more likely that the pose of the queen, with her left hand on the king's arm, is one of deep ritual significance. As heiress of the royal blood she appears to protect and present her brother, on whom she has conferred the kingship by marriage. The base and back of the statue were left unfinished and this is further evidence for the haste attending the completion of the last of Egypt's great pyramids.

Plate 56

Apart from all other evidence, the alabaster head of Shepseskaf in the Boston Museum shows by sheer family resemblance that he was the son of Menkaure and Khamerernebti II. He was the last pharaoh of the Fourth Dynasty and possibly married to his sister, Khentkaues. However, Shepseskaf broke with the Fourth Dynasty tradition and, instead of erecting a pyramid, built for himself a sepulchre at Saqqara, to which the

Fig. 29

Arabs gave the name of Mastabat Fara'un. It has the shape of a large sarcophagus, but is not nearly as imposing as a pyramid. The base is only 100 m. long and 72 m. wide, with a total height of about 20 m. The burial chambers are reached by a polar passage and there was a modest mortuary temple at the east with a causeway to an unexcavated valley temple.

Another similar, but rather smaller, tomb was built for Queen Khentkaues between the causeways of the Khafre and Menkaure pyramids at Giza. It seems that she carried her half of the royal blood into the Fifth Dynasty, since in her tomb she is described as 'mother of two kings' but there is no mention of the father who sired them. Khentkaues was venerated throughout the Fifth Dynasty as its founder, and it is clear that the father may not have been Shepseskaf.

With Menkaure a period in the history of Egypt and, we would suggest, a significant era in our civilization, had drawn to a close. Within less than a century the four largest pyramids had been built, employing something like 100,000 people, quarrying, shaping and moving over 20 million tons of stone. Nobody knows why the Pyramid Age came to this sudden end from one reign to the next. However, before we can speculate on the reasons for the end of an era we first have to find out how, and why, this era ever came into being.

3 The Unsolved Problems

Excavation, accurate measurement and their correlation with inscriptions have provided a large body of information about the pyramids, the gist of which has been recorded in the previous chapter. Nevertheless, the number of questions that have been answered is matched by at least as many new questions which have arisen from this research. The great antiquity of the pyramids has taught us to be very careful about the evidence which the archaeologist's spade is turning up. The pyramids are separated from our own time by almost 5000 years and a lot has happened to them during this interval. Much of the vital evidence has been destroyed or irretrievably lost, but equally dangerous is, as we shall presently see, the extraneous evidence which has been added.

Again and again we have had to use the words 'robbed in antiquity'; in fact, it appears that all the great pyramids had already been entered and despoiled almost a thousand years before Tutankhamun was laid in his tomb. The solid confidence in the eternity of divine power which the pharaohs of the Fourth Dynasty expressed in their gigantic pyramids did not outlast them for more than three centuries. Towards the end of the Sixth Dynasty one king, Pepi II, reigned for no less than ninety years. It seems that during the last decades of his long life corruption and regionalism gained the upper hand in an already decadent administration. After Pepi's death the woman of the royal blood, Nitokerti – Queen Nitocris of Herodotus' history – had herself proclaimed pharaoh in the hope of saving the dynasty. However, she failed in her efforts and the different lists now mention a host of kings who may have reigned for very short times and probably simultaneously. The historical record becomes hopelessly blurred as the country entered into what the Egyptologists call 'the First Intermediate Period'. It lasted for about two centuries and evidently was a time of internecine warfare and general civil disorder. In spite of Manetho's list of four dynasties covering this interim period, it is fairly certain that no central authority operated during this time.

The contemporary account of one Ipu-wer, preserved in a Middle Kingdom papyrus at Leiden, is a long list of lament, revealing a state of turmoil and revolt. 'All is ruin,' he said, 'A man kills his brother. Blood is everywhere. A few lawless men have ventured to despoil the land of the kingdom. The laws of the judgment hall are cast forth. Officials are slain and their records are taken away. The secrets of the kings of Upper and Lower Egypt are divulged. What the pyramid concealed has become empty and the palace is destroyed'.

When the pharaohs of the Fourth Dynasty secured their tomb chambers with blind passages and portcullises, they felt that their mummies and their treasures had been well guarded against the thief who might sneak in at night, and even against an armed band of robbers who would overpower the watchman. They evidently had not envisaged any long period of lawlessness during which local chiefs had leisure to mount sustained and large-scale operations against the royal sepulchres. During this Intermediate Period not only the pyramids but practically all the tombs of the princes, the high officials and the rich were rifled. Moreover, it seems that knowledge of the secret location of the tomb chambers had, in many cases, been preserved. When after several unsuccessful attempts Petrie and Wainwright found the tomb chamber hidden in the bulk of an immense mastaba – No. 17 – at Meidum, they discovered that it never had an entrance. It had been completely sealed after the burial and the mastaba had then been built up above it. Nevertheless, the tomb had been robbed and, as Wainwright noticed, the thieves must have known exactly where the burial chamber was located since they had tunnelled straight for it by the shortest possible route.

Plate 13

After Wainwright and Petrie had explored the tomb, they closed it again and filled in the shaft that they had dug into the mastaba. The only way in now is to crawl through the narrow tunnel which the thieves had bored into the mud brick of the structure. It cannot be recommended to anyone suffering from claustrophobia, and the crumbling dry mud is an unpleasant reminder that the tunnel may fall in. It was the only place into which our Bedouin guides did not accompany us. However, the visit was well worthwhile. Through a small hole one enters the T-shaped tomb chamber of smoothly dressed limestone which bears no inscription. In it stands an immense sarcophagus of pink granite with its lid swivelled aside, as the tomb robbers left it 4000 years ago. It is the earliest granite sarcophagus ever discovered and its completely unadorned bulk is deeply impressive.

Plate 14

Plate 15

It is significant that here, as in other tombs of the period, after the sarcophagus had been opened the body of the occupant was thrown on the floor where the archaeologists found it. The thieves had only been after his treasure. It is interesting to note that the bodies recovered from these early tombs were not mummies in the generally accepted sense.

The art of embalming, that is, of preserving the human body as a whole, as practised in later times, had evidently not yet been perfected in the Fourth Dynasty. Instead, the skeleton was defleshed and the bones reassembled with linen bandages soaked in resin. Wadding was put into the body cavity and by the use of more bandages the figure of the dead was faithfully reconstructed. Two fingers, which were missing from the Meidum skeleton, had been carefully replaced by rolled-up linen. The effigy of the dead person, built up around his skeleton, was re-created to such detail as the male sex organs and the breasts and nipples of the women. Again there is a parallel with West African custom where the corpse of the king was defleshed and then articulated with gold wire.

The systematic robbing of the pyramids and of all rich tombs, lasting for two centuries, has deprived us of practically all the evidence connected with the burial of the kings and their families. We do not, of course, know whether somewhere under the desert sand of Saqqara or Giza some undisturbed tomb still awaits discovery. The trouble is that, unlike the carefully hidden rock burials of the New Kingdom, the Old Kingdom tombs, and particularly the pyramids, were built to be conspicuous. However, there are exceptions. When in 1925 Reisner cleared the sand around Khufu's pyramid he came across a number of paving stones which had been concealed with plaster. They turned out to cover the mouth of a shaft, 32 m. deep and entirely filled with stones. At its bottom *Plate 35* the American archaeologists found a tomb chamber with the alabaster sarcophagus and tomb furniture of Queen Hetepheres I, the mother of Khufu and wife of Snofru, the woman who had carried the royal blood from the Third into the Fourth Dynasty. The magnificent gilded tomb furniture was carefully restored by the expedition members and stands *Plate IX* today in the Cairo Museum, with a replica set in the Boston Museum of Fine Arts.

In the tomb was also found an alabaster canopic chest containing the viscera that had been removed from the Queen's corpse. The sarcophagus, however, was empty. Reisner suggested that this was a reburial after the Queen's tomb at Dahshur had been rifled and that her body was stolen, the latter fact having been concealed from Khufu. When, 45 years after Reisner's explanation, I asked a surviving member of the team, Dows Dunham, whether he still believed in it, he was hesitant, saying that it was the best story they could think of at the time. However, Dunham pointed out to me the important fact that the inside of the sarcophagus showed brown stains which he took to indicate that it may once have contained a body. In any case, the shaft tomb of Hetepheres is so far the only royal burial, even if it was merely a reburial, which has survived intact from the Old Kingdom.

Figs. 11, 12

Thirty years after Reisner's find another discovery of undisturbed Old Kingdom relics was made close by. These are the two huge boat pits, adjacent to the Great Pyramid, of which only one has been opened. It contained the complete parts of a large ship which was found in the same state as when Djedefre buried it there after Khufu's death four and a half thousand years ago. These two discoveries of untouched subterranean cavities in the rock at Giza show that the sand of the pyramid area may still hold surprises. While cosmic ray investigation has shown that the bulk of the Khafre pyramid contains no hidden chamber, we know nothing, as Emery once pointed out to me, about possible chambers *below* the pyramids. It is, indeed, a curious fact that large subterranean galleries and magazines have been found only under the first three step pyramids, of which they formed an important feature. No such underground stores have been discovered at the Meidum structure which originally, too, was a step pyramid, or at any of the subsequent pyramids. Access to the step pyramid stores was from the entrance passages and, as we have pointed out, the entrance to the Meidum pyramid deviated from the earlier pattern, even in its original stepped form. In fact the whole pyramid complex at Meidum differs from the large enclosures of the Third Dynasty, indicating a conceptual change in the structure of the royal tomb which came in with the Fourth Dynasty. We do not, of course, know whether from then onward the dead pharaoh could dispense with the thousands of stone vessels that were formerly buried with him in his stores. On the other hand it is not inconceivable that such subterranean galleries also exist under the later pyramids but that they had separate and well-concealed entrances which have as yet not been found.

Fig. 8

Although the existence of the ascending passage in Khufu's pyramid was revealed only when the Caliph Ma'mun's battering rams caused the concealing roof slab to fall, the robbers of the Intermediate Period would have known of another access to the King's chamber. They seem to have made use of it 3000 years before the Caliph. In order to allow the escape of the workmen who had originally sealed the ascending passage from within, a narrow shaft had been constructed which connects the bottom of the Grand Gallery with the unused subterranean tomb chamber. The men who left last then allowed a prepared block of limestone to drop into its place so as to cover the entrance to the shaft from the Grand Gallery. Probably the shaft as well as the underground chamber were subsequently filled with masonry. The block concealing the top of the shaft is now missing and one might suspect that the ancient thieves removed the masonry and then ascended through the shaft into the sealed interior.

While the marauders in the long period of unrest plundered the tomb chambers of the pyramids and of the Old Kingdom mastabas very thoroughly they appear to have done little damage to the structure of the monuments. Their object was to unearth the buried treasure and, as the example of mastaba 17 at Meidum showed, they knew where to look and how to get there by the shortest route. Otherwise, the fabric of the pyramids was evidently of little interest to them.

Things unfortunately changed for the worse after order was restored throughout the country by a series of Theban princes, who, for a span of about 500 years, again held undisputed rule over the two kingdoms. This period of Egyptian history is called the 'Middle Kingdom' and the pharaohs of this era were powerful monarchs who, understandably, were bent on erecting impressive tombs. At first they governed the country from Thebes which thus for the first time became the capital of Egypt. There they also constructed their tombs, and one of these, that of Mentu-hotep I, embodied a small pyramid as its central feature. After about 200 years of Theban rule the next dynasty, the Eleventh, returned to the north, establishing a new administrative capital a few miles south of Memphis. Influenced by the pyramids of the Old Kingdom in their close proximity, they decided to provide themselves also with pyramid tombs. However, they evidently did not command the strong labour force needed for large-scale quarrying which their early predecessors had at their disposal and therefore they began to re-employ the masonry of the Old Kingdom tombs.

The pharaoh Amenemhat I, in particular, showed a superb disregard for the monuments of the past, and he used stonework, much of it with relief sculpture, from the earlier tombs. It has been seriously suggested by Egyptologists that it might be worthwhile to dismantle completely Amenemhat's pyramid at Lisht, which already is much ruined, in order to recover the Old Kingdom sculpture which it contains.

Stone robbery from ancient monuments continued for many centuries throughout the New Kingdom and archaeologists have singled out the great Pharaoh, Rameses II, as one of the main perpetrators. Even so it seems that the Giza pyramids were not seriously damaged when in the fourth century BC they were described by Herodotus. He refers to an inscription on the surface of the Khufu pyramid which shows that the outer limestone casing was then still in existence. It seems certain that this casing was eventually removed by the Muslims who used the well-polished outer blocks to build the large mosques and the city wall of Cairo.

Herodotus gives a quite fantastic description of the interior of Khufu's pyramid, referring to a subterranean lake under the building with an island in it on which the pharaoh was buried. This indicates that the pyramid, which certainly had been entered during the First Intermediate Period, had been closed up again. Moreover, the original entrance must still have been well concealed and all knowledge of its existence had evidently been lost when in the ninth century AD the Caliph Ma'mun drove his tunnel into the building in order to discover the tomb chamber and its hidden treasure.

The final closing of the pyramids which had been pillaged in ancient times probably took place during the latest period of Egyptian independence under the Saïte dynasty which ruled the country in the seventh and sixth centuries BC. Whereas we have had to deal so far with the destruction of evidence by treasure seekers and stone robbers we now have to discuss an entirely different aspect: the fabrication of misleading evidence. In spite of the neglect and wanton destruction of the Old Kingdom edifices in later times the pyramids retained their aura of sanctity and, with the passage of the centuries, veneration of the Old Kingdom returned. It became a mark of distinction and an insurance for a man's afterlife to be buried in or near the ancient tombs. The earlier of these 'intrusive' burials, to use an archaeological term, bear so clearly the stamp of their own age that they can easily be recognized for what they are. However, more difficult problems for the archaeologists were created by the pharaohs of the last Egyptian dynasties.

Towards the end of the pharaonic empire the priests of Amun at Thebes gained an ever-increasing political power which, in keeping with the ancient matrilineal tradition, was exercised in the name of a royal princess who held the title 'wife of the god'. She was never the pharaoh's wife but the spouse of Amun and her succession was ensured by adoption of further royal princesses. Thus the pharaoh now held power in a less direct manner – not as husband of the 'great wife' but as father of his daughter. The central power had slipped from the hands of the king into those of the priests who, in order to maintain it, began to employ foreign mercenaries. These, however, were no match for any powerful aggressor, such as the Assyrians who overran Egypt without much difficulty at about 650 BC. The Assyrians' victory was of short duration because they, in turn, had to defend themselves against Media.

As the Assyrians' power in Egypt crumbled, the man whom they had installed to govern the country on their behalf turned against them. He was Psammetichus who declared himself pharaoh and legitimized his position by having his eldest daughter, another Nitokerti, adopted as 'wife of the god'. Enthroned at his capital of Saïs, Psammetichus and his successors in the Twenty-Sixth Dynasty tried to restore the splendour of the ancient traditions, and the Old Kingdom of 2000 years before their time became their model. Their sculpture and architecture imitated that of the early dynasties so closely that at first Egyptologists were frequently misled. It seems that the Saïtes also cleared the pyramids and resealed them after having buried their own dead there. When in 1837 Perring discovered sixty mummies in a large gallery under the Step Pyramid at Saqqara he took them naturally to be the dead retainers of Zoser. Only later was it discovered that not only did the mummies belong to the Late Period but that the gallery itself had been newly excavated by the Saïtes.

Recently both the wooden coffin lid, inscribed with the name of Menkaure, and the mummy found in the pyramid were recognized as late substitutions. Some doubts have therefore arisen about the authenticity of Menkaure's basalt sarcophagus, which unfortunately had been lost at sea. The existing drawing of it does not make it appear impossible that this sarcophagus too was a Saïte production, despite the fact that it reproduces the 'palace façade' decoration.

Plate 41

Summarizing all these facts and taking into account early pillage and late restoration, it becomes clear that the evidence presented by the pyramids today is often confusing and, to some extent, perplexing. The complexity is further increased by the existence of the small subsidiary pyramids which were attached to each big pyramid, dating from that at Meidum onward. The interior chambers of some of these are too small to have served for the burial of a human body, and it has been suggested that they may have been the repositories of the canopic jars, holding the pharaoh's viscera. In that case this 'ritual' pyramid should be regarded as an integral part of the standard pyramid complex, together with the mortuary temple, causeway and valley building.

The matter, however, becomes more complicated by the fact that the pyramid complexes of Khufu and Menkaure each contain three of these small pyramids. A pointer concerning their occupants is given by Herodotus. According to the priests from whom he obtained his information, the pharaoh, Khufu, wishing to raise funds for the building of his pyramid, induced his daughter to sell her charms. The lady, who wished to erect a memorial to her filial devotion, asked each man to give her one stone, and she was eventually buried in the small pyramid collected in this manner. Quite apart from the fact that Herodotus could have rejected this preposterous story on numerical grounds – the pyramid contains at least 20,000 stones – it is hardly in keeping with the position of a royal princess of the Fourth Dynasty. However, even the most unlikely legends usually contain a grain of truth and it seems probable that some, at least of these subsidiary pyramids were the tombs of the 'great queens'. Indeed, according to a late stela, the southernmost of Khufu's small pyramids was built for Queen Henutsen, one of Khufu's wives and the mother of Khafre. The details about all these subsidiary pyramids are best given in tabulated form.

Table 3

Table of subsidiary pyramids

Main Pyramid	Number of subsidiary pyramids	Remarks
MEIDUM	I	Too small for burial.
BENT PYRAMID	I	Too small for burial.
RED PYRAMID	—	Undiscovered.
KHUFU	3	*Southern*, built presumably for Queen Henutsen; empty. *Central*, burial chamber empty. *Northern*, burial chamber empty.
KHAFRE	I	Entrance too small to enter.
MENKAURE	3	*Eastern*, burial chamber with red granite sarcophagus; empty, built possibly for Queen Khamerernebti II. *Central*, burial chamber with small granite sarcophagus; containing skeleton of young woman. *Western*, burial chamber empty.

One of the problems that has exercised the minds of many people is the significance of the angle of elevation of the pyramids. Most of them rise at an angle of about $52°$; only the Red Pyramid and the upper part of the Bent Pyramid, both at Dahshur, are built at the same lower angle of $43\frac{1}{2}°$. We have mentioned that for the Khufu pyramid the angle ($51°52'$) leads to the ratio $1/2\pi$ with an accuracy that cannot comfortably be dismissed as fortuitous and has given rise to strange esoteric speculations which are mentioned in the Appendix to this book. Since this geometric relation was first noticed, more than a century ago, a number of very careful triangulations of the Giza plateau have been carried out. From each of these measurements the ratio $1/2\pi$ emerged with increased accuracy. Since it is known that more than a thousand years after Khufu the Egyptians still did not know the ratio of circumference to diameter of a circle to a greater accuracy than 3, the accurate use of the factor $1/2\pi$ in pyramid construction remained somewhat uncanny. A great number of mathematical explanations have been suggested and even one, made by a noted archaeologist, that the builders by accident used a ratio of $14/11$, remains lamentably unconvincing. In spite of brilliant constructional skill and superb workmanship, we have no evidence that the Egyptians of the Old Kingdom had more than the most rudimentary command of mathematics. Any acceptable solution must therefore have a practical, rather than a theoretical, basis, and that suggested to me by an electronics engineer, T. E. Connolly, fulfils this condition.

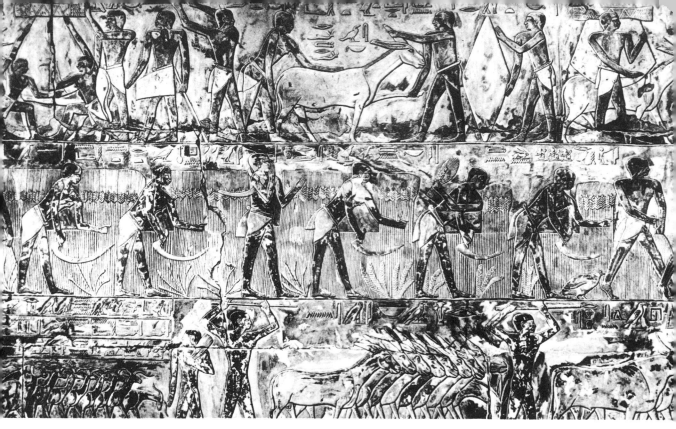

1, 2 The Egyptians believed that the afterlife was a continuation of their existence on earth. They endeavoured to make sure of it by entombing with the dead the possessions which he had enjoyed in his daily life. In his mastaba at Saqqara (*above*) the vizier Mereruka was surrounded by workers reaping corn and tending the herds on his estate. Dancers and muscians (*below*) accompanied the nobleman Khai on his last journey.

3 A relief in the mastaba of the high official Tiy (*left*) shows the owner in his boat as he watches the cook catching fish for his table and other servants hunting hippopotami. The thicket on the shore is teeming with fowl and wild animals.

4 Figures of domestic servants, too, were placed in the tombs of the rich (*see also* Plate X). The woman (*below*) is shown grinding corn for the household.

5   The earliest known statue of a pharaoh is that of Kha-sekhem (*left*) of the Second Dynasty wearing the crown of Upper Egypt. At the base are shown the contorted corpses of his defeated enemies.

6   Remains of the outer wall (*below*) of the Saqqara tomb of the pharaoh Uadji of the Second Dynasty. It shows the recessed panelling of the period and clay bull-heads, carrying natural horns, on the podium of the edifice.

7–10 Details of Zoser's Step Pyramid complex at Saqqara (*see also* Plate II and Figs. 9 and 10). The arrow (*left*) points to the smoothly dressed wall of the original mastaba, revealed by the ruin of the south-east corner of the pyramid. The roof of the tomb chamber (*below*), at the bottom of the central shaft, has a granite stopper closing its entrance. The temenos wall (*opposite above*) surrounding the complex is entirely composed of fortress-like buttresses built of dressed limestone. It has a total length of 1·7 kilometres and was originally 10 metres high. The building overlooking it is the mysterious South Tomb. Adjoining the Step Pyramid on its north side is the *serdab* (*opposite below*) seen here from above, with the seated statue of Zoser.

11, 12   A sealed but empty alabaster sarcophagus (*left*) was found in the tomb chamber of Sekhemket's pyramid. The unfinished state of the building (*below*) shows the arrangement of inclined buttress walls (*see also* Plate 42 and Figs. 9, 11, 20, 21 and 25).

13-15   The large mastaba 17 (*above*) at Meidum never had an entrance passage since it was built over a sealed burial chamber. The only access to it is through a narrow tunnel (*below left*) dug by tomb robbers who opened the large granite sarcophagus (*below right*) by swivelling the heavy lid to one side.

16 Part of the famous painted frieze of geese found in the mastaba of the princess Atet at Meidum.

17 The reconstructed carrying chair of Queen Hetepheres I, Great Wife of Snofru and mother of Khufu, found in her tomb at Giza (*see also* Plate IX).

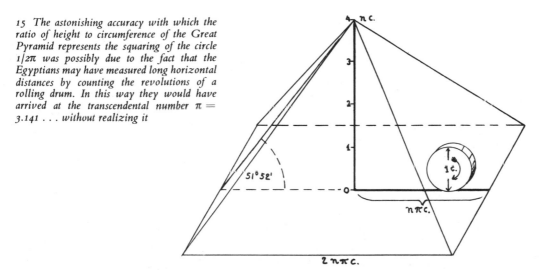

The explanation is based on the assumption that the ancient Egyptians had not yet formed the concept of isotropic three-dimensional space. In other words, whereas to us measures of height and vertical distance are the same thing, namely a length for which we use the same unit, this may not have been regarded as natural by the pyramid builders. They used as height measure the royal cubit, based on the upward distance from elbow to fingertips, which in the Old Kingdom had already been standardized to a length of 52 centimetres. Since ropes of palm fibre tend to stretch, a much more accurate way of measuring long horizontal distances as, for instance, the base of a large pyramid, was required. One such method is to roll a drum and count the number of revolutions. The royal cubit, already used for height measurement, would immediately suggest itself as the standard diameter of the drum, and one revolution – we may call it a 'rolled cubit' – corresponds to the circumference of the drum stretched out horizontally.

Fig. 15

It appears that, using this system of measurement, the Egyptian architects never did anything more sophisticated than to build pyramids according to the simple gradients of $4:1$ and $3:1$. Taking the former first, the height of the pyramid will be $4 \times n$ cubits, where n is the number chosen to determine its size. The horizontal distance from the centre of the building to its side will then have to be $1 \times n$ rolled cubits or, in our mathematical terms, $n\pi$ cubits. Since this distance is half the side length of the pyramid, the latter's circumference comes to $8 \times n\pi$ cubits. Therefore, the ratio of height to circumference is $4 \times n/8 \times n\pi$ cubits or, by dividing this fraction by $4 \times n$ cubits, simply $1/2\pi$. This is the mysterious ratio used in pyramid construction and which, at the same time, leads inevitably to an angle of elevation of $51°52'$. In other words, the pyramid builders discovered the transcendental number π (3.141 . . .) without trying and without knowing. The explanation is made even more likely by the fact that using in this way the lower gradient 3:1 instead of 4:1, the angle of elevation comes out correctly as $43\frac{1}{2}°$.

Having disposed of the idea that the Egyptians of more than 4000 years ago revealed in building pyramids an enigmatic command of advanced mathematics, we can return to the generally accepted interpretation that the pyramids were pharaonic tombs. However, while the funerary function of the pyramids cannot be doubted, it is rather more difficult to prove that the pharaohs were ever buried inside them. Although it is known that the pyramids were all entered and robbed in the First Intermediate Period this leaves a disturbing number of unexplained features. In particular, there are too many empty sarcophagi and, what is worse, rather too many empty tomb chambers, to make the idea of actual burials unchallengeable. It is worthwhile to assemble the existing evidence in tabulated form:

Table 4

Pyramid	Number of chambers	Sarcophagi	Remarks
ZOSER	2	Burial pits	Empty except for one foot.
SEKHEMKET	I	I	Sealed but empty.
KHABA	I	—	
MEIDUM	I	—	
BENT	2	—	
RED	3	—	
KHUFU	3	I	Lidless, empty.
DJEDEFRE	I	—	
KHAFRE	I	I	Empty.
MENKAURE	3	I	Sarcophagus lost at sea.

Leaving out Zoser's Step Pyramid, with its unique burial chambers, the nine remaining pyramids contain no more than three authentic sarcophagi. These are distributed over no fewer than fourteen tomb chambers. Petrie has shown that the lidless sarcophagus in the Khufu pyramid had been put into the King's chamber before the latter was roofed over since it is too large to pass through the entrance passage. The sealed but empty sarcophagus of Sekhemket also was evidently brought in before the pyramid was finished. Even if we assume that the pyramids of Khaba and of Djedefre were left unfinished at an early stage, we still have to account for the disappearance of at least four, and possibly as many as eight, sarcophagi. The magnificent and large granite sarcophagus in mastaba 17 at Meidum shows that even at this early age substantial and heavy sarcophagi were customary, and this is borne out by the sarcophagi in Khufu's and Khafre's pyramids. One would like to know what has happened to the missing sarcophagi. The robbers might have smashed their lids but they would hardly have taken the trouble of stealing a smashed sarcophagus. In spite of careful search no chips of broken sarcophagi have been found in any of the pyramid passages or chambers. Moreover, it has to be remembered that from the Meidum pyramid onward the entrance was well above ground level. At the Bent Pyramid even the lower corridor is located 12 m. above the base and bringing a heavy sarcophagus in or out would have necessitated the use of a substantial ramp. At Khufu's pyramid the sarcophagus had been, as we have seen, put in the tomb chamber while the monument was still under construction, and the pyramids of Khafre and Menkaure were both provided with entrances at the base, in addition to the polar passage.

The fact that the sarcophagi in the Khufu and Khafre pyramids were found empty is easily explained as the work of intruders, but the empty sarcophagi of Sekhemket, Queen Hetepheres, and a third one in a shaft under the Step Pyramid, pose a more difficult problem. They were all left undisturbed since early antiquity. As these were burials without a corpse, we are almost driven to the conclusion that something other than a human body may have been ritually entombed.

We have already referred to the fact that Snofru seems to have had two, or even three, large pyramids, and he can hardly have been buried in all of them. This brings us back to the awkward problem of multiple tombs which we encountered when discussing the royal burials of the first two dynasties in Chapter I. There we came across the existence of two tombs for many of the early pharaohs with the added possibility of a third which may have sunk into the silt of the Delta. It was for this reason that, when first introducing the pyramids, we referred to them as 'funerary monuments' rather than as 'tombs'. If some of the royal tombs, including the pyramids, were not the burial places of the body but cenotaphs, it should be noted that nevertheless they *all* had tomb chambers. The question arises as to who or what was interred in them.

Most Egyptologists agree that some of the dead person's spiritual attributes, such as the *ba* and the *ka*, were closely connected with his eternal house. The *ka*, in particular, was thought to dwell in the tomb, which it could enter or leave by a false door, the closed-up replica of a real entrance. Mastaba tombs usually contain a *ka* chamber with a statue of the dead occupant. It is also clear that the statuary found in the valley buildings of the pyramids was not meant to be seen and did not serve the same purpose as a present-day monument. These royal statues, which were often combined with those of gods, or the royal spouse, all in an attitude of protecting the dead pharaoh, had purely ritual significance. They were to be animated by his *ka*, for which the pyramid may have been primarily built.

Turning again to West Africa, we find burials of the soul in proper graves whenever the person has died far away from his home. Since in a hot, humid climate the corpse tends to decompose rapidly, it has to be buried forthwith and cannot be transported. However, the corpse's hair and fingernails are cut off and sent for burial to his home. Since these features often show some growth after death they are believed to be associated with the spirit of the dead person which is reluctant to leave the body. It is not impossible that some sort of token burial played a part in the funerary arrangements of ancient Egypt.

Even if we concede that the bodies of the pharaohs have long since disappeared, the riddle of the missing sarcophagi remains. They may, of course, not only exist but even be well-known. Who, we may ask, for instance, was the unnamed man buried in the large mastaba 17 at Meidum?

Plate III   His tomb stands in a prominent position in front of the pyramid which was still being built when he was laid to rest in a completely sealed tomb. He had been buried in the large granite sarcophagus which has remained undamaged in his tomb chamber to this day. It would be tempting to think that he may be the pharaoh whose pyramid – without a sarcophagus in it – rose behind his tomb, as the abode of his soul.

Thoughts like these could be dismissed as idle speculation but for a stela found by Petrie at Abydos. It records a reply of the pharaoh Ahmose, founder of the Eighteenth Dynasty to his wife, Queen Ahmose-Nefertari. The passage is important enough to be quoted verbatim in translation:

His sister spoke and answered him: 'Why have these things been recalled? What has come into thy heart?' The King's own person said to her: 'I have recalled the mother of my mother and the mother of my father, king's great wife and king's mother, Tetisheri, deceased. A tomb chamber and a sepulchre of hers are at this moment upon the soil of the Theban and Abydene nomes, but I have said this to thee because My Majesty has wished to make for her a pyramid and a chapel in the Sacred Land close to the monument of My Majesty' . . . His Majesty spoke thus, and these things were accomplished at once.

We are thus faced with the contemporary statement of a New Kingdom pyramid builder that Queen Tetisheri, consort of the pharaoh Senakhtenre Tao, already possessed two tombs, in one of which she must have been buried, when a pyramid was built for her as well. For once we have the words of the pharaoh himself to state the facts.

While very few people will dispute that the pyramids had some connection with the afterlife of the pharaoh, the general statement that the pharaohs were buried in them is by no means indisputable. The complexity of the evidence before us does not, unfortunately, permit such a simple categorical statement. Quite possibly each pyramid once housed the body of a pharaoh, but there also exists, as we have seen in this chapter, an unpleasantly large number of factors that speak against it. It is on the basis of these complexities and contradictions that Egyptologists had to try and find a solution to the most difficult problem of all: why were these immense pyramids built in the first place?

When the Step Pyramid at Saqqara was erected, pharaohs who were rulers of Upper and Lower Egypt had been buried, evidently to the satisfaction of all concerned, in palatial tombs. These, however, had demanded only a small fraction of the labour required for Zoser's funerary complex. The true unification of the country can be cited as a good reason, but then it was in a way a false dawn as the next two pyramids were never finished. Later, with the enigmatic change of plan at Meidum, pyramid building truly got into its stride and in the space of just about one century almost 25 million tons of limestone were quarried, dressed, moved and piled up into man-made mountains. Then, within one generation, this fantastic activity was brought to an end. Pyramids were still provided for the pharaohs for another thousand years, but they were small and soon became cheap and shoddy. They were well within the ordinary budget of the country. The short spell of what appears to us as the magnificent madness of the Fourth Dynasty was never repeated.

Plates 42–44

Egyptologists have looked in vain for a convincing solution of this riddle in a change of religious belief. Such changes did, in fact, take place, but they cannot explain the employment of up to a hundred thousand people for a century on what, on the face of it, is a useless expense of labour. The main difficulty which Egyptologists face is the re-creation of a state of mind of human society 5000 years ago. Our own approach, which was triggered off quite accidentally, deals with constructional mishaps and their causes. The conclusions are of a purely technological nature and it is due to this nature of our approach that we enjoy a peculiar advantage over the Egyptologist. Whereas in the last 5000 years man's spiritual world-picture and his moral laws have changed out of all recognition, the laws of physics have remained unaltered. The knowledge that these same laws were operative and had to be obeyed 5000 years ago in exactly the same way as today provides a reliable link between the pyramid builders and ourselves. We can follow their decisions, analyze their mistakes and recognize their corrections with absolute certainty. For the technologist a return to the mind of the Old Kingdom presents no difficulty. Whatever Imhotep's religious beliefs and spiritual motives may have been, his work was governed by the same laws of stability to which we are subject today. It is not that the scientist sees more than the Egyptologist – he merely sees different things. His conclusions do not supplant the Egyptologist's work but may complement and, one hopes, enrich it.

4 A Clue at Meidum

The crucial observation which eventually led us to understand the reason for pyramid building was made at Meidum. It was the realization that almost 5000 years ago a technological disaster of immense dimensions had overtaken the building and the thousands of people working on it. The site became deserted and was even shunned by those who meant to be buried there. They left their tombs unoccupied so as not to be associated in their afterlife with this place of ill omen. Meidum, the location which a pharaoh had selected for his eternal abode, remained desolate ever after.

By virtue of its size and its serene simplicity, the pyramid at Meidum can easily qualify for being the most impressive ruin in the world. It is also one of the oldest. Seen from the lush vegetation of the Nile valley it rises as an immense square tower of more than 40 metres on the top of what appears to be a hill on the western desert plateau. This is how the first European traveller who described it saw the monument. He was Captain Frederick Lewis Norden, F.R.S., who journeyed to the Sudan on orders of the King of Denmark, and he made three excellent sketches of the pyramid from a distance. They show the building in its ruined state, very much as we see it today, except that the rubble surrounding it seems to be a little, but not very much, higher. That was in 1737, and a little later in the same year another Fellow of the Royal Society, Edward Pococke, also made a note of seeing the Meidum pyramid. A famous orientalist, much interested in Arabic history, he recorded that the Arabs called the building 'el Haram el Kaddab', 'the false pyramid'. Pococke also saw the pyramid only from a distance.

Plates III, VI

The next visitor was W. G. Browne of Oriel College, Oxford, who in 1793 explored the actual site and, digging into the debris, found some casing stones of the pyramid. He concluded, correctly, that the tower was not standing on a natural hill, but that it was the rubble surrounding the building which gave this impression.

A few years later Denon, with other members of the scientific expedition accompanying Napoleon's army, came to Meidum, and some of his colleagues may have climbed the building. Denon made an excellent drawing which was published in the expedition's records. There is a curious discrepancy between this sketch and Denon's description, to which we will return later. Visits to the Meidum pyramid by a number of noted Egyptologists followed, among them Perring in 1837, Lepsius in 1843, and Mariette in 1871. The latter discovered close by the tomb the statues of Prince Rahotep and his wife, Nofret, as well as the famous 'panel of geese', now among the principal treasures of the Cairo Museum. Then in 1882 the Head of the Antiquities Services, Gaston Maspero, opened the pyramid but found it empty.

Plate 61
Plate 16

Perring's visit is of particular interest, since he not only provided an excellent sketch of the building but also investigated its base by sinking trial pits at the north-east corner and on its western side. From these he concluded that the base was that of a true pyramid, although he felt that, owing to the short time at his disposal, this suggestion had to remain tentative. He also mentioned that the huge amount of debris covered the whole base in an irregular fashion. Only the north-east corner of the pyramid was not covered with rubbish and from here stones had been removed. Perring, in fact, suggested that casing blocks from the pyramid had been used to build the bridge at Tahme.

It appears that on the previous day Perring had had ample opportunity to examine what was evidently the same bridge because his boat had fouled it. Fortunately a number of Arabs were at hand to free the craft but not, as Mr Perring was at pains to point out, until a suitable remuneration had been agreed upon. All this took time and it delayed his visit to Meidum by one day. It was a small, if irritating, incident which, however, was to acquire far-reaching importance. By innocently mentioning the pyramid masonry in the bridge at Tahme, Perring drew a red herring across the trail of all future investigation which was to deflect his successors from the obvious conclusion for well over a century.

More recently four explorations of the Meidum pyramid have been carried out, all of which have some bearing on my own observations. After a cursory visit to the site in 1883, Petrie returned in 1891 to undertake serious excavations. He cleared some of the debris from the east face and discovered the existence of a small mortuary temple at its centre. He also discovered the causeway but found that any valley building which may have existed had sunk deep into the mud. As for the pyramid itself, he realized that its present state revealed the three distinct building stages to which we have already referred. The first two of these were step pyramids – one of seven, and the next of probably eight steps. Finally, the second step pyramid was covered with an outer mantle of which only the lowest part surrounding the two lowest steps now remains. The next two steps, the third and fourth, have disappeared, leaving the core of the

Plates 20, 22

Fig. 16

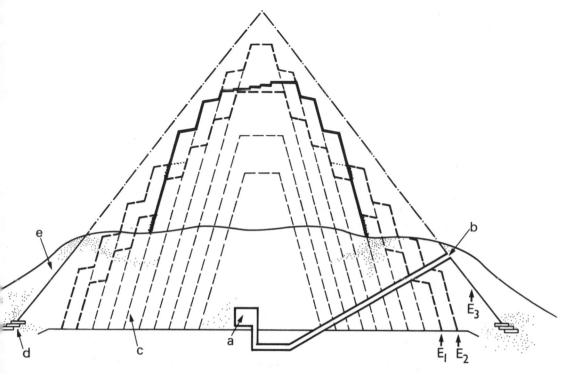

16 Schematic section of the Meidum Pyramid in the north-south direction. The first two phases of construction were step structures E_1 and E_2, built consecutively, on which finally a true pyramid E_3 was superimposed. The tomb chamber (a) is entered through a passage (b), pointing to the celestial North Pole. The building contains ten buttress walls (c) which stand on a rock foundation, whereas part of the outer pyramid mantle E_3 rests on sand (d). The lower part of the building is covered by debris (e) and the existing visible part is shown in heavy outline. The top of the steps was slightly sloping and not, as has generally been assumed, horizontal

fifth step standing, surmounted by the intact sixth step and remnants of the seventh. It is this freely rising core which gives the building its tower-like appearance. The remaining part of the outer mantle shows that the third building phase was to be a true pyramid, the first of its kind. Because the complexity of this heavily ruined structure tends to be somewhat confusing, we shall use the notation introduced later by Borchardt, which has since been generally accepted. He calls the first step pyramid E_1, the second step pyramid E_2, and the outer mantle of the true pyramid E_3.

In 1909 Petrie, accompanied by E. Mackay, G. A. Wainwright and others, returned to Meidum to carry out further work, which included clearing the mortuary temple completely and also the causeway. Within the peribolus wall they discovered the ruin of a small subsidiary pyramid to the south and a mastaba tomb to the north. Wainwright drove a tunnel under the whole pyramid and, when working inwards from underneath the base of the mantle (E_3), he found the foundations of ten successive buttress walls. His tunnel ended up in the rock near the tomb chamber, showing that the Meidum pyramid was not based on a mastaba such as at Zoser's monument. This is quite in keeping with discoveries at the Sekhemket and Khaba pyramids which were excavated after Wainwright's work. These two edifices were built as step pyramids right from the start and it is therefore not surprising that the Meidum pyramid followed the same constructional pattern. An interesting feature of Wainwright's excavation was the investigation of the outermost buttress wall of the second step pyramid (E_2), underlying the mantle of the true pyramid (E_3). He showed that this buttress wall was dressed down to ground level, indicating clearly that the second step pyramid (E_2) was intended as the final stage before the transformation of the monument into a true pyramid (E_3) was undertaken.

Fig. 18

Further proof that the two step pyramids (E_1 and E_2) were each for a time regarded as ultimate before the next phase was started is provided by Petrie's observations in the passage descending into the pyramid. The internal masonry lining of this corridor shows clear discontinuities at those places which correspond to the original entrances of the successive step pyramids E_1 and E_2. Beyond these the passage was subsequently continued outwards to the final entrance in the pyramid mantle (E_3). Altogether, the thorough work of Petrie and Wainwright at Meidum covered all essential features of the pyramid, leaving, as it turned out, comparatively little to the three following explorations.

The next exploration, carried out by Ludwig Borchardt in 1926, only lasted one day and a half. As Borchardt points out, even this was unnecessarily long since he found what he was looking for within the first thirty minutes. He had made two even shorter visits to the site before, one together with Reisner in 1897, and the second with Ricke – earlier in 1926. Borchardt had evidently evolved some very clear ideas about the structure of the Meidum pyramid in the thirty years separating his two visits, and all that now remained was to prove his theory correct. If Borchardt's exploration was short, the same cannot be said about his publication. There are 30,000 words of concise and detailed information, supported by many diagrams, setting out his theory, its proof and many other problems of pyramid construction, to which we shall return later. His report is a veritable mine of information.

Plate VI

Borchardt's main object was to explain the 'rough bands' which intersect vertically the otherwise smooth pyramid core. They had been regarded as possibly a decoration by Petrie and Wainwright who, however, had not much faith in their own explanation and admitted that they were at a loss for a sensible interpretation of this feature. Borchardt

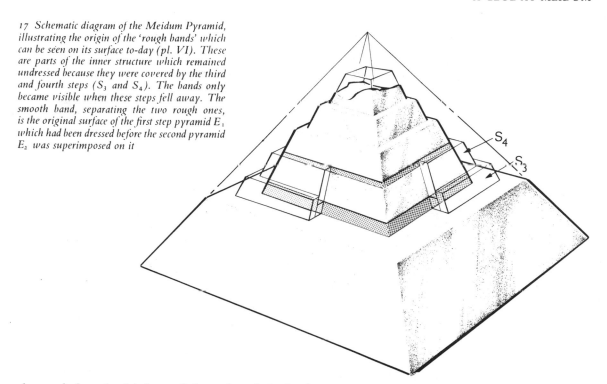

17 Schematic diagram of the Meidum Pyramid, illustrating the origin of the 'rough bands' which can be seen on its surface to-day (pl. VI). These are parts of the inner structure which remained undressed because they were covered by the third and fourth steps (S_3 and S_4). The bands only became visible when these steps fell away. The smooth band, separating the two rough ones, is the original surface of the first step pyramid E_1 which had been dressed before the second pyramid E_2 was superimposed on it

showed that the higher of these bands is, in fact, part of the second step pyramid (E_2) which had been laid on top of the steps of E_1. In other words, when the original step pyramid (E_1) was extended to larger dimensions, the height of the new steps did not coincide with the old ones; the latter had first been raised by about 4 m. each. The reason for this change is simple. At the first step pyramid (E_1) the entrance of the passage had been located at the level of the first step. With the enlarged version, i.e., the second step pyramid (E_2), this entrance would have emerged 4 m. above this step level. In order to bring the entrance up to the level of the first step of E_2, this step and all others had to be raised. However, there was no need to dress the outside of these heightened steps of E_1 since their surface would be covered by the steps of the new E_2. Only when the third and fourth steps of E_2 were eventually removed did these undressed parts of the buttress walls become visible as 'rough bands'. There can be little doubt that Borchardt's explanation is correct but it tells us nothing about the reason why steps three and four disappeared.

Figs. 16–18

The third exploration of the Meidum pyramid was undertaken by Alan Rowe, who had worked with Reisner, on behalf of the Pennsylvania University Museum. The excavations were carried out in the winter 1929/30 and part of the results were reported promptly in the Museum's Journal in 1931. Unfortunately the rest of the work has still to be published,

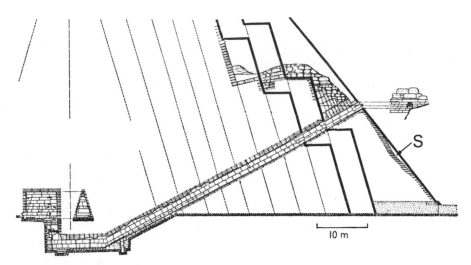

18 Part of the north–south section of the Meidum Pyramid given by Rowe, showing the tomb chamber and the entrance passage. The subsidence (s) of the exposed part of the outer pyramid mantle should be noted

after more than forty years. Inside the pyramid Rowe went over much the same ground as his predecessors, only discovering a short blind shaft near the bottom of the passage and two slight changes in its slope, amounting altogether to less than 3°. By far the most important of the published results concern excavations in and near the mortuary temple which we shall discuss later in this chapter.

The fourth exploration of the site is part of a very much larger work by V. Maragioglio and C. Rinaldi of the Turin Museum. Their survey, which has now reached the seventh double volume, does not deal with any special problem but is designed to cover all the Memphite pyramids. Their stated aim is to collect and critically review all data about these monuments, a task which also includes the production of detailed and exact diagrams. Such additional information of interest to us which they have given on the Meidum pyramid will presently be discussed.

It is most astonishing that none of these four detailed investigations made any comment on the cause of the unusual shape of the Meidum ruin, which is so completely different in its aspect from any of the other six large pyramids. It seems that Perring's mention of the stones robbed for building the bridge at Tahme had done its work as an explanation. Petrie picked it up again and said that the pyramid had become the quarry of the neighbourhood; nobody was buried without a tombstone stolen from the pyramid. He mentioned cart-tracks and even Arabs carrying away stones on little donkeys. Borchardt faithfully followed this lead and he, as well as Petrie, noted the disappearance of stones seen on earlier visits. Comparing Borchardt's photographs covering an interval of thirty years, a serious loss to the archaeologist is noticeable but this loss is minimal when compared with the bulk of the pyramid. However, his ire against the local fellahin was roused and he darkly hinted at the nefarious intentions of a few whom he found standing on the top of the rubbish heaps. On being asked what they were doing there, they replied that they were supervising their fields. This was probably quite true since the hill provides an ideal vantage point for spotting stray animals. Nevertheless, Borchardt comments with somewhat heavy Teutonic sarcasm: 'I did not see their stone mallets.'

We have mentioned earlier that its immense bulk makes it virtually impossible to steal a pyramid. In fact, the impossibility of such an undertaking has been proved by a direct experiment. The Arab historian, Abd al Latif, reported that during his own lifetime, in AD 1215, the Caliph Malek al Azis Othman gave orders to destroy the pyramids and with a large force of labourers, collected from all over the country, set to work on the Menkaure pyramid. They had to give up after eight months of hard and continuous work and with very little success. Al Latif said: 'Considering the vast masses that have been taken away, it might be supposed that the building would have been completely destroyed, but so immense is the pile that the stones are scarcely missed. Only on one of its sides can be noticed any trace of the impression which it was attempted to be made.'

Plate XII

The fairly simple geometry of the Meidum ruin permits a good estimate of the lost quantity of stone. It amounts to about 250,000 tons, and that is a lot of limestone to cart away with little donkeys. Even if this huge quantity had been stolen for some building purpose it had to appear conspicuously elsewhere. Unlike the much smaller loss of stone from the great pyramids at Giza, to be re-employed for the large mosques and the city wall of Cairo, there never existed a sizable town near Meidum for which this immense quantity of building material could have been used.

As a matter of fact, those 250,000 tons of limestone never left the Meidum site at all. They lie heaped up in the huge accumulation of debris *Plates III, IV, 22* which is so large that the early travellers mistook it for a natural hill. Walking on little paths, as I did, up and down these hillocks, it was only after seeing, more than two years later, pictures of the slipped mine tip at Aberfan that I realized what had happened at Meidum. The pyramid had collapsed!

At this point our story of scientific detection really starts. The unusual appearance of the Meidum ruin, so different from the other great pyramids, had now found an explanation, but this was only the beginning. There is all the world of difference between saying that the pyramid debris looks like a landslide and proving it really was one. From now on it becomes a search for evidence that a disaster really took place. We must now find out why, how and when this catastrophe occurred. Did the disaster affect the design of later pyramids and, if so, in what way?

Before discussing the reasons for the catastrophe, its nature and the time of its occurrence, it is worthwhile proving that stone robbery cannot have played any essential part in it at all. A look at the other great pyramids shows that the pattern of stone robbery is quite consistent. First of all, it has to be noted that the robbers were interested only in the smoothed casing blocks of fine Tura limestone. Even at Giza, the robbers never touched the beautifully squared building blocks backing the casing stones, although they were easily accessible at ground level. Even at the corners

Plate 31

of the Great Pyramid, where these blocks could simply have been pulled away without any danger of stone falls, they have remained in their original position. The planed casing stones, on the other hand, were removed even from the very top of the pyramids. It evidently was not the already quarried stone which attracted the robbers but the smooth surface finish and the superior material of the outer casing.

The method of robbing these casing stones also followed a definite pattern. Ease of access and the avoidance of stone falls were the guiding principles, as is shown by the way in which stones were taken from the

Plate 26

Bent and Khafre pyramids. The attack started at the base and the corners of the building and continued inwards and upwards across the faces. If the Meidum pyramid had been ruined by stone robbers, they would also have attacked it in the same manner. This, however, was not the case.

When Browne saw the pyramid in 1793, the outer mantle was completely covered with debris and only by his exploration was the pyramid character of the base revealed. He removed the rubble from two of the corners and there discovered the existence of the outer casing which he found completely intact. He stated that 'The stones and cement may be observed to the very bottom.' Until then the local fellahin evidently knew nothing about this hidden treasure of building material, but it seems that Browne's discovery encouraged them to extract some of these readily available casing stones. They evidently used them for the bridge at Tahme and, as Petrie points out, as gravestones. Neither use can have contributed much to the loss of 250,000 tons. In fact, when Petrie surveyed the Meidum pyramid a century after Browne had shown the local inhabitants where to quarry, the pillage was still not at all significant. Only small inroads of 7 to 10 m. had been made at three corners while the south-east corner remained buried under the debris. Petrie excavated it and found it completely untouched.

Apart from the four corners, there are only two small areas where the pyramid mantle (E_3) has been laid bare. The rest of its surface remains buried under the debris. In 1909 Petrie and Wainwright, when freeing the small mortuary temple adjoining the eastern face of the pyramid, cleared the centre of this face down to the foundation level. They found the exposed casing perfectly intact and there was no sign of any attempt to remove casing blocks. A smaller clearance, not going down to foundation level, was made by Maspero in 1881 when he opened the entrance of the descending passage located in the north face about 20 m. above the base and just below the present level of the debris. This free surface of E_3 also shows the original casing in position.

Plate 20

None of these findings admit any suggestion that the mantle of the Meidum pyramid had ever been attacked by stone robbers before it became covered with large quantities of debris. In fact, the supposition that the pyramid owes its heavily ruined state to the activity of stone robbers can be confidently rejected. The evidence further shows that whatever calamity overtook the building occurred while the outer casing was still undamaged. It is also evident that the collapse of the pyramid was not a gradual one. The nature and the distribution of the debris leave no doubt that a sudden disaster took place in which the masonry was thoroughly broken up, cascading down from a great height. The angle of repose of the rubble and the considerable distance to which the fragments had travelled show that they came down with great speed, indicating a high kinetic energy. This fact precludes a slow disintegration of the edifice and points to an instantaneous catastrophe which must have ruined the structure in a matter of a few minutes. Having arrived at this conclusion, our next task must be to estimate when in the history of the Meidum pyramid this sudden destruction occurred.

Plates 22, 23

For a number of reasons we must assume that it took place before the third building phase, the transformation of a stepped monument (E_2) into a true pyramid (E_3), was completed. Evidence – especially Wainwright's investigation obtained by tunnelling under the structure – makes it clear that two successive building phases, resulting in the step pyramids E_1 and E_2, had each been meant to represent the final form of the monument. This is also shown by the well-planed surfaces of these two step pyramids and by the discontinuities in the passage, corresponding to the original entrances of E_1 and E_2. The latter even shows grooves for metal bars to hold the final casing stone by which the step pyramid was to be closed.

Fig. 18

Another indication that the collapse took place before the pyramid was finished is provided by the fact that the building was abandoned and evidently never used. In the little court of the mortuary temple stand the

Plate 20

two stelae which traditionally were to bear the name and titles of the king. However, they remained uninscribed. The temple itself was not completed, as is shown by the fact that the lower courses of its limestone walls were left undressed whereas their upper portions were already smoothed.

Further evidence that the pyramid was never completed is provided by the internal state of the monument. The entrance lies a little below the present level of the outer mantle (E_3) from where it has to be negotiated, and there is the unpleasant prospect of missing it and sliding down the smooth surface of the pyramid which offers no hold. A low and slippery passage, just over 1 m. high, descends at a gradient slightly steeper than 1 in 2 for about 60 m. At its end there is a horizontal corridor of 10 m. length, from the end of which a vertical shaft, $6\frac{1}{2}$ m. high and just wide enough to climb through, rises to the floor of the tomb chamber. The chamber itself was clearly left unfinished. The large limestone slabs

Plate 18

forming the corbelled roof are perfectly fitted together but have remained undressed, and the wooden bulks, used during construction, were never removed. Comparison with the beautifully finished interiors of mastaba

Plates 14, 15, 29

17 and the Red Pyramid leaves no doubt that work on the tomb chamber of the Meidum pyramid was interrupted before completion.

The sudden abandoning of the Meidum site is also demonstrated by the considerable number of mastabas, built for courtiers, which were never occupied or were left unfinished. It is significant that no tombs of mortuary priests, who usually liked to be buried close to the pyramid complex which they served, have been found at Meidum. On the other hand, there are a number of tombs of such priests at the Dahshur sites.

While all the evidence cited so far indicates that the disaster occurred during the third building phase of the monument, we have so far not discussed the stage which the outer mantle (E_3) had reached when the

Plates VI, VIII

building collapsed. Traces of mortar can be seen adhering to the smooth walls of steps 5 and 6 – that means, practically to the full height of the remaining core. This shows that the outer mantle was at least 60 m. high, and the question arises whether it had extended further. Since the top of the edifice is missing, this might appear an insoluble problem but here we are fortunately helped by a chance observation recorded in 1899 by A. Robert of the Egyptian Survey Department. He ascended the top of the structure to set up a marker – a pole with a flag attached – to serve as a reference point. On this occasion he not only noted some Greek and hieroglyphic *graffiti* but also found that the highest existing step, the seventh, was never completed.

Before discussing the reasons for structural failure, we will first examine the effect of Robert's observation on the accepted ideas about the

18-20 The slabs forming the corbelled roof of the tomb chamber in the Meidum Pyramid (*above left*) are perfectly fitted but remained undressed. This, and the un-inscribed stelae in the mortuary temple (*below*), show that the pyramid was abandoned before completion. The arrow indicates the intact outer casing which was covered by debris when the pyramid collapsed. The internal masonry blocks (*above right*) are badly squared.

21-23 Plastic flow under gravity. The small pyramid model (*left*), made of a highly viscous material, collapses under its own weight. The development of lateral forces (*see also* Fig. 19) is shown by the outward 'bulging' of the structure. The similar collapse of the Meidum Pyramid is best seen in aerial photographs (*opposite*). The flow of debris from the pyramid mantle and the missing lower steps is apparent in the shape of the rubble heaps surrounding the core (*opposite above*). It is obvious that the base of the latter is the only place from which robbers can have taken stone. The picture also shows the excavated mortuary temple (Plate 20) and causeway. To its left are the remains of a building ramp. The view from above (*opposite below*) shows the even spread of the flow in all directions from the core, reaching as far as the temenos wall. The building at the lower left is mastaba 17.

24 It has been suggested that the pyramid as a solar emblem may have originated from the rays of the sun when they break through the clouds in the morning.

25 The roof in the Bent Pyramid's upper chamber remained unfinished and the horizontal cedar wood beams were probably spacers used during construction (Fig. 14).

26-28   The Bent Pyramid (*above*) owes its name to a change in the angle of elevation which was deemed prudent in order to avoid a collapse similar to the Meidum disaster. The arrow indicates the entrance to the western passage. The northern entrance (*below*) is 12 metres above ground and access requires a ladder. The casing stones are sloping inwards (*see also* Plate VII and Fig. 25).

29, 30   Unlike the ceilings of the tomb chamber of the Meidum Pyramid and the upper chamber in the Bent Pyramid (*see also* Plates 18 and 25), those in the Red Pyramid (*left*) are smoothly dressed. The Red Pyramid (*below*) is built entirely at the 'safe' lower angle of $43\frac{1}{2}°$.

31 In order to guard against collapse, the packing blocks of the Khufu Pyramid (*right*) are very large and well squared. Only the casing was removed by stone robbers who left the packing blocks untouched.

32 Aerial view of the pyramids of Khufu, Khafre and Menkaure at Giza (*below*) seen from the north-east. East of Khufu's pyramid are the mastabas of members of the royal family (*see also* Plate 35) and to the west those of high officials.

33, 34   The entrance to the polar passage in the north face of Khufu's pyramid (*above*) is protected by huge gabled limestone blocks. Caliph Ma'mun's hole can be seen below it, slightly to the right. The remains of the casing stones (*below*) of white Tura limestone are closely fitted and dressed smoothly.

Meidum pyramid. It has so far been generally believed that the two successive step pyramids (E_1 and E_2) were fully completed before the next building phase was embarked upon. This theory was based mainly on the smoothly dressed surfaces of E_1 and E_2 and on the provision made for the entrances of both these phases. Since the upper part of E_1 is completely enclosed in the present remains of E_2, nothing can be said about the final stage of this first step pyramid. However, we now know that the second step pyramid (E_2) was never completed, which clearly means that the decision to transform the monument into true pyramidal shape was taken before E_2 was finished. In that case the architect would have waited for the mantle of E_3 to reach the present height of E_2 before proceeding to the construction of the apex. The premature collapse clearly did not allow for this plan to be pursued and the whole pyramid complex at Meidum was abandoned.

In this context we should also remember the unfinished state of the tomb chamber. If either E_1 or E_2 was ever considered as a completed sepulchral monument, the slabs in the tomb chamber would have been dressed. Instead, we must now assume that there was never an inactive interval between plans E_1, E_2 and E_3. Each of these two changes must have been decided upon at a time when the previous phases were still building. There are technological implications of this overlap of constructional phases to which we shall return later. For the Egyptologist the main interest in this conclusion lies in the fact that there never existed a completed step pyramid tomb at Meidum in which a burial was likely to have taken place before the monument was changed into a true pyramid.

Another conclusion derived from our evidence answers a much wider question of pyramid construction which has been much debated in the past. It concerns the problem of that stage in building operation when the outer casing was laid on and when it was dressed. Although, as we now know, the mantle of E_3 had never reached its full intended height, the casing at the lower part had been both laid and smoothed from the very beginning. The same argument, of course, applies to the casing of the underlying step pyramids E_1 and E_2. This is of particular interest in the case of E_2 which, as now appears certain, was never completed.

Turning now to the structural reasons for the collapse of the monument, something has to be said about the stability conditions governing a large building such as a pyramid. There is little chance that the mere weight of the monument, large as it is, will by itself cause its collapse. This is, of course, attested to by the success with which Zoser's Step Pyramid and all the other great pyramids have withstood both constructional inadequacies as well as the ravages of millennia. In fact, they

97

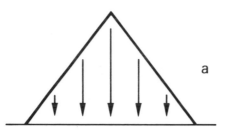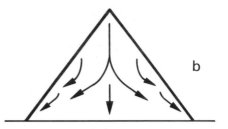

19 *Direction of the gravitational force acting within a well-built pyramid* (a) *and in one composed of badly squared stones* (b), *leading to the development of lateral components*

have proved to be remarkably stable structures, in spite of their immense size. The pressure exerted by its own weight at the base of a pyramid, such as that at Meidum, amounts to about 25 kg/cm² (25 atmospheres). This is high for a building but not excessively so. It certainly would not cause crumbling of limestone in a well-built edifice.

Taking the case of an ideally constructed pyramid, built with perfectly squared blocks, the pressure everywhere within the structure acts only downwards. At each horizontal face of any building block the force of the superincumbent weight acts vertically downward on the face of the underlying block. It is balanced by the rigidity of the building material and will not cause any deformation, except for the negligibly small elastic compression of limestone. However, once we depart from the ideal cube form of the blocks, these conditions change. If the surface of the blocks is somewhat irregular, they will touch at a few points only and consequently the pressure at these points of contact may rise to hundreds, or even thousands, of atmospheres, which is large enough to cause crumbling and serious deformation of the blocks. The result will be a movement of the building material in a direction to avoid this pressure – and that is sideways and out of the building. In other words, in a pyramid containing stones of irregular shape, the vertically downwards acting force will develop lateral components, favouring a break-up and flattening of the structure. It is therefore significant that the large hole in the north side of the Meidum pyramid core (E_1) discloses the imperfect nature of the masonry underlying the smooth casing. The blocks are relatively small and only roughly shaped, with large and irregular gaps between them.

In a well-built pyramid, on the other hand, any lateral components developing from a weak spot in the structure will remain localized and a small deformation is likely to be taken up by the surrounding material. All that will happen in this case is a slight 'settling' of the building, for which evidence exists in nearly all the pyramids. It seems that Imhotep

Fig. 19

Plate 19

was fully aware of the danger of lateral forces and therefore introduced a stabilizing internal structure which we have mentioned when discussing the shape of Zoser's monument. This stabilizing device is the buttress wall.

In the first large stone building which he designed, Zoser's mastaba, Imhotep used horizontal building courses and the feature which he introduced to ensure stability was an inward inclination of the outer walls. This was simply achieved by cutting the outermost building blocks of each horizontal course at a slope. This type of construction, however, offers very little resistance to lateral forces. There is nothing to counteract an outward sliding of the courses except the friction of one building block lying upon another. This system, however, was completely changed in the subsequent design of the step pyramid built above and around the original mastaba. The core of the pyramid was given an internal structure of buttress walls at intervals of 5 cubits – about 2.5 m. – all leaning inward at an angle of about 75°. The blocks forming these walls were of regular shape, giving them strength to prevent the masonry enclosed by them from moving outward.

Such inclined buttress walls, but made of mud brick, had evidently been used with success in some of the tombs of the earlier dynasties. The

Fig. 20

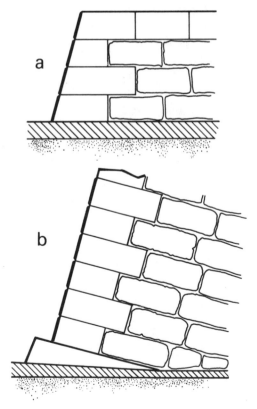

20 *Position of building blocks in Zoser's original mastaba* (a) *and the buttress walls of his Step Pyramid* (b)

construction of a whole mastaba in stone must have convinced Imhotep that, by using this new and hard building material, he could erect a far more impressive monument than anything which had been attempted before. His aim was to raise a structure of unprecedented height which should be as steep and commanding as possible. He decided on the buttress wall as the essential building element.

From the crumbling of earlier mudbrick buildings Imhotep must have been fully familiar with the undesirable development of lateral forces. Although at that stage the labour force at his command was clearly able to quarry, cut and transport limestone in huge quantities, he evidently could not count on obtaining one million tons of limestone in the form of perfectly squared cubic blocks. His pyramid would therefore not correspond to the ideal conditions outlined earlier and he knew that he would have to contend with the development of sizable lateral forces. He decided on counterbalancing these forces with inwardly inclined buttress walls of sufficient strength and in sufficient number. Although the

Fig. 9

sequence of building operations was, of course, quite different, the basic design of his monument can be described as a high tower rising to a height of 60 m. at an angle of about 75°. Such a tower would naturally not be stable and so he had to support it with a series of surrounding buttress walls. Admittedly, the resulting structure would not be as steep and imposing as the tower, but by grading the height of the buttress walls outwards he still could achieve an imposing edifice. The result was Zoser's Step Pyramid, and its stability and solidity are ample proof of Imhotep's superb design.

His successor at Meidum was not so fortunate in his efforts. Nevertheless, it is interesting that by a curious chance the ruin now provides us with the aspect of Imhotep's basic design, the tall and impressive tower. However, Imhotep wisely decided to hide its grandeur by the strengthening outer buttress walls. These, of course, also existed at Meidum but fell away when disaster overtook the building. Our next task is now to discover why the Meidum building collapsed whereas Imhotep's Step Pyramid at Saqqara still stands.

Neither the size nor the original foundation of the Meidum step pyramids (E_1 and E_2) can be held responsible. The projected building was not much higher than Zoser's and as regards its foundation, the design at Meidum was sounder than at Saqqara. Instead of forming a structure superimposed on a mastaba with horizontal courses of masonry, the Meidum pyramid consists of buttress walls built directly upon a rock foundation. Nevertheless, the Meidum pyramid exhibits a number of design faults which nowadays, to us, are so obvious and dangerous that the catastrophe can be traced with remarkable certainty. Most, though

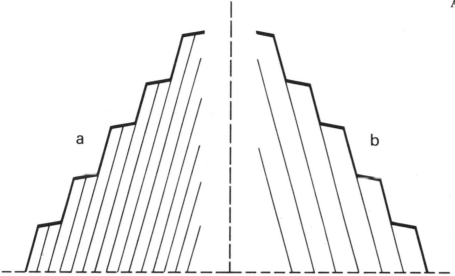

21 *Schematic diagram showing the number and position of buttress walls in Zoser's Step Pyramid* (a) *and in the Meidum Pyramid* (b)

not all, of these faults were introduced when the step pyramid E_2 was changed into the true pyramid E_3.

One serious departure from Imhotep's original design concerns the number and spacing of the supporting buttress walls. In Zoser's monument the spacing of buttress walls is 5 cubits (about 2.5 m.), which means that there are two buttress walls for each step. The same spacing was employed in the unfinished step pyramids of Sekhemket and Khaba. At Meidum the architect evidently economized by increasing the spacing between the buttresses to 10 cubits, which allowed for only one wall per step. He was possibly encouraged to effect this saving because he considered Imhotep's design as unduly cautious. Nevertheless, the lateral forces against which the buttresses had to protect the pyramid were twice as large at Meidum as at Saqqara. In all fairness it should be remembered that E_1 and E_2 did not collapse spontaneously as long as they were left alone. The disaster was triggered off by the addition of E_3, and it is conceivable that a major catastrophe might have been avoided by twice the number of buttress walls supporting the building.

The real trouble was the decision to superimpose E_3 on a completely unsuitable substructure. Both E_1 and E_2 had their outer surfaces planed when the masonry of the mantle E_3 was laid on. The smooth surfaces represented very dangerous slip planes and the ruin shows that the E_3 masonry was not anchored to these surfaces by anything better than a layer of mortar. Much the same can be said of the lack of adherence of E_2 on E_1. A conspicuous feature of the ruin are the unscarred surfaces of

Fig. 21

Fig. 16

Plate VIII

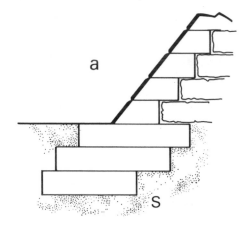

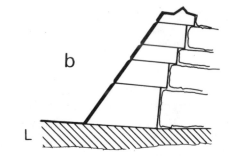

22 *At Meidum* (a) *the outer mantle of the pyramid rests on limestone blocks embedded in compacted sand* (s) *whereas at the Bent Pyramid* (b) *the casing was supported by a prepared inward sloping limestone base* (L)

E_1 and E_2 which indicate that the outer material was sheared off in bulk, simply falling away when the mishap took place.

However, we may assume that the primary failure occurred in E_3 which, presumably due to the novelty of its design, suffered from two serious structural errors. First of all, Wainwright's tunnel has revealed that, whereas E_1 and E_2 were firmly laid on the rock bed, this was only partly true in the case of E_3. In fact, much of its foundation, particularly near the periphery, simply rested on the underlying desert sand and its casing was merely supported by three rows of fairly thin slabs of limestone which, in turn, had only been loosely embedded in sand. Maragioglio and Rinaldi mention this fact but considered it as harmless since, as they state, the weight of stone at the periphery of the pyramid is not large. This argument, reasonable as it may appear at first sight, is, as we shall see, unfortunately fallacious.

The process of transforming E_2 into a true pyramid was carried out by first filling up the steps so that a pyramidical shape resulted. However, these packing blocks did not rest as securely on the steps as was hitherto believed. When Robert ascended the building, he noticed that, although the underlying masonry courses of the buttress walls slope inwards the

Fig. 22 a

two remaining top surfaces, those of steps 5 and 6 of E_2, were laid sloping outward. This design is similar to Zoser's pyramid and served the purpose of letting rain water run off the monument instead of seeping into its structure. This outward slope had not been levelled when packing blocks were laid on to the steps. The blocks were therefore less stable than they would have been on the horizontal steps drawn in Borchardt's and Rowe's reconstructions. The lower steps were destroyed in the disaster but there can be little doubt that they, too, had an outward slope and the accepted reconstruction has therefore to be modified.

Fig. 25 a

Fig. 18

For some reason the builders were not satisfied with merely filling up the steps but extended the mantle outward by about 6 m. beyond the structure of E_2. Since the top of the building has disappeared we do not know what motivated this design but it was probably necessitated in order to achieve the intended angle of 52°, i.e., an elevation of 4 in π. Whatever the cause, it constituted the most serious threat to the stability of a building which already suffered from a number of design faults. The filling blocks resting on the sloping steps received only a limited amount of support from the buttress walls and this was not even the case for the mantle as a whole. The packing blocks and those used in the outward extension of the mantle were not well squared and the force exerted by their weight acted not merely downwards but to a large extent along the surface of the mantle itself. In other words, the force acting on any point in the mantle was very much larger than the weight of the blocks immediately above it. This force rose steadily as the accumulated weight of the mantle increased until it caused its structure to bulge out of the pyramid. As a result, the whole mantle slipped and crumbled, taking the third and fourth steps of E_1 and E_2 with it.

Fig. 16

How and where the catastrophe was triggered off cannot at this stage be determined with certainty. It may have started on one of the slip planes but it seems equally or even more likely that the initial failure occurred in the mantle itself. Owing to the serious structural faults of the building there was no chance of any local failure to right itself by 'settling'. Wherever the first breach in the structure took place, it was bound to become immediately cumulative, resulting in a sudden and large-scale disaster. Examination of the casing of E_3 near the mortuary temple shows the lowest courses of casing stones to be smooth and in perfect condition. Higher up, the casing becomes progressively more scarred, and this is quite consistent with a landslide of rubble careering down over the pyramid casing in which more material will pass across the higher than across the lower courses. When Petrie examined the casing in 1910 he tried to explain its damaged state as due to 'weathering', but nevertheless described it as 'chipped'.

Plate 20

I The face of the Sphinx at Giza is the portrait of the Pharaoh Khafre, the builder of the second of the three large pyramids.

II Zoser's Step Pyramid at Saqqara, seen from the south-east. This view from inside the enclosure wall shows some of the reconstructed dummy buildings of the ceremonial Heb-Sed Court.

III The ruined Pyramid of Meidum seen from the Nile. The steep core seems to stand on a natural hill; this is, in fact, the mound of debris which completely covers the base of the monument. The hillock to the right is mastaba 17 (*see* pl. 13).

IV The 'Bent' Pyramid (left) and the 'Red' Pyramid (far right) of Dahshur seen from across the Nile.

V The Meidum Pyramid surrounded by the debris from its collapse, seen from the north-west.

VI The core of the Meidum Pyramid, showing the smoothly dressed surfaces of the original step pyramids and the 'rough bands' separating them.

VII Casing of the lower section of the 'Bent' Pyramid. The inward slope of the casing blocks is clearly visible (*see also* fig. 25b).

VIII Surface of the core of the Meidum Pyramid, looking upward; showing the smooth finish of the step pyramid walls and adhering mortar.

II

III

IV

V

VI

VII

VIII

Whether the slip of the mantle was aided by the poor foundation of E_3 is not clear since, except for the two small clearances mentioned above, the rest of the casing is completely covered with debris. It may be significant, however, that the diagram given by Rowe shows the casing at the north clearance to have sagged heavily. Any decision on this point will have to wait until the rubbish can be cleared from the base of the pyramid, and this would require very extensive work. Such clearance may also be interesting for a different reason. If, as seems likely, the disaster took place very rapidly, equipment, and even bodies, may be buried underneath the rubble. They might furnish valuable information, having been left undisturbed since the beginning of the Fourth Dynasty.

Fig. 18

The average size of the fragments visible in the debris indicates that the material coming down from the higher reaches of the building had been broken up rather thoroughly. This is not surprising in view of the irregular shape of the building blocks, and it may also be due to the poor quality of the local limestone. As to the latter, Rowe states that many of the tombs surrounding the Meidum pyramid have fallen in because of the softness of the stone. One of the causes triggering off the catastrophe may have been a heavy rainstorm, such as occurs occasionally in Lower Egypt. In fact, most of the Old Kingdom buildings show provision to cope with large amounts of rainwater; but during the laying on of the outer mantle, the Meidum structure would have been completely un-protected. As is well-known from natural landslides, water can act as a dangerous lubricant; it certainly did so in the case of the Aberfan minetip. Owing to the softness and the irregular shape of the limestone building blocks, most of the rapidly descending material was quickly ground down into a rubble of fairly small pebbles. Their average size is clearly visible in those parts of the debris from which the blown sand has been cleared during excavation. This rubble cascading down the sides of the pyramid had the dynamic properties of a fluid rather than that of large-scale solid debris. In fact, it exhibited the well-known characteristics of plastic flow, behaving very much like a stream of treacle. This means that it would not destroy the stelae or the temple at the foot of the building but rather flow around and over them. Any large packing blocks that remained unbroken did not hurtle down but were carried engulfed in the stream of rubble, like crumbs in treacle. When first excavating the temple, Petrie found such blocks deeply embedded in the rubble.

Plates VI, 20

By far the best illustration of the flow of rubble is provided by the aerial photographs of the Meidum site. They show how the debris spread out from the ruin in all directions until it finally came to rest as a result of its own internal friction. The blown sand held by the rubble provides excellent contrast with the darker surrounding soil. In particular

Plates 22, 23

the picture taken directly overhead reveals the circular area around the monument to which the flow extended.

Plastic flow of this kind seems to have menaced the pyramid of Pepi II four centuries later. It was a badly built edifice constructed of small stones bonded with mud, and overlaid with a limestone casing. The base of this pyramid, after its construction had proceeded to an advanced stage, was then surrounded by a massive dyke of 8 m. thickness which dammed it in completely. It appears that lateral forces must have developed in its poor construction to such an extent that they threatened to flatten out the building. Another case of plastic flow occurred fairly recently when excavators removed the stone covering from some sections of the large Pyramid of the Sun at Teotihuacan in Mexico. The core of the structure, built of adobe brick and clay, began to flow after heavy rain, and rapid emergency action had to be taken to save the edifice. Because of their enormous mass, pyramids are especially prone to this type of destruction by plastic flow which never became dangerous in later, and very much lighter, buildings.

Plate 21

Finally, we have to examine what happened to the Meidum pyramid between the fatal day of its catastrophic collapse and the present time. A number of attempts have been made to reconstruct its history, all of them based on the idea of the gradual destruction of a perfect building by stone robbers. Maragioglio and Rinaldi have tried to trace this decay through the height of inscriptions on the walls of the monument, starting with the hieroglyphic and Greek *graffiti* near the present top of the core. This is, of course, at variance with our own deduction that the pyramid collapsed while still under construction. Their conclusion also ignores the tendency of tourists to carve their initials, not necessarily at the contemporary level but at the highest point to which they had climbed. Equally misleading is the frequently repeated statement that five steps of the structure still existed at Napoleon's time. It is based on an ambiguity in translation of Denon's famous account into the English language. The French *gradin* means 'tier' rather than 'step', and Denon's own drawing leaves little doubt that he referred to the separation due to the 'rough bands' on the smooth core. His sketch of the Meidum pyramid was based on observations from a distance by means of binoculars. It gives a very faithful picture of the pyramid core as we see it today, but he was not as accurate as Norden or Perring in sketching the wide distribution of the debris.

Denon was the first to comment on the large hole in the north face which is now about 10 m. above the height of the debris but which he thought could then be reached from the rubble. However, it has to be recalled again that his observation was made from a distance and Robert comments on steps which the local fellahin had cut into the north wall to reach this hole. They are clearly visible today and enable the local population to harvest from the cavity bats' dung which is valued for its curative properties. The villagers told Robert that neither in their, nor in their forefathers' memory, had anyone ever scaled the pyramid to a greater height.

Another frequently quoted account of five still existing steps is that of Sheikh Abu-Mohammad Abdallah who visited Meidum in 1117–19 and whose observation was recorded by Makrisi in the fourteenth century. It is to be noted, however, that the Arabic word used by Makrisi translates correctly as 'storeys' and not as 'steps'. Small remnants of a third step of E_2 may possibly have existed after the disaster close to the present core. The aerial photographs indicate that this is the only place from which stones appear to have been removed by the fellahin and archaeologists, and it comprises only a very small section of the ruin.

Plate 2

The most reliable information of the history of the debris is provided by Wainwright's excavation in 1910. He found two figures of the Twenty-second Dynasty 'in the highest part of the rubbish, just below the present surface, showing the rubbish to have been practically as high in the XXII dynasty as it is today'. He, and later Rowe, found a number of intrusive burials in the debris, presumably of roughly the same date or later. Summing up all this evidence, we must conclude that the Meidum site presents today much the same aspect as it did 3000 years ago.

Going back still further towards the day of the pyramid's collapse and its abandonment, we are hampered by the fact that, except for the corners of E_3, the entrance and the mortuary temple, the base of the building is still completely covered by debris. Almost certainly the tomb chamber and the temple were entered during the First Intermediate Period; Petrie found in the corridor some pieces of a destroyed wooden coffin of plain style, possibly an early intrusive burial. The paved floor of the tomb chamber has been torn up and a hole cut into one of the walls, and this damage, as well as beams and pieces of ancient rope found by Maspero, indicate the activity of thieves.

As mentioned earlier, the roof slabs of the tomb chamber had never been dressed and it seems unlikely that the chamber ever contained a stone sarcophagus. Access to it from the corridor is by the vertical shaft described earlier, which enters the floor of the chamber and is only 117×85 cm. wide. A sarcophagus would have had to be placed in the chamber at the time when this was being built and it could not have left the chamber by the narrow shaft, except if broken into pieces. Apart from the fact that such destruction would be useless, no granite fragments were found, either in the chamber itself or anywhere in the corridor.

Plate 18

Fig. 18

The mortuary temple, first uncovered and investigated by Petrie, was thoroughly excavated by Rowe, and from his work the following sequence of events emerges. First of all, after the disaster the little building served as a habitation of shepherds, as is shown by a fireplace and animal dung and also by a grain silo constructed outside the temple door. *Graffiti* on the temple walls indicate that it was visited by tourists down to the Seventeenth or Twentieth Dynasty when somebody was buried in it and the doorway was bricked up. Still later, *graffiti* indicate that the outer court must have been accessible after the burial but it appears from Wainwright's excavation that it had become covered with sand and debris at the time of the Twenty-second Dynasty.

It is quite impossible to say whether the temple was cleared immediately after the catastrophe or during the First Intermediate Period, or whether it was spared in the original avalanche. Whereas scientific analysis has no difficulty in determining the causes of the collapse and its final result, it is unable to give evidence on the immediate state of the structure after the initial disaster. The debris may have settled in its ultimate state straight away but it is also quite possible that for some time parts of the masonry remained in a precarious position at higher levels only to crash down eventually – perhaps again after heavy rains. Regard-

Plate 23

ing the geometry of the building and the wide spread of the rubble, our own opinion is that the temple was engulfed instantaneously and subsequently dug out again. Such an operation would not have been too difficult, as was shown by Petrie who, in 1891, accomplished this task with only twenty-five men in under two months.

Not much useful indication about the state of the ruin can be gleaned from the *graffiti* at the temple and the pyramid entrance appended by tourists of the Eighteenth Dynasty, more than 1200 years after the catastrophe. One of these, the 'son of Amen-mesu, Scribe and Ritualist of the deceased King Tutmose I', said that he 'came to see the beautiful temple of the Horus Snofru. He found it as though heaven were within it and the sun rising in it'. These words mean nothing since they are a standard phrase used by tourists on ruins all over Egypt at that time. However, it is interesting that the scribe mentioned Snofru as the owner of the building although this attribution cannot, after the enormous lapse of time since the erection of the pyramid, be regarded as conclusive.

Summarizing the observations described in this chapter, we conclude that the heavily ruined state of the Meidum pyramid cannot be attributed to the activities of stone robbers, but that the building collapsed during the third phase of its construction. This collapse occurred as a sudden catastrophe and can be traced to a number of design faults. When the disaster took place, the outer pyramid mantle (E_3) had reached a height of about 60 m., and not only this third phase but also the underlying step pyramid (E_2) was never completed.

The Meidum structure was only the second monument which had attained a considerable height and one may wonder why a catastrophe of such colossal dimension did not discourage the architects of the Old Kingdom from erecting further edifices of enormous size. The answer to this question is simple. When the Meidum pyramid collapsed in its final building phase, the next pyramid, planned on more than twice as large a scale, had already reached a height of 50 m. at Dahshur.

5 Confirmation at Dahshur

Plate 26

The rhomboid shape of the southern stone pyramid at Dahshur, which has earned it the name of the 'Bent Pyramid', is the direct consequence of the disaster at Meidum. There are two stone pyramids at this site which is just south of Saqqara and 45 km. north of Meidum. It is now certain that chronologically the Bent Pyramid followed that of Meidum and that the northern Red Pyramid was the successor of the Bent Pyramid. Owing to certain architectural features which will be discussed presently, the Bent Pyramid was, until recently, thought to predate that of Meidum. Recent excavations have also shown without doubt that the Bent Pyramid has to be ascribed to Snofru. The same is true for the Red Pyramid, and there exists an important decree by King Pepi I of the Sixth Dynasty, exempting the priests of the 'two pyramids of Snofru' from certain taxes and services. This stela of Dahshur was found in the cultivation near the Red Pyramid and may have belonged to that monument's valley building. However, owing to the confusion over dating these pyramids, that of Meidum was first believed to be the 'southern pyramid of Snofru'.

Plate V

Unlike the deserted Meidum site, the Dahshur pyramids seem to have been places of active worship for a long time and the Dahshur necropolis bears witness to a long line of funerary priests whose tombs unfortunately attracted the attention of Arab treasure seekers in the Middle Ages and, even more so, that of the nineteenth-century hunters for *objets d'art*. There is a good deal of evidence that the pyramids were entered and robbed of their contents in the First Intermediate Period and, while their treasure did not survive the time of unrest, the cult of Snofru did. The Dahshur pyramids remained a site of worship for well over a thousand years and Snofru's cult was alive throughout the New Kingdom, and possibly down to Ptolemaic times. The pyramids may have been re-sealed in the Saïte period or even earlier but, if so, they were opened again by the Muslims. European travellers of the seventeenth century entered the Bent Pyramid and its first exploration was carried out by the indomitable and ever-active Mr Perring in 1839.

Perring, in fact, invented scientific archaeology a century in advance. In spite of later work at Dahshur by such noted Egyptologists as Lepsius, de Morgan, Barsanti and Jéquier nothing superseding Perring's original observations on the Bent Pyramid was found until after World War II. Then, in 1948 Abdulsalam Mohammed Hussein began serious work at the Bent Pyramid on behalf of the Antiquities Department. His first great discovery was the name of Snofru on the corner stones of the building and also in the upper chamber. This settled the question as to whom the Bent Pyramid belonged. Hussein also discovered the cedar beam frame- *Plate 25; Fig. 14* work in the upper chamber which had been hidden by a great number of small squared stone blocks with which the chambers of the Bent Pyramid, like those at Meidum and the Red Pyramid, had been partly filled. The purpose of this packing, in which nothing seems to have been hidden, is not known. Neither can one be sure that it formed part of the original design. Hussein died suddenly in 1949 on a trip to the United States and his notes have never been found. His work was continued by Ahmed Fakhry, to whose discoveries we have already referred. There is a lingering suspicion that the Bent Pyramid may contain some so far undiscovered passage or chamber. When in 1839 Perring broke through the choked northern entrance, there occurred a rush of fresh air down the passage into the inner chambers, which continued for two days so strongly 'that the lights would with difficulty be kept in'. Since the western entrance was at that time still sealed he concluded 'that the apartments must have had some other communication with the outside air'. Fakhry reported that on windy days a noise, sometimes lasting for ten seconds, can be heard in the connecting passage between the two chambers.

In order to understand the reasons for changing the angle of elevation when building the Bent Pyramid, we have to return to the problems of pyramid design and construction. Imhotep had discovered the method of erecting a tall stone building by appreciating the inward thrust of a buttress wall, and this ingenious device seems to have dominated the construction of all large pyramids. The buttress walls can be seen openly at the step pyramids of Zoser, Sekhemket and Khaba and, owing to its collapse, also at the Meidum pyramid. Because of their immense bulk and their good state of preservation, nothing can be said about the internal structure of the two stone pyramids at Dahshur or the Khufu and Khafre pyramids at Giza. However, we may safely assume that they, too, were designed in the same way since the hole cut into the Menkaure pyramid in 1215 by Caliph Malek clearly discloses the step structure of this building. *Plate XII* Moreover, buttress walls can also be seen in the subsidiary pyramids at Giza and in the more heavily ruined pyramids of the Fifth Dynasty at Abusir. It appears therefore that Herodotus' statement that 'the pyramids *Plates XI, 42* were built in tiers, battlementwise, as it is called, or according to others, stepwise', is correct.

There is another reason why it is not feasible to build a true pyramid, gradually rising but without first constructing a central core. Whereas in a step pyramid slight errors of alignment are hardly apparent and can always be corrected at the next step, the same is not the case for a true pyramid. Its edges must be straight and, at the same time, meet in one point which, in the early phases of construction, is high up in the sky and unattainably far from the building operations. It seems quite impossible that the Egyptians could have been in possession of sophisticated surveying methods or instruments to carry out this task. For a building of the size of the great Giza pyramids a tiny error of only 2° in the alignment of the edges will result in a mismatch of over fifteen metres at the top. Since the edges had to be straight from the outset, they could not be corrected later and had to be accurate to a fraction of a degree. The only feasible explanation would be the existence of a tall core building with a central marker set up on the top. That this, in fact, was the case, was proved by Robert who, in 1899, scaled the unfinished top of the Meidum step pyramid (E_2) to set up a flagpole, a marker for the Egyptian Survey Department. He found the place already prepared by a 30 cm. deep hole in the centre of the structure which, he concluded, had held a mast. Somebody had set up a marker there more than 4000 years earlier. It had evidently served as the required reference point in the sky on to which the pyramid edges of E_3 could be sighted accurately.

Fig. 23

Fig. 24

This fact and some of the observations mentioned in the preceding chapter allow us to trace the sequence of operations in erecting a large

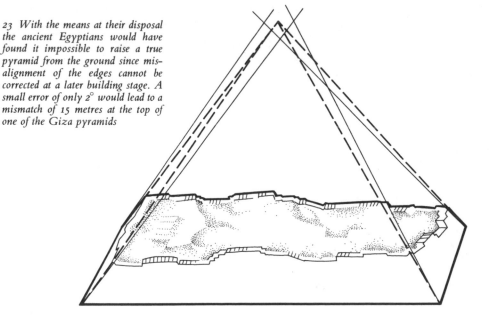

23 With the means at their disposal the ancient Egyptians would have found it impossible to raise a true pyramid from the ground since misalignment of the edges cannot be corrected at a later building stage. A small error of only 2° would lead to a mismatch of 15 metres at the top of one of the Giza pyramids

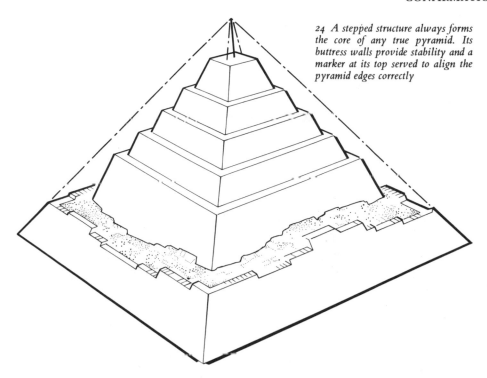

24 *A stepped structure always forms the core of any true pyramid. Its buttress walls provide stability and a marker at its top served to align the pyramid edges correctly*

pyramid. First the site would be levelled and aligned in the cardinal directions by methods thoroughly discussed by I. E. S. Edwards. Then the erection of a step pyramid, consisting of core masonry held by a series of buttress walls, would begin. As this structure gradually rose, an ever-increasing number of the buttress walls would be discontinued with increasing height, leading to a succession of steps. Building material for the core would be brought on to these steps by building ramps, the relics of which exist to this day at the Meidum and Sekhemket pyramids. After the completion of the whole step pyramid, the marker was set up on top and packing blocks were laid on to give the building its pyramidal shape, the correct angle being checked by sighting on the marker. Subsequently, or possibly at the same time, the outer casing would be laid on, starting at the bottom, and finally it would be dressed to a plane smooth finish. The nature of the Meidum ruin suggests that workmen were engaged on these last operations simultaneously, since we see there the outer casing dressed and finished at the bottom while packing stones were still added at the higher steps.

At the Bent Pyramid the core had reached a height of about 50 m. when it was decided to lower the angle of elevation from $54\frac{1}{2}°$ to $43\frac{1}{2}°$, reducing its ultimate height from approximately 130 to 100 m. Two explanations have been proposed to explain the alteration as a *reduction in height* whereas in our opinion lowering of the edifice was not primarily important but the concomitant *decrease in the angle of elevation* was the really decisive factor. At this stage there will have existed only the unfinished central core with probably four steps, and buttress walls rising at an angle of roughly 75°.

The first explanation for the rhomboid shape was given early in the nineteenth century by Sir J. Gardner Wilkinson who suggested that the monument had to be completed in haste because the king died prematurely. Perring supported this view since he thought that the smaller packing blocks and less careful work in the upper part suggested a hurried construction. For two reasons this explanation is not convincing. In the first place, owing to the geometric shape of a pyramid, the quantity of stone that can be saved in changing the top part is not large. In the present case it amounts to only 9 per cent of the total masonry, an economy hardly worthwhile. Secondly, the next pyramid, the Red one, was *entirely* built at this lower angle.

The second explanation given for the change in angle is that the superincumbent weight had to be reduced because cracks had developed in the building. It has also been argued that the cedarwood beams in the upper chamber were introduced in order to shore up the structure against lateral pressure. Reasonable as this explanation might appear at first sight, the technological evidence is quite unconvincing. First of all, as was mentioned in the last chapter, the effect of pressure due to the weight of stone on the rest of the building is not serious and, moreover, the reduction in weight on lowering the angle of elevation amounts in this case to no more than 23 per cent. The cracks in the Bent Pyramid are small and could easily be plastered over. They are no worse than the cracks due to 'settling' in any other pyramid. As regards the cedar beams, they are at right angles to the acting force and, in any case, would have been easily broken by the forces involved. It is our opinion that they were not introduced later to save the structure, but that they were used as horizontal spacers while the pyramid was being built. They were not removed because, as the shape of the roof shows, the upper chamber was never finished. Far from being damaged, this corbelled roof presents the same aspect as the undressed roof slabs in the Meidum pyramid. There, incidentally, cedarwood spacers had been employed, too, and their remnants are still *in situ*. Altogether there existed in the Bent Pyramid itself no reason to reduce the superincumbent weight of masonry.

On the other hand, we have ample evidence that it was primarily the angle of elevation and not the weight which was considered perilous, and that the danger envisaged was not a crushing of the interior chambers but a slip of the outer mantle. It was this slip which had caused the disaster

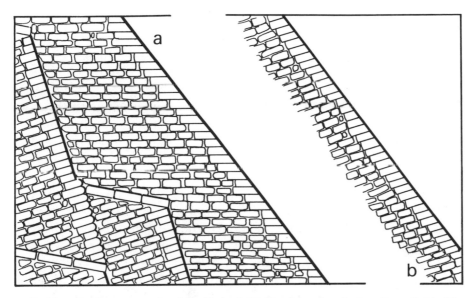

25 *Position of casing stones and packing blocks at Meidum* (a) *and at the Bent Pyramid* (b). *The inward slope of the Bent Pyramid's casing was chosen to provide the same stability as the underlying step structure at Meidum. This stabilizing feature was missing in the horizontal packing layers of the Meidum Pyramid, a factor which must have contributed to its collapse. Moreover, the packing did not rest securely on the slightly outward sloping steps and the outer part of the mantle was not at all directly supported by the steps*

at Meidum and it appears an inescapable conclusion that the change in design of the Bent Pyramid was an effort to avoid a similar catastrophe at Dahshur. At the time when the Meidum pyramid collapsed, nothing could be altered at the half-finished Dahshur structure, except the construction of the packing and the outer casing. And for this there is, indeed, clear evidence. When the step pyramid at Meidum (E_2) was transformed into a true pyramid (E_3), packing blocks had been put onto the steps in horizontal layers. Moreover, these layers had been continued for about 6 m. beyond the outer limits of the supporting buttress walls. It was evidently here that the disaster occurred and the builders at Dahshur had to make sure that any repetition of it should be avoided. They were fully aware of Imhotep's stabilizing device of inwardly inclined buttress walls, composed of layers of masonry sloping towards the centre of the structure. In order to assure similar inward thrust by the outermost layers of the Bent Pyramid, they laid the packing blocks and also the casing stones not horizontally but in courses which slope inward at an angle of about 6°.

Fig. 25

Plates VII, 27

It is this apparently archaic feature in design, reminiscent of the structure of Zoser's Step Pyramid, which induced the archaeologists for some time to date the Bent Pyramid before that of Meidum. From the evidence since discovered, revealing the name of Snofru in the Bent

Fig. 22 b

Pyramid and its valley building, we now know that it was the successor of the Meidum monument. The return of the builders to the earlier system of inward sloping courses was simply the result of their knowledge that this was a method ensuring increased stability. Moreover, the casing stones at the lower and steeper part of the Bent Pyramid are much larger than those employed at Meidum. Finally, whereas at Meidum the outer casing rested simply on sand, that of the Bent Pyramid is firmly supported by a limestone base which itself slopes inward. Thus everything was done to safeguard against plastic flow in the already existing part of the monument whose steep angle of elevation could not be lowered.

As for the upper part of the pyramid, the building-up of the core could now be done less steeply, at a gradient of $3/\pi$ instead of $4/\pi$, which appreciably reduced the danger of slip for the packing blocks and casing. The somewhat laborious laying of inward sloping courses of masonry could here be dispensed with, nor was it necessary at this safe angle of elevation to employ large fitted casing stones. We therefore find, in the upper part again, horizontally laid packing blocks and small casing stones.

Plate 26

These were the features which appeared to Perring and his successors as indications of less careful and hasty building. However, this impression is mainly caused by the selective activity of stone robbers who, after having scaled the lower part along the edges, found it much easier to remove casing stones resting on horizontal packing layers than at the steep lower section. There, the difficulty of dislodging large casing stones, lying at a camber, has saved larger areas of intact outer casing than at any other pyramid.

All these features – the reduced angle of elevation, large blocks of inward sloping casing, and the firm foundation – render the Bent Pyramid a strongly confirmatory testimonial of the catastrophe which overtook the Meidum monument. These three structural changes turned the Bent Pyramid into a hybrid edifice which had been started as a steep true pyramid, outshining that at Meidum, but which then had to be converted midway in search of greater structural stability. It is interesting to follow the technological lessons which had been learnt at Meidum and were applied at Dahshur.

Plate 30

The wish to play safe, even at the cost of a less impressive appearance, completely dominated the design of the next monument: the Red Pyramid. Its height is similar to that of its southern predecessor which, however, it exceeds in volume, for the Red Pyramid was built throughout at the safe angle of elevation of $43\frac{1}{2}°$. Owing to its good state of preservation and its great bulk, we know nothing about the underlying internal structure. It is, nevertheless, to be assumed that this too was constructed as a step pyramid on top of which was placed the marker needed to obtain the straight edges of the casing. While its main structure is well preserved, almost nothing is left of the casing. Owing to the gentle slope, this pyramid became an ideal quarry for stone robbers who were able to remove the blocks of dressed white limestone safely and without much difficulty. Today its appearance is characterized by the underlying packing blocks of reddish local stone which have given the building its name.

As in the upper part of the Bent Pyramid, the packing blocks of the Red Pyramid are laid in horizontal courses. These blocks are well-shaped, though not as carefully squared as those of the next pyramid at Giza. Altogether the two Dahshur pyramids show a transition from the small-scale masonry of the early step pyramids to the megalithic stonework at Giza. This distinction between the two different types of masonry was emphasized by Clarke and Engelbach in their standard work on ancient Egyptian masonry. As they point out, entirely new methods of handling had to be adopted as soon as the blocks employed became too heavy to be lifted by a few workmen; the use of lifting tackle was unknown in the pyramid age. These special skills had been needed in the Third Dynasty only sparingly, but we witness their employment on a very large scale at the Giza Pyramids.

Even when compared with Zoser's Step Pyramid the very much larger Red Pyramid loses by being less steep. Fakhry's suggestion that the new form of the upper part of the Bent Pyramid 'must have appealed to the architect' somehow seems to lack conviction. As we have seen, the lowering of the angle of elevation was purely a safety precaution and it is likely that only for this reason was it chosen for the Red Pyramid. How keen the Egyptian architects were to erect again a steep, imposing building is shown by the fact that they returned at Giza to the original gradient of $4/\pi$ and that they retained this shape for all future pyramids. On the other hand, they were fully aware that this steeper angle had caused the disaster at Meidum and that, in order to avoid a repetition, they would have to introduce structural modifications in any new venture of this kind. Our next step, therefore, must be to look for these modifications in the structure of the great Giza pyramids and find out what was done to overcome the defeatist attitude of the cautious builders we have seen at Dahshur.

Plates XI, 32

The new features introduced at Giza show, like the modifications of the Bent Pyramid, an amazing clarity in the analysis of the stability failure at Meidum. The stability of the Giza pyramids, which has preserved them structurally intact for more than four and a half thousand years, bears witness to the acute understanding of the basic physical and technological problems with which the builders of the Fourth Dynasty approached their task.

Since earlier and later stone pyramids relied on a basic core of buttress walls it is more than likely that the same design was used in the great Giza pyramids. Borchardt has drawn attention to the existence of 'girdlestones' in that part of the ascending passage of the Khufu pyramid which was cut through already existing masonry at the first alteration of the interior design. These are large vertical slabs through which the new corridor passes at intervals, and he has taken them as parts of internal buttress walls. This view has been disputed by Clarke and Engelbach, who have pointed out that it would be wholly fortuitous for the passage always to have encountered whole stones. They also maintain, rightly, that the walls of this passage are made of fitted stones. Probably both sides are correct. The passage was evidently lined with new masonry and the girdlestones, while not being part of the original buttress walls, were placed to mark their positions. This seems the more likely since the girdlestones are spaced at intervals of 10 cubits (about 5 m.), which is the distance between buttress walls in the Meidum pyramid. This indication of internal buttress walls shows that no novel features seem to have been introduced in the core structure of the Giza pyramids.

Plates 31, 33

On the other hand, the builders clearly improved the stability of the outer skin in order to make a pyramid with the steep gradient of $4/\pi$ proof against slip. They had evidently recognized that the right way to prevent the appearance of lateral forces was the use of well-squared packing blocks. These blocks are not only carefully shaped but also very large, each weighing approximately $2\frac{1}{2}$ tons. In addition to the size and good shape of the packing blocks the builders of the Khufu pyramid introduced an additional measure to ensure stability. In each horizontal row of blocks a gentle grading was carried out by which the blocks at the edges were very slightly higher than those in the middle of the face. In this way the corners of each layer of packing blocks was somewhat lifted, making the whole layer slightly concave towards the apex. This method provided an additional inward thrust which further counteracted any tendency of lateral forces to develop.

Fig. 26

This last-mentioned safeguard was clearly a laborious and time-consuming device, requiring selection and grading of the blocks before they could be laid. It seems to have been regarded as an unnecessary precaution and was not employed at the next Giza pyramid, that of Khafre. Its place was taken by a new method of preventing slip in the casing. This consisted of fashioning the lowest layer of casing stones out of granite blocks which, owing to their hardness and strength, formed a reliable base for the outer mantle. Granite blocks in the same position were also employed in Djedefre's pyramid at Abu Roash whose reign immediately followed that of Khufu. At the last of the Giza pyramids,

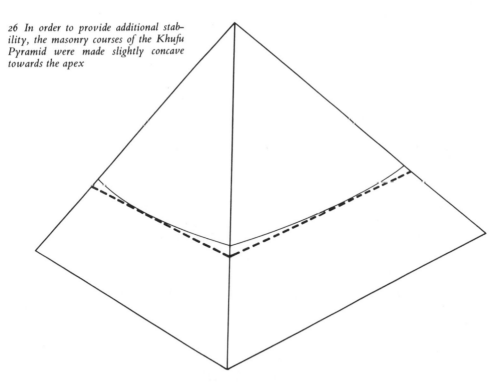

26 *In order to provide additional stability, the masonry courses of the Khufu Pyramid were made slightly concave towards the apex*

Plate XII

that of Menkaure, the sixteen lowest layers of the casing are of pink granite. This feature had always been regarded as an embellishment. However, since clearing the sand from the base of the Djedefre and Khafre pyramids has revealed single layers of granite, which were hardly visible, its seems justified to assume that their function was structural rather than artistic.

The Menkaure pyramid, too, was built with large, well-squared blocks. Vyse and Perring said that 'The bulk of the pyramid has been more carefully built than the two larger and the stones have been better finished, and are of greater size'. Moreover, the hole cut into its eastern face by the Caliph Malek al Aziz Othman reveals a substantially built buttress wall. On the other hand, the mortuary temple, the causeway and the valley building were finished with inferior materials by Menkaure's successor, Shepseskaf. There is a strange contrast in Menkaure's mortuary temple of immense limestone blocks, weighing as much as 200 tons each, and the use of mud brick and plaster. All these signs of a sudden lack of interest and saving of labour are part of the abrupt end of the Pyramid Age. The surprisingly large number of granite courses at the Menkaure pyramid casing may be another indication of this decline. Possibly the granite quarries at Assuan, which began only after Khufu to produce in large numbers casing stones for pyramids under construction and future ones, were taken by surprise at the sudden drop in demand. It almost looks as if the quarry masters found themselves with an excessive number of casing blocks on their hands which were then all used at the Menkaure pyramid, the last one of the Fourth Dynasty.

Other architectural innovations on the pyramids of the Giza period concern the design of the interior passages and chambers. The only corbelled roof at Giza is that of the Grand Gallery in Khufu's pyramid. This high and sloping passage provides interesting evidence for the fear of slip which seems to have been ever present in the mind of the Egyptian architects after the Meidum disaster. The roof slabs are made to lie individually against notches in the top of the walls and not against each other. This was to ensure that the weight of the slabs did not accumulate at the lower end of the sloping ceiling. The roof of the Queen's chamber in the Khufu pyramid and those of the tomb chambers in the Khafre and Menkaure pyramids consist of very large gabled blocks of limestone which have stood the test of time. We do not know whether, above these roofs, there are relieving chambers similar to those above the King's chamber of Khufu.

The efforts made by the Giza architects to erect large pyramids with a gradient of $4/\pi$ mainly involved the development of megalithic building on an immense scale. Even if we assume that the large squared blocks were confined to the packing only, this required the preparation of about 700,000 carefully shaped limestone cubes, weighing roughly $2\frac{1}{2}$ tons each. To these will have to be added something like one million m.² of well-built buttress walls and 200,000 m.² of smooth planed casing consisting of large blocks of Tura limestone. The remaining examples of this casing show that the stones were made to fit so closely that a postcard cannot be inserted between the blocks. All these various types of stone had to be quarried, transported, laid and dressed in the form of units which were

Fig. 27

Plate 34

Fig. 28

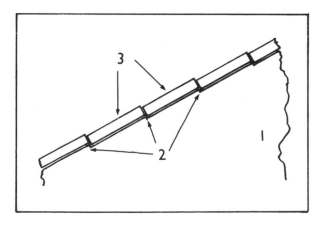

27 *After the Meidum disaster the danger of slip was ever present in the mind of the pyramid architects. The walls (1) in the 'Grand Gallery' of the Khufu Pyramid had a sawtooth edge (2) on top, so that the roofing blocks (3) rested individually against it. This prevented their weight from becoming cumulative*

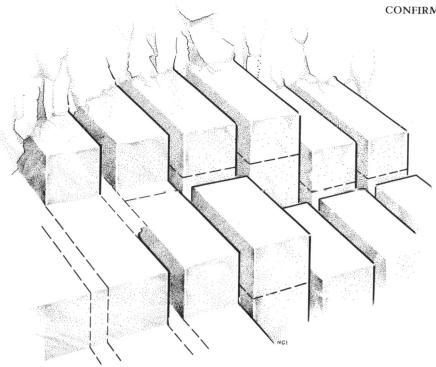

28 When quarrying limestone blocks for the pyramids, vertical cuts were made with copper chisels or by pounding with diorite balls. The blocks were then detached with wedges, often made of wood which would expand when soaked with water

too large to be lifted by men. In each case they had to be handled by levers, the only machine known to the builders of ancient Egypt.

Any such task had to rely not only on a stupendous labour force but also on a superb and highly developed technological organization. The problems that had to be solved on the administrative level far exceed those usually discussed, such as the piling up of building material to a great height. The most impressive feature is the persistence and escalation of pyramid building after the Meidum disaster. Moreover, the insistence on the true pyramidal shape of the monuments must be regarded as significant. The Egyptian architects knew full well that it had been the fatal decision to superimpose a pyramid mantle on the step structure at Meidum which had caused the catastrophe. At Dahshur they could have reverted to the old and tried design of step pyramids. The fact that they embarked on the difficult and hazardous course of building true pyramids indicates that this particular form had become essential to the development of their society.

Who were the people that issued the orders for this immense enterprise, and who executed them? Who were the members of the Egyptian 'establishment', to use contemporary parlance? First and foremost it was, of course, the pharaoh, but his position seems to have undergone a considerable change during the first four dynasties. Arising from a tribal society, the early pharaohs evidently held a divine kingship as it has survived to our day in Africa. The welfare of the people depended on the health and vigour of the king, who originally was not allowed to lose his powers with advancing age but had to be killed ceremonially when his strength waned. In historic times the slaying had been replaced by a magical rejuvenation ceremony, the *heb-sed* festival which soon came to be regarded as a regnal jubilee.

It was evidently during the four centuries covering the first two dynasties that the position of the king changed from a wizard with magical powers into the institution of the crown. The unification of the two kingdoms of Upper and Lower Egypt required the beginnings of a central administration, based on the capital, which had to be more rational and more permanent than the somewhat haphazard activities of a tribal chieftain. It was probably a gradual, though not necessarily a smooth development, but always tending towards centralization. As the heresy of Peribsen indicates, this was a period still perturbed by religious schisms, the origin of which lay in the past. It was a time when the local gods were both relegated to a secondary position and absorbed into a remarkably unadjusted pantheon. The Egyptians were extremely conservative and never threw anything away. So they kept all the tribal fetishes without making much effort to integrate them into a unified religious system. All that happened was that some of the local gods attained some specific, and generally accepted, minor function. So, for instance, the cow totem of Dendera, Hathor, and the cat Bast of Bubastis became the universally acknowledged goddesses of love, and the hippopotamus Toueris the goddess of childbirth.

Fig. 6

The invading dynastic race conquered Egypt under the standard of the Horus falcon, and their leader, finally to become king of Upper and Lower Egypt, was personally identified with this totem bird. The most important of the king's titular names was his Horus name which is inscribed in the 'serekh', an image of the palace façade surmounted by the falcon. It was incidentally from this representation of the royal palace, the Great House, in Egyptian 'per-o', that the Hebrew word 'pharaoh' was derived. The royal name had become taboo and 'the Great House' was the standard circumlocution used in reference to the king. The local gods had their temples and priesthoods but Horus stood high above them, his supremacy challenged only by the indigenous god Seth of Ombos. As mentioned in the first chapter, Seth succeeded under the Second Dynasty pharaoh, Peribsen, in supplanting Horus, but Horus was re-installed later during this same dynasty. It is significant, however, that eventually, under Kha-sekhemui, a compromise was reached with both the Horus and Seth emblems surmounting the serekh. Subsequently a judicious division of the world was instituted by the priesthood, in which Seth received the heavens and Horus the earth. This permitted the king, as the personification of Horus, to rule unimpeded over the land of Egypt.

With the consolidation reached at the turn of the Second Dynasty, the capital, as the seat of the central administration, gained in importance and it was inevitable that the priesthoods of the local gods were the most likely sources to provide the civil service. The local god of Memphis was Ptah, who had become the patron of learning and the scribes, which marked out his temple as a suitable sanctuary for the members of the administration. It appears that the kings, especially the early ones, relied heavily on this institution which they fostered and endowed. Another even more ancient sanctuary existed 30 km. north-east of Memphis at On, which was called Heliopolis by the Greeks. As the name indicates, it was a shrine of the sun god Re and its emblem was a conical stone, the *ben-ben*, representing the rays of the sun falling on earth. The temple of Heliopolis was also the home of astronomy, mathematics, the measurement of time and the calendar. Such little information as we have indicates a certain amount of rivalry between the priesthoods of Ptah and of Re for a leading part in advising and guiding the monarchy.

It seems that during the first two dynasties the influence of Ptah was decisive but with the beginning of the Third Dynasty Heliopolis took an ever-increasing share. Imhotep was a high priest of Heliopolis and there can be little doubt that the scientific and architectural expertise manifested in the building of the Step Pyramid of Saqqara emanated from the mathematics school of the sun god. Apart from the novel design of Zoser's tomb, the Step Pyramid complex itself is still dominated by the ancient tribal traditions with a stone replica of the *heb-sed* court, laying stress on the pharaoh's rejuvenation by magic. A similar enclosure around the pyramid of Sekhemket shows that this tradition was maintained in the Third Dynasty.

Then, however, a fundamental change in the position of the pharaoh seems to have taken place at the turn of the Third Dynasty. Our evidence for it is the departure in the lay-out of the Meidum pyramid. Even before it was decided to transform the original step structure into the pyramidal emblem of Re, important changes in design had taken place. The tomb chamber was not at the bottom of a shaft; there was a polar passage laid out from the beginning of the plan and the large *heb-sed* enclosure was omitted in favour of an unadorned small temenos wall with a causeway and a valley building. The meaning of the Egyptian monarchy was

Fig. 13

127

taking on a new form under the guidance of the Heliopolitan priesthood.

The pharaoh was gradually becoming closely connected with Re and, after death, was going to accompany the sun god on his daily journey across the sky. After Khufu the name adopted by the pharaoh contained the syllable 're', and the tutelage of Heliopolis, which was to come into full force in the Fifth Dynasty, began to make itself felt in the affairs of

Plate 61

state. For instance, Prince Rahotep who, with his wife Nofret, was buried at Meidum, was a 'son of the king' (probably Huni), commander of the army and high priest of Heliopolis. Meanwhile the Heliopolis priesthood had established a cult by which Horus was worshipped as 'Harakte', a variant of Re. It was in this era, which had evidently begun with Snofru, that the influence of the solar cult made its first impact on the monarchy. For entirely different seasons, the use of the pyramidal emblem of Re and its exaggeration into fantastic proportions went hand in hand. The building of pyramids had become the foremost activity of the country as a whole and it was evidently sustained by the Heliopolitan priesthood. This possibly also had an effect on the structure and recruitment of the civil service.

From early times the Egyptian civil service was of a dual nature, with offices corresponding to Upper and Lower Egypt, the Red and the White House. The highest official, who was the representative of the pharaoh, was the vizier to whose office the other departments, such as the Treasure House and the Store House, were responsible. The vizier and the heads of the other essential departments were usually sons of the king; during the first two dynasties royal princes also replaced local dignitaries as governors of the provinces. It seems that the vizier as supervisor of 'all the king's works' was in charge of pyramid construction which, as we shall see, was of paramount importance in the economy of the Fourth Dynasty. While Imhotep himself was evidently not a king's son he may have been connected to the royal house by marriage.

The Fourth Dynasty viziers were all sons of the pharaoh and their titles and offices are known from their mastaba tombs. The first vizier in charge of building operations who is known to us was Nefermaat, the son of a king, probably Huni, and who was buried at Meidum. His successor was a son of Snofru's, called Kanefer, whose tomb is at Dahshur, and who may have been in charge of the work when the Meidum pyramid collapsed. However, the disaster did not harm his career since we know that Kanefer continued in office into the reign of Khufu. He

Plate 58

was succeeded by his own son, Prince Hemon, Khufu's cousin and his great architect, whose impressive and forceful portrait statue is in the Hildesheim Museum. Hemon is generally credited with building Khufu's pyramid but there exists no definite proof for it except that the work

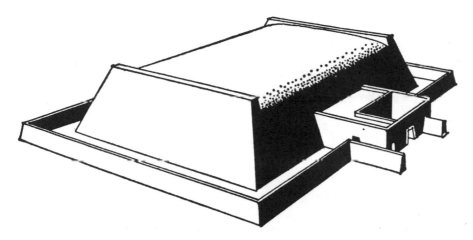

29 *The Mastabat Fara'un at Saqqara. Shepseskaf, the last Pharaoh of the Fourth Dynasty did not build a pyramid for himself but set up a more modest structure of archaic design* (after Edwards)

seems to fall into Hemon's term of office. It is possible that the vizirate was then conferred on Baufre and perhaps on Djedefhor, both sons of Khufu by Queen Merytyetes. However, there is a suspicion that they were eliminated in one way or another by Djedefre, whose vizier was another Nefermaat, a grandson of Snofru's by his daughter Nefertkau.

While the tombs disclose to us the names and even the portraits of the leading officials, and of many lower ones, who formed the administration of the Fourth Dynasty, they tell us nothing about the meaning of the change which the influence of the Heliopolis priesthood created in the Egyptian monarchy. This change evidently brought greater power to the priests of Re and it was intimately connected with the building of enormous pyramids. With Menkaure, this phase came to an end, and it is possible that his pyramid is nothing better than a left-over from the previous gigantic effort. It almost looks as if existing material was used up, as the labour force was being drastically run down.

There is a suspicion that at this time the hold which the priests of Re had over the monarchy was declining and it may be significant that Shepseskaf, Menkaure's son and successor, did not build a pyramid for himself. He also forsook the Giza necropolis, erecting a tomb in the shape of a large sarcophagus at the ancient necropolis of Saqqara. This heavily ruined building, called by the Arabs 'Mastabat Fara'un', though much larger than the mastaba tombs of the princes, is quite small in comparison with the Giza pyramids. It contains only about 3.5 per cent of the masonry of the Khufu pyramid. Egyptologists have regarded the departure from the pyramid shape which Shepseskaf decreed for his monument as reflecting a weakening of the Heliopolitan influence on the status of the

Fig. 29

pharaoh. Early Memphite texts describe Ptah as protector of Horus, i.e. of the king, and it may be significant that the first known high priest of Ptah was Ptahshepses, a son of Shepseskaf.

However, more important than abstract religious considerations or even the shape of the tomb appears to us the sharp decline in building effort which may have been foreshadowed by Menkaure's monument. We have to remember that pyramid construction was by far the most important activity for the Egyptians of the Fourth Dynasty. When dealing in the next chapter with the economic effects of this large-scale technological enterprise we shall see that, by the time of Khafre, pyramid building may have exhausted its usefulness, becoming a burden on society rather than a benefit to it. The servants of the sun god who seem to have fostered the channelling of the country's efforts towards gigantic representations of the solar emblem had possibly pushed the power of Re too far, and this may have turned the monarchy in its own interest towards the worship of the less exacting Ptah.

If this was the case, the establishment at Heliopolis did not take it lying down. There is no record of any serious disorders at the end of the Fourth Dynasty, but when Queen Khentkaues, Shepseskaf's sister, became the founder of the Fifth Dynasty, she brought Re and his Heliopolitan priesthood back with her. However, the priests had now significantly changed the position of the pharaoh from god into son of god. It seems to have been a fairly smooth take-over, in which Ptah and his priesthood were not victimized, but simply relegated to their former dignified but innocuous position. The sun god was re-installed by a famous legend which has come down to us in the Westcar papyrus in the Berlin Museum. Although the papyrus dates from the Middle Kingdom it clearly goes back to an Old Kingdom source. According to it a magician, Dedi of Meidum, who had been brought before Khufu to demonstrate his supernatural powers, prophesied the future of the royal house. The descendants of Khufu, he predicted, would rule over Egypt for three more generations, but then the three next kings would be triplets, begotten by Re himself, and borne by the wife of his high priest.

The legend, even in its corrupted form, bears the stamp of a priestly mythos, created to glorify the new dynasty of children of the sun god. The advantage of the new cult is immediately apparent. Being merely the son of Re, the pharaoh no longer required a monument of stupendous dimensions. It still had to be a pyramid to agree with the traditional pattern of solar worship, but it could now be on a more modest scale. In fact the pyramids of the Fifth and Sixth Dynasties are all of fairly uniform size, each being about one-thirtieth of the Khufu pyramid's bulk. In addition, the much smaller masses of these monuments did not require the stringent and costly precautions against collapse which had followed the Meidum disaster and which we have discussed above. Consequently, while the constructional pattern of using buttress walls was maintained, the internal masonry consists merely of roughly quarried rubble. Therefore, these small pyramids, because of their shoddy construction, did not stand the ravages of time as well as the giant edifices of Giza and Dahshur. Their ruins are of interest to us because they disclose not only poor workmanship, but also the existence of internal buttress walls.

Plate 43

Considering the greater ease of construction due to their smaller size and the saving effected by poor materials, it can be estimated that the labour force, which had to be devoted to these pyramids, amounted to no more than 2 or 3 per cent of that lavished on the Giza structures. As far as the communal effort was concerned, the Pyramid Age had definitely come to an end, and although still shoddier pyramids were erected for almost another thousand years after Khufu, their building never again became the primary occupation of the Egyptian people.

Plate 44

In order to compensate the pharaoh and his court for the loss of immense tombs, the Heliopolitan priesthood devised an entirely new place of solar worship for the king. This was an imposing sanctuary built for each pharaoh at the very edge of the desert plateau just north of Memphis, near the present village of Abu Gurob. These sanctuaries

Fig. 30

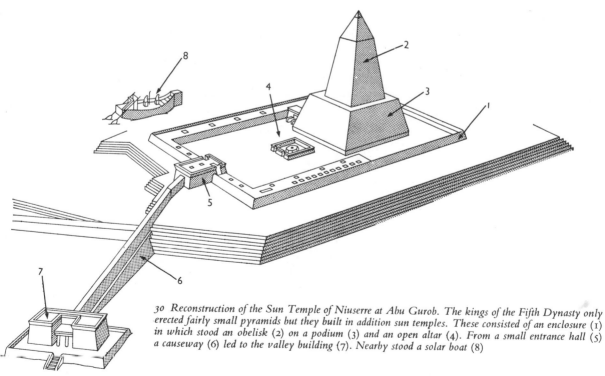

30 *Reconstruction of the Sun Temple of Niuserre at Abu Gurob. The kings of the Fifth Dynasty only erected fairly small pyramids but they built in addition sun temples. These consisted of an enclosure (1) in which stood an obelisk (2) on a podium (3) and an open altar (4). From a small entrance hall (5) a causeway (6) led to the valley building (7). Nearby stood a solar boat (8)*

could be reached by a covered causeway from a landing stage at the Nile which led to a sacrificial enclosure. This contained an altar and a series of alabaster basins to receive the blood of the slaughtered animals. The main feature of these temples, however, was a novel structure which, in due course, came to replace the pyramid as the emblem of Re. It was an obelisk. The original obelisks of Abu Gurob, were, unlike their mono-lithic descendants, squat and massive structures, closer in concept to the Pyramid Age than the slender spires in the New Kingdom temples. Again it should be noted that the amount of labour required to build these solar sanctuaries was minimal when compared with that lavished on a pyramid.

35, 36 Boat pits and royal family mastabas (*above*) seen from the top of Khufu's pyramid. The arrow indicates the position of the shaft leading to Queen Hetepheres I tomb. The granite casing (*below*) of Menkaure's pyramid was fitted but only partly dressed (*see also* Plate XII).

37   The King's Chamber (*opposite*) in Khufu's pyramid
with the lidless granite sarcophagus.

38, 39   Khafre's valley building of rose granite (*right*)
and the cosmic ray 'telescope' (*below*) set up in the tomb
chamber of his pyramid. It established that the monument contains no hidden upper chamber.

40, 41 A granite sarcophagus with its lid broken (*above*), let into the floor, was found in the tomb chamber of Khafre's pyramid. On opening the tomb chamber of Menkaure's pyramid (*left*), Vyse and Perring discovered a basalt sarcophagus with panelled outer surfaces. It was unfortunately lost at sea when shipped to England. Although the ceiling of the chamber gives the impression of a barrel vault, it is constructed of gabled straight granite slabs.

42, 43 The pyramids of the Fifth Dynasty were not only much smaller than those of the Fourth but also of inferior workmanship. That of Neferirkare at Abusir (*above*) has crumbled so heavily that the internal buttress walls indicated by arrows, have become visible. The masonry of Sahure's pyramid (*right*) is very roughly quarried and the blocks are not squared.

44, 45 The pyramids of the Middle Kingdom became even shoddier. That of Amenemhat III at Dahshur (*above*) was built of mud brick and has crumbled into a shapeless black heap. The latest pyramids at Meroe in the Sudan (*left*) were built of stone but they are quite small and erected at a steep angle.

46-48   Among the royal portraits the relief of Zoser (*right*) shows this king's aquiline features, while that of Snofru (*below left*), from his funeral stela, is marked by a strangely weak, receding chin. The only likeness we have of Khufu (*below right*) is a small ivory statuette whose face is distinguished by high cheekbones and a firm mouth.

49-51   Many portraits of royalty are provided by the strange 'reserve heads' found in their tombs. *Above left* is Khufu's Great Queen Merytyetes and *below*, one of his sons with his wife, whose features leave no doubt that she was a negress. The much married Queen Hetepheres II (*above right*) with her daughter Meresankh III were both spouses of Khafre (*see also* Table II).

6 The Solution

The results of our investigation so far lead to two main conclusions. The first is the destruction of the Meidum pyramid through a building disaster. The second is an explanation of the rhomboid shape of the Bent Pyramid as a direct consequence of this disaster. In the preceding two chapters we have adduced a considerable number of further observations and correlations to prove the correctness of these two main conclusions. Moreover, this research, like all investigations, has led to other results besides the main line of thought which it is customary to call the 'fall-out' of the work. These were the realization that the stepped phase of the Meidum pyramid was never completed, that a true pyramid always had to have a stepped core, and that pyramid casings were dressed from the bottom of the structure while the top was still building. This fall-out, as well as the two main conclusions, will be of some interest to Egyptologists but are unlikely to engage the attention of a wider public. They could be adequately accommodated in papers submitted to learned journals but by themselves they would hardly justify a book addressed to the general reader.

It was not until I realized the existence of a third conclusion, based on the two earlier ones, that the subject suddenly acquired a very much wider significance. Up to this point my interest had been entirely focussed on the immediate consequences of the initial discovery that an immense building catastrophe had occurred almost 5000 years ago. It proved an absorbing investigation into technological problems of ancient building construction but at no stage had it touched on the intriguing riddle of why the pyramids were built at all. The third conclusion completely changed the aspect of this originally fairly narrow study into an exciting quest for the answer to the riddle. As was made clear in the preface, it had never been my intention to solve this central problem and when its solution came, it was a complete surprise.

The third conclusion concerns the timing of building operations of successive pyramids. We have seen that the sudden decision to change the shape of the southern pyramid at Dahshur resulted from the catastrophe at Meidum. The disaster, as could be proved conclusively, took place in the middle of the third constructional phase at Meidum. On the other hand, the pyramid at Dahshur had reached about half of its projected height when the angle of elevation had been changed. This means that roughly 70 per cent of the masonry of the Bent Pyramid had already been placed in position when the previous pyramid at Meidum was still under construction. The inescapable conclusion is that the building periods of these two pyramids overlapped very considerably.

This, of course, conflicts with the opinion generally held so far that each pharaoh, on ascending the throne, began the building of his pyramid which it was his aim to finish well before his death. It means that the pyramids would have been built consecutively in the succeeding reigns. The discovery of strongly overlapping building periods came at first as a surprise. However, once we consider the technological effort involved, it soon becomes apparent that consecutive construction is an economic and organizational impossibility. Owing to their immense size, the building of pyramids on the scale undertaken in the Fourth Dynasty had to become an activity in its own right which demanded its own economic rules. It essentially dominated the pattern of life and, once started, tended to continue and escalate like a self-sustaining chemical reaction. It was the pyramid and not the pharaoh that ruled Egypt and new pyramids had to be erected, irrespective of whether a pharaoh was ready for burial or not. Once it is realized that the continuous construction of pyramids had become compulsive, the strange fact that Snofru should have built no fewer than three large pyramids acquires new meaning. These assertions must necessarily appear somewhat sweeping and it will now have to be shown how they were derived from our conclusion that the building periods of the large pyramids were overlapping.

First of all, we must take a closer look at the technological and economic implications of the construction of large pyramids. A great deal has, in fact, been written about methods of pyramid construction – in particular about the type of ramps and the way in which the blocks were quarried, transported and placed. Much of this has, of necessity, been mere conjecture, and almost nothing has been concluded from these discussions as to the size of the working force employed. Here the estimates have varied from a few thousands to a third of a million. The only historical figure is that given to Herodotus by his Egyptian informants 2000 years after the Pyramid Age. Herodotus mentions a labour force of 100,000, working in shifts of three months. His own wording on this point is ambiguous but it is generally assumed that the labourers worked for three months each year during the time of the annual inundation of the Nile when no agricultural work could be done. As will be shown, the labour force required for building the pyramids was very large and it seems unlikely that all these men could have been spared from the food production process by employing them continuously.

Only two serious attempt have been made to estimate the size of the labour force during the Fourth Dynasty. One, by Croon, was made at Borchardt's suggestion and assumed the use of ramps with a 20° inclination. It dealt with the Meidum pyramid only, but the assumptions made are reasonably well founded. The other, by Kozinsky, discusses the work on the Khufu pyramid but, unfortunately, the assumptions made in this study are not realistic enough to be of much value. It is clearly quite useless to try and arrive at the strength of the labour force employed through detailed models of the work process that was involved. About this process we know nothing beyond the fact that it succeeded and that it must have been extremely well organized in order to do so. In view of the superb planning shown by the Egyptians, we may assume that they made use of the most economic methods at their disposal. They may, for instance, have employed long approach ramps for the lower levels of a pyramid, only to switch to spiral embankments for the upper reaches; it does not really matter.

While, with the paucity of our knowledge, speculations on the exact methods of pyramid construction must remain idle, it is, by simple technological reasoning, relatively easy to arrive at an estimate of the total working force which should be correct within an order of magnitude. We know that in the space of about one century roughly 25 million tons of material, mostly limestone, but also mortar and brick, were piled up at the desert plateau above Meidum, Dahshur and Giza. Since the force exerted by one man in dragging up, together with others, a laden sledge amounts to 10 or 15 kilograms, we can calculate the average number of workers in the Pyramid Age, provided we can put in a figure for the speed of the operation. Assuming, as seems not unreasonable, that the time needed for one crew to bring building material from the quarry to the pyramid and putting it into place there varied between one to three days, we end up with a work force of about 50,000 men. Naturally, this time depended on the height to which the block had to be raised, but we have already accounted for this by making the time for the journey variable.

Our calculation includes the workers who had to build and dismantle the approach ramps but not the effort in quarrying and dressing the stone. A similar order of magnitude estimate yields about 10,000 or 20,000 men, counting all the auxiliary workers who had to keep the transport lines under repair, supplying lubrication water for the sledges, bringing food and water for the workers, etc. These 70,000 or so men were all seasonal workers who would be fully employed during the whole century under the assumption of steady work for three months. It cannot be emphasized too strongly that such an order of magnitude calculation can never give an accurate figure, but we are unlikely to have gone wrong by more than a factor of two, one way or the other.

In addition to the seasonal, and essentially unskilled, labour force there had to be employed skilled and semi–skilled masons who would cut, fit and smooth the casing stones. These, incidentally, are practically the only stones which bear quarry marks and, in some cases, dates. All the casing stones came from the underground quarries at Tura in the Mokattam hills on the east bank of the Nile and had to be transported, not only across the river but also a considerable distance overland. It is likely that these skilled masons were not seasonally employed but were working at Tura and on the pyramid site all the year round. Petrie found workmen's huts near the Khafre pyramid which he estimated as providing sufficient accommodation for 4000 people. A rough calculation of the labour involved in providing the casings and also the sculptured causeways would lead us to a somewhat higher estimate for the permanently employed artisans, which may have numbered close to 10,000. However, this force was not critical in the effort as a whole.

As set out above, our estimate represents an average figure for a labour force of constant strength employed with maximal efficiency and at a steady rate for the span of a hundred years. This certainly must be regarded as a gross simplification but it should be remembered that it is a minimum figure, since fluctuations in employment would cause an increase and not a decrease in the aggregate number of workers. For reasons to be discussed later, we may suspect that the actual labour force was less than 70,000 to begin with, increased to more than this number in the middle of the period, and was probably run down fairly rapidly at its end.

Considering these large numbers, we now begin to see why the building period of the Meidum pyramid and the Bent Pyramid had to overlap so heavily, and why the old concept of consecutive building periods under successive pharaohs was quite impossible. While it is true that, since the work was carried out during the inundation period, the drain on food production in the Pyramid Age was not serious, its general economic effect on the country must have been profound. We can best *Fig. 31* illustrate the pattern of work by a simple and highly idealized diagram. Let us consider first the accepted idea that on his accession to the throne the pharaoh started on the construction of his pyramid. He then would make use of the maximum available labour force in order to ensure that the monument should be completed as speedily as possible. This means that the maximum number of workers available for the project will have

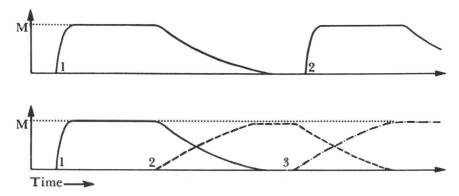

31 Idealized diagram of the maximum employable labour force as a function of time when building pyramids consecutively (above) and with overlap in construction (below). Overlapping construction of the pyramids could be phased in such a manner that the employable labour force was always equal to the maximum available labour force M. In this simple form the diagram takes no note of changes in the available labour force which during the Fourth Dynasty probably rose gradually and tapered off fairly rapidly after about a century

been run up as rapidly as possible and they would all be employed season after season for ten or twenty years. Throughout this time they were busy quarrying, transporting and placing the blocks. Then, however, the stage was reached when the pyramid had grown so high that access to the working area was becoming restricted and also slow. This means that the working force had to be run down during the next seasons until the pyramid was finished and all building activity ceased.

Nothing now happened until the next pharaoh started his reign, when the same process had to be gone through all over again. Since there would have been an interval between the building periods and also a gradual run-down of the force at the end of each period, our original calculation of the labour force is too low and about 150,000 workers had to be employed seasonally for, say, fifteen years, after which they would be idle for a similar period. It does not require much imagination to see that this type of employment pattern is utterly unrealistic and economically not feasible.

Even the lower figure of 70,000 workers will have represented a colossal army in the Egypt of 5000 years ago. Its communal feeding, clothing and upkeep for three or four months each year must have completely revolutionized the pattern of life of the whole country. In the course of ten or twenty years of construction, a large section of the working population came under the jurisdiction of a central administration which completely regulated its life. It was this new central administration which had now become responsible for their livelihood and to whom they had become answerable instead of to their tribal council and their village elders. The whole exercise involved far too drastic a change in the life of everybody to be reversed to the original pattern after a span of twenty years. No economy in the world, not even that of ancient Egypt, could have survived such a switching on and off of this immense working force. In other words, consecutive construction of large pyramids was simply not practicable.

Going back to our diagram we see that a critical stage for the maintenance of the working force was reached when limitation of access to the pyramid demanded its reduction. At this stage there was only one way out of the economic dilemma; the surplus workers had to be shifted to the start of the next pyramid. From then on not one but two pyramids were under construction, as indeed we have discovered in the simultaneous work on the Meidum and Bent Pyramids. It is also clear that pyramid building had to become essentially independent of the length of a pharaoh's reign since it had to continue unabated in order to maintain the employment pattern once it had been instituted. With construction periods running heavily into each other and the total labour force probably increasing all the time, the fact that there exist more large pyramids in the Fourth Dynasty than pharaohs who could be buried in them becomes understandable. Since the average reigns of Snofru, Khufu and Khafre seem each to have been about a quarter of a century, it is not surprising that they ended up with four, or possibly five, large pyramids.

The difficulty of gearing the construction of a pyramid to the length of a prospective reign had already occurred to the great German Egyptologist, Richard Lepsius, in the middle of the nineteenth century. How, he asked, could a pharaoh provide a completed or nearly completed monument at the time of his death when he could not possibly foresee how long he still had to live? Lepsius' answer was his famous accretion theory, according to which the king would start with a tomb chamber over which he would then erect a gradually increasing pyramid. Its final size would therefore be determined by the length of his reign.

When it was eventually discovered that the layout of the large pyramids had been determined at the outset, Lepsius' theory had to be discarded. However, it appears that by then his critics had forgotten the real reason for Lepsius' proposal and the problem of correlating pyramid construction and length of reign remained unsolved. The suggestion that the successor would finish the previous king's monument turns out to be a semantic argument. If a pharaoh died halfway through the completion of his monument, his successor would have had to finish a sizable structure when starting on his own pyramid, which would be indistinguishable from the pattern of continuous construction outlined above.

There exists in fact further evidence for the simultaneous construction of more than one pyramid at a time. We have mentioned earlier the quarry and date marks on the casing stones from the Tura quarries. A good deal of confusion has been caused by trying to use these dates in determining the sequence of pyramid building, and the results of these attempts have been baffling. Such difficulties are now removed since we know that at any time more than one pyramid was under construction. The blocks were dated either at the quarries or at the assembly points, and it was decided only later at which of the simultaneously rising pyramids they were to be employed.

Much has been said about procuring the immense labour force required for pyramid building and the cruelty of the Fourth Dynasty kings under whom this work was undertaken. In one of his learned publications Borchardt interrupts his discussion on building ramps with an account of toiling Egyptians dragging up stones on sledges under the lashes of the whips of overseers. He clearly felt that in no other way could such a prodigious achievement be sustained. However, Egypt of the Old Kingdom knew no slaves except for some prisoners-of-war. Moreover, the idea that large numbers of workers can be compelled by force makes little sense for an age in which the absence of superior weapons made it impossible to control many by a few. It is quite inconceivable that year after year an unwilling labour force could have been levied from scattered and distant villages. In other words, we have to assume that pyramid building was an essentially voluntary activity.

The most obvious incentive is believed to have been a religious one and based on the self-interest of the individual. We know far too little about the spiritual concepts prevailing 5000 years ago to say exactly what motivated the average Egyptian farmer to give his time and labour to pyramid construction. However, it is known from African divine kingship that obedience and service to the monarch confers benefit on the tribe as a whole, whose well-being and maintenance depend on him. It is likely that the beliefs originating in Egypt's Archaic Period included similar demands on the community. In particular, we may assume that the resurrection of the pharaoh, ensured by a suitable burial, was essential also for the afterlife of the common man. Personal sacrifice by each individual for the good of the community has been a generally accepted duty in primitive societies and has been retained by many highly civilized communities throughout the world. We ourselves have, since the Renaissance, tended to idealize individual initiative, but even our own society has submitted to the concept of sacrifice for the common good in patriotic wars.

Although the Egyptian's concern for his afterlife was of absorbing interest to him, it is probable that other aspects of pyramid construction also played an important part. Man does not live by faith alone, and it is quite possible that even 5000 years ago the provision of food by a central authority may have given villagers a new and much-needed sense of security. The story in *Genesis* of Joseph's prediction of seven fat years to be followed by seven lean ones clearly refers to fluctuations of the Nile inundation which made the setting up of governmental grain stores imperative. In fact, we find in the Giza tombs titles of officials who were responsible for the pharaoh's granaries. It is clear that the concentration of a large labour force for pyramid building also necessitated the institution of large-scale food storage. These grain stores had to be extensive enough to ensure supplies even in lean years and therefore they acted as an important buffer against the fluctuations of the Nile. Once instituted, this security against famine would certainly not be discontinued and must have acted as a powerful argument for retaining the labour pattern of steady pyramid building.

Another important aspect of the pyramid project is provided by the tally marks on the casing stones delivered from the quarries. They give the titles of the individual work teams who were to be credited with the supply. These names which have come down to us read: 'Stepped Pyramid Gang', 'Boat Gang', 'Craftsmen Crew', indicating special duties. We also find teams called: 'How vigorous is Snofru', or 'The powerful White Crown of Khufu', telling us the reign under which they worked. Of particular significance, however, may be such descriptions as: 'Vigorous Gang', 'Enduring Gang' and 'Sound Gang' which seem to refer to expressions of pride and competition. In fact, it looks as if participation in the pyramid project had created a sense of comradeship among the workmates, and that people who before had been strangers to each other had found a new basis for friendship. It is a phenomenon which I have encountered in modern China where huge labour forces are brought together to build a dam or a bridge. There is never any difficulty in obtaining sufficient workers because, in addition to good pay, kudos is attached to being selected for an important and much publicized project. When the men go back to their villages, they are the heroes of the community who, in the evenings, tell the story of how they built the dam.

Altogether one begins to wonder whether esoteric religious concepts were really more important in bringing about the Pyramid Age than such down-to-earth issues as assured food supply and a new dimension in neighbourliness. To answer this question we have to go back to the days of Imhotep and to his design of King Zoser's funerary monument. After four centuries of fitful attempts at unification and almost constant internal strife, the stage had been reached when the gods Horus and Seth were finally at peace. The new pharaoh was the son of the king of Upper

THE SOLUTION

Egypt, Kha-sekhemui, and of the heiress of Lower Egypt, Nemathap, who thus became the first 'great queen' of the united kingdom of the Nile. King Zoser not only inherited peace throughout his land but also the opportunity of utilizing this new potential provided by the most civilized nation in the world. The stage was set for the next great step in the development of human society, the creation of the state. The pyramid was going to provide the means of achieving it.

It would be unrealistic to think that, with almost fiendish cunning, Imhotep devised the method of mass employment to attain this aim. In fact, we can easily prove that this was not the case. When Zoser ascended the throne, there existed the capital of Memphis and a few other fortified towns, all of them probably with a rather limited urban population. The great mass of the Egyptians lived in tribal units, engaged in village agri-culture, separated from each other and possibly not always on friendly terms. The idle season of the inundation provided the villagers with a good opportunity to raid neighbourhood communities for cattle and women. This is a tribal custom practised all over the world. Some taxes were evidently gathered, but this activity too was probably somewhat hazardous.

Imhotep set out to build at the desert edge above Memphis a mag-nificent monument for the living god, the Horus Neterkhet Zoser. We shall never know whether his foremost aim was the grandeur of the construction or the idea of employing troublesome villagers during the inundations. One thing, however, is certain: the problem of large-scale organization must have been foremost in his mind. He used it to an unprecedented degree and was evidently, besides, the creator of an efficient and complex civil service. This had to be the basis for all his operations. From then onward the central administration of Egypt increased steadily, and it had to be closely tied to the construction of pyramids since this became the foremost centralized activity in the country.

It is almost uncanny that after 5000 years the technological evidence should allow us to follow the way of Imhotep's mind after he had taken the first crucial step. However, this is exactly what we can do. The first monument was a stone mastaba erected above the tomb shaft. It was the first stone structure of any size ever built, 63 m. square and 8. m. high, covered with dressed limestone from Tura. For this, almost 10,000 tons of stone had to be quarried, to say nothing about the large surrounding wall, also of stone. Perhaps a labour force of three to five thousand men were working on it all the time. It certainly was a larger number than had been employed on any earlier tomb, but it was only the beginning. As mentioned in an earlier chapter, the mastaba then underwent three

149

Fig. 9

small successive alterations, and after that something completely unfore-seen took place. Above the mastaba was erected a pyramid of four steps, containing no less than 200,000 tons of limestone.

Evidently, with the building of the stone mastaba Imhotep was feeling his way in building with a new material as well as with procuring and transporting it. Mud brick had given way to limestone. He and his staff must have discovered, during the construction of the mastaba, a number of salient facts. First of all they found that limestone could be quarried and transported in large quantities provided labour was available. Secondly, their organization was able to master the complex tasks of the various working processes and enlist the labour required. Thirdly, they began to realize the building potentialities of the new material. Correlating all these factors, they suddenly saw that they might be able to build a tower reaching to heaven that would dominate the capital below them. To a young and growing society this must have been an exhilarating prospect of unlimited possibilities, and so they decided on building a pyramid, a man-made mountain.

One more problem had to be solved; it had to be a mountain which would not collapse. They knew that they had to embark on a venture into the unknown but they set out on it full of confidence in a magnificent invention. It was Imhotep's stabilizing buttress wall. As the future was to show, this invention carried the Egyptian architects through a period of unparalleled achievement.

The next problem was the labour force. Imhotep must have felt pretty confident in the ability of his administration to provide him with a labour force twenty or thirty times larger than that used for the stone mastaba. It was most likely at this juncture that mainly seasonal labour began to be employed, leading to the beginning of a new economic pattern.

When the pyramid of four steps had been completed, Imhotep and his colleagues knew that their stability calculations had been correct. They also knew by this time that the new employment pattern was not only feasible but that it was eminently successful. Unless they had been satisfied on this last issue, they would hardly have embarked on the next two enlargements of the pyramid, the first by widening it, and the second by heightening it to six steps. The quantity of stone required in these succes-sive operations amounted to no less than 650,000 tons, more than three times that already invested in the four-stepped pyramid. This fantastic escalation of effort, all in one and the same project, leaves little doubt that seasonal mass employment was proving its worth, not only at the building site but also probably in the government of the emerging state structure. With this final enlargement, pyramid building had passed from the stage of a daring experiment to the basic work-pattern of the Egyptian society.

It is a pity that the technological evidence of the rest of the Third Dynasty does not allow us to follow the decisions of builders and administrators with the same clarity as in the construction of Zoser's pyramid. The two unfinished pyramids of Sekhemket and Khaba show that pyramid building continued during their short reigns. We do not, of course, know whether Zoser's pyramid was finished in his own lifetime. If not, it may have been decided that the available labour force had primarily to be employed in its completion, leaving a rather smaller number of workmen for the two new monuments. However, the reason why they were never finished has probably nothing to do with the labour supply. Something had happened to the direction of the administration in using the royal power.

At the end of the Third Dynasty a profound change in the position of the pharaoh seems to have taken place. Again, the evidence for this is entirely technological. The next pyramid, that at Meidum, departed, as we have already seen, in several ways drastically from the Third Dynasty pattern. Even before it was to be transformed from a step structure into a true pyramid, a number of significant alterations had been made in the basic layout of the monument as a whole. The large enclosure was omitted, as were the extensive replicas of the king's palace and of his ceremonial *heb-sed* court. The southern tomb which exists in both Zoser's and Sekhemket's monument is missing and instead there appeared a small subsidiary pyramid south of the main structure. Together with the change into a true pyramid, the pyramid complex with mortuary and valley buildings and with a causeway to the Nile was instituted, which became the standard pattern for the rest of the Old Kingdom.

Fig. 13

There is no doubt that this revolutionary change had religious significance but the implied re-orientation in the people's basic beliefs has perhaps been over-estimated. They went on erecting pyramids as they had been doing since the days of Imhotep. The possible ascendancy of the priests of Re has been mentioned but perhaps this was a power struggle within the top rank of the administration rather than a popular movement. Conceivably there was an attempt in the palace to stop pyramid building since it tended to transfer initiative from the divine king to the heads of administration. Whatever happened there is no record of serious troubles at the end of the Third Dynasty, and the first pharaoh of the Fourth, Snofru, became the greatest pyramid-builder of all. By omitting the archaic trappings of the ritual rejuvenation court from his pyramid complex, he was the first pharaoh to step into a new era of kingship. Under the influence of the Heliopolitan priesthood, Snofru changed from a supernatural being endowed with magical power into a head of state.

Snofru's escalation of the pyramid project far outshines Imhotep's example. We have more than once referred to his two, or even three, pyramids which surpassed Imhotep's effort at Saqqara. We have also dealt with the misfortune that befell Snofru's attempt to build a tall true pyramid. The magnificence of this huge and shining emblem of the sun god has obscured another aspect of this architectural change which may have an important technological significance. The new type of pyramid complex differed from that of Zoser and Sekhemket, not only in the shape of the monument itself. The Third Dynasty complexes contained, besides the central pyramid, a great number of dummy buildings and a very extensive temenos wall with recessed panelling. All these structures required a large number of skilled masons. At the Fourth Dynasty pyramids, these subsidiary buildings were reduced to a minimum while at the same time the bulk of the monuments increased more and more.

This signifies a steady increase in the force of unskilled seasonal workers in comparison with the permanently employed craftsmen whose number, if anything, may have diminished. It all points to a conscious encouragement of the employment of agricultural villagers without at the same time augmenting the permanently occupied people. In other words, the central administration constantly increased their hold over the population as a whole without training correspondingly more specialists. It thus appears that their motives were purely political by creating a progressively growing economic dependence of the common people on what was now becoming the state.

It would be quite wrong to assume that this increasing power of the civil service and the steadily rising involvement of the villagers in the pyramid project impoverished the country. Such evidence of the period of Snofru's rule as has come down to us indicates an age of expansion and rapidly increasing prosperity. The fragments of the Palermo Stone list temples and palaces that were built in Snofru's reign, and in his thirteenth year he organized an expedition into the Sudan which brought home 7000 men and women as captives and 200,000 oxen and sheep. He also secured the southern frontier with a number of fortified garrisons. In the following year he sent another expedition, this time a fleet of forty seagoing ships, to Lebanon to procure cedar wood. It set the pattern for an important trade, since Egypt has hardly any timber, and it is likely that the cedarwood beams inside the Bent Pyramid were part of this consignment. Military campaigns were mounted against the neighbouring tribes in the western and eastern deserts. Snofru also secured the caravan route into Sinai and his exploits were commemorated by inscriptions at Wadi Maghara, where turquoise and copper were mined to be sent across the desert to Egypt.

Throughout Egypt's long history Snofru was remembered as a benevolent king and for the first time there is a record of the pharaoh as a human being instead of an almost abstract god. The Westcar papyrus mentions that the king addressed his courtiers as 'comrades' and from another source we learn that he called the old vizier of his father 'my friend'. While the person of the king of Upper and Lower Egypt remained forever beyond the reach of ordinary mortals, Snofru appears here as not a god but a man among other men. The priests of Heliopolis had newly decreed that the pharaoh would become divine only after his death. In his lifetime he was the supreme head of a new form of society, which we call the state.

The pyramid project was creating a type of community which had never existed before. Tribal villagers were welded by common work into people with the consciousness of nationhood. It was probably for the first time that they thought of themselves first and foremost as Egyptians. Working together, under one administration, their differences and mutual suspicions were bound to lessen. With this unifying labour on three large pyramids in the reign of Snofru it may have become of secondary importance in which of them he was eventually buried. In fact, it was not even important whether his body was buried in any of his three pyramids. Those puzzles which beset Egyptologists for a long time: in which pyramid the pharaoh was buried, and whether any pyramid ever contained a body, are not solved by our considerations but they have lost much of their former significance. Once it is realized that the main object of pyramid construction was a work programme leading to a new social order, the religious meaning and ritual importance of the pyramid recede into the background. If anything, these man-made mountains are a monument to the progress of man into a new pattern of life, the national state, which was to become his social home for the next 5000 years.

After Snofru two even larger pyramids were to come and another 14 million tons of stone were to be piled up on the desert plateau. One cannot help feeling that the Egyptians gloried as much in this stupendous achievement, towering over their living world, as over having sent off their pharaohs to accompany the sun. Pyramid building was now getting on for a century; for three or four generations of Egyptians it had become their normal life. By then, we may assume, the social object of the gigantic technological project had been attained. The country had now lived for so long in its new social and political environment that the old tribal existence was largely forgotten. It was time to give up what had become an unnecessary and wasteful occupation, and it is remarkable that the running down of the pyramid project should have been achieved with what appears a minimum of trouble.

153

As happens with any large and heavily entrenched programme, the pyramid age may have gone on for just a bit too long. The administration had evidently manoeuvred itself into a vortex of pyramid construction from which it was difficult to escape. A large section of the civil service, reaching down into low levels of administration and comprising several thousand officials, derived and justified its livelihood from pyramid building. It represented a large vested interest. Keeping this in mind, certain upheavals in the dynastic orbit which we have already touched upon and which have usually been explained as a palace revolt, acquire a more profound aspect.

There was obviously some trouble at Khufu's death. The legitimate heir, Kawab, was dead and the succession should have passed to one of his full brothers, all sons of Khufu and Queen Merytyetes, who alone carried the royal blood. Instead, the throne was usurped by Djedefre, who then married the great queen of the next generation, Hetepheres II, the widow of Kawab. So far it all looks like a harem intrigue, except for one point. Djedefre, although he put the finishing touches to Khufu's monument, had all further work at Giza stopped. Since we know that at that time Khufu's pyramid was essentially finished, work must have been well advanced on the next large pyramid, eventually to be used by Khafre. However, Djedefre did not complete this Giza pyramid for himself but selected for his own burial a site at Abu Roash, and it is significant that the pyramid which he planned there for his own use was almost ten times smaller than that of Khufu.

Far from being the seizure of power by the son of a concubine, it very much looks as if Djedefre's succession to Khufu was based on a movement to break away from the pyramid building establishment of Heliopolis. He occupied the throne for only seven years and we do not know how he died. During Djedefre's reign a gradually decreasing labour force was probably employed on the construction of the immense causeway at Abu Roash. Such a reduced force would have been quite capable of building the small projected pyramid as well at the same time with no undue difficulty.

With Khafre's accession, work at Giza was resumed but it is obvious that it never regained its original strength or impetus. Khafre's own pyramid, which, when he became pharaoh, was probably in the last phase of construction, was completed, though not with the same care as that of Khufu. In fact, it is even doubtful whether after Djedefre's death the number of men employed again at Giza were brought up to anything like the original strength. It would be more rational to assume that the labour force was not appreciably increased again and it was evidently run down to a low strength for building the last Fourth Dynasty pyramid, that of Menkaure. For the next monument, Shepseskaf's Mastabat Fara'un, a quite modest number of workmen will have sufficed.

One certainly would not wish to claim that our analysis of the end of the Pyramid Age will be correct in detail. However, these last conclusions were arrived at by correlating the technological evidence with the known succession of kings at the end of the Fourth Dynasty and, on the whole, they seem to make sense. It is also interesting to compare these deductions with the legends concerning the pyramid builders that were handed down through Egyptian history. While Snofru was always remembered as a beneficent pharaoh, the same cannot be said of Khufu and Khafre. Herodotus records a story that Khufu and Khafre were hard and wicked kings who suppressed the people and closed the temples, and that it was Menkaure who opened them again and was beloved. Popular legends, while they can hardly be regarded as established historical accounts, often contain a grain of truth. In the present case they fit rather too well to be discounted.

It is not unlikely that the vested interest of the administration tended to prolong the pyramid project beyond the stage when its usefulness had been exhausted. Moreover, bringing the villagers together to a common, and remunerative, task will at first have brought about friendly relations between strange tribesmen. On the other hand, this fusion must eventually have had the effect of turning them into an organized force which was capable of discovering common interests other than those in the mind of the establishment. In other words, once a homogeneous nation had been created, it was likely that paternalism gave way to a trade union spirit. The newly established state of the Egyptian people may have taken on a life of its own.

The core and driving force in the administration was the Heliopolitan priesthood of Re who had initiated and sustained the pyramid project. Starting with Imhotep's escalation of the labour force, the programme had proved eminently successful. The enterprise had spawned an immense and well-organized civil service which permeated and regulated all aspects of life. Its close connection with the pharaoh was ensured by the fact that the vizier and the highest officials were royal princes. Thereby the administration was fully integrated with the religious leadership of the nation and opportunity was provided for consultation on all important decisions. The pharaoh himself had become the spiritual figurehead of a large and highly efficient administrative machine whose directives came from the priesthood of Re, who were the real government of Old Kingdom Egypt.

However, there was still the priesthood of Ptah with its hold on the scribes and learned men, and, as evidently happened at the end of Menkaure's reign, the pharaoh, in this case Shepseskaf, may have felt assured of popular support against the pyramid diehards of Heliopolis. He evidently brought it off, at least for the time being. There is an echo of priestly schism in the legend that Khufu and Khafre closed the temples. Possibly these were the temples of Ptah. One thing is quite certain, Shepseskaf's refusal to build a pyramid brought the Heliopolitan priesthood to their senses. They eschewed further construction of gigantic pyramids and settled for a new and relatively inexpensive solar emblem, the obelisk. A period of greater influence of the Ptah priests may have temporarily intervened during Shepseskaf's reign but again the reorientation towards the solar cult of the Fifth Dynasty appears to have taken place without spectacular disorders.

A similar mastaba to Shepseskaf's was constructed for Queen Khent-kaues, the carrier of the royal inheritance. However, whereas Shepseskaf forsook the Giza necropolis for Saqqara, his sister Khentkaues returned to Giza with a tomb built between the causeways of the Khafre and Menkaure pyramids. In one way or another, probably by marriage to the *Table 2* high priest of Heliopolis, Userkaf, she became the founder of the Fifth Dynasty. It is interesting to note that Userkaf was probably not a usurper but may have had his own share of the royal blood. However, it seems that he inherited it, not through the branch of the royal family represented by Khafre, Menkaure and Shepseskaf, but from his mother Neferhetepes who was the daughter of the much married great Queen Hetepheres II by the renegade Djedefre.

We cannot leave the Pyramid Age with its stupendous achievements in both buildings and social change without having a look at its life and people. As for the pyramid builders themselves, a seated statue of Zoser *Plate 10* was found in a small chamber attached to the north side of the Step Pyramid. Unfortunately, its face was badly damaged by thieves who broke out the eyes which were probably made of rock crystal. Even so, the features reveal the high cheekbones, characteristic of some of his successors. There exist a number of good profile representations in the *Plate 46* reliefs of the underground chambers, which show a man with strong features and an aquiline nose.

Until recently we did not know what Snofru looked like, but the post-war excavations at Dahshur have yielded a stela with the king's *Plate 47* portrait. His profile shows a surprisingly weak face with receding chin. Only one likeness of Khufu has been found so far. It is a small ivory *Plate 48* figure and, although it is not too well preserved, the king's features are clear enough to indicate determination, underlined by high cheekbones and tight lips. The same high cheekbones and firm determined mouth *Plate 55* characterize the life-size quarzite head of Djedefre in the Louvre Museum.

52 Head of the diorite statue of Khafre from his valley building. He is protected by the wings of the Horus falcon.

53, 54 The double statue of Menkaur
and Khamerernebti II (*left*) shows th
queen's arm encircling her husband
waist, which is usually regarded as
mark of affection. However, it may b
a symbolic pose of presenting th
pharaoh on whom she, as royal heires
has conferred the crown. Compariso
of their profiles (*above*) leaves no dou
that they were brother and sister.

55-57 Djedefre's high cheekbones and firm mouth (*right*) resemble those of his father Khufu whom he followed on the throne. There is again close family resemblance between Shepseskaf (*below*), the last pharaoh of the Fourth Dynasty, and his parents shown on the opposite page. Userkaf (*below right*), the first king of the Fifth Dynasty was possibly a grandson of Djedefre and Hetepheres II (*see also* Table II).

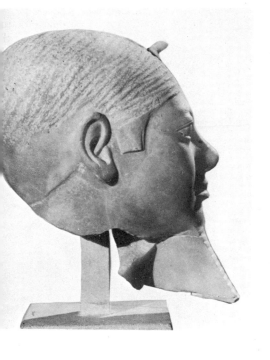

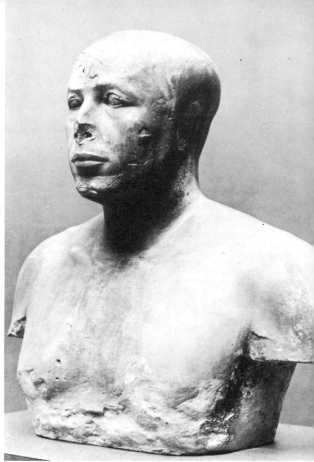

58-60 Portraits of the great officials leave no doubt that they were powerful executives. Hemon (*above left*) was Khufu's vizier and may have been the builder of his pyramid. Ankhaf (*above right*) was possibly a son of Snofru and was vizier in the time of Khafre. Often high civil servants liked to be portrayed at work as scribes (*left*).

61-63 Double statues and family groups were often placed in the tombs. Prince Rahotep, commander of the army under Huni (*right*) is shown with his wife Nofret, and the dwarf Seneb (*below*) with his wife and children. Dwarfs, because they are conspicuous, were in demand as custodians of treasure. The ethnic type in the Nile valley has remained unchanged for thousands of years and when the statue of Ka-aper was found (*below right*), the fellahin were struck by his resemblance to their village elder.

64, 65 At the small Aztec pyramid at Santa Cecilia (*above*), the only one whose sanctuary is preserved, the steepness of the stairs is enhanced by rising banisters. The same impression is produced at the Maya pyramid of Kukulcan in Chichen Itza (*below*) by making the banisters diverge towards the top. The effect is only noticeable when seen from a distance.

66-68   The circular cult mound at Cuicuilco (*above*) had to be partly excavated from the engulfing lava. The ornate facade of the temple of Quetzalcoatl at Teotihuacan (*below left*) was only discovered when a superimposed later phase of the building was removed. Mexican pyramid steps (*below right*) have to be negotiated with caution and fatal accidents can occur.

69 Reclining figures, called Chacmols, are typical of the Toltec civilization. The bowl he holds served as a receptacle for the hearts of sacrificed victims.

70 The excavated remains of a ceremonial cannibal feast at the pyramid of Cholula.

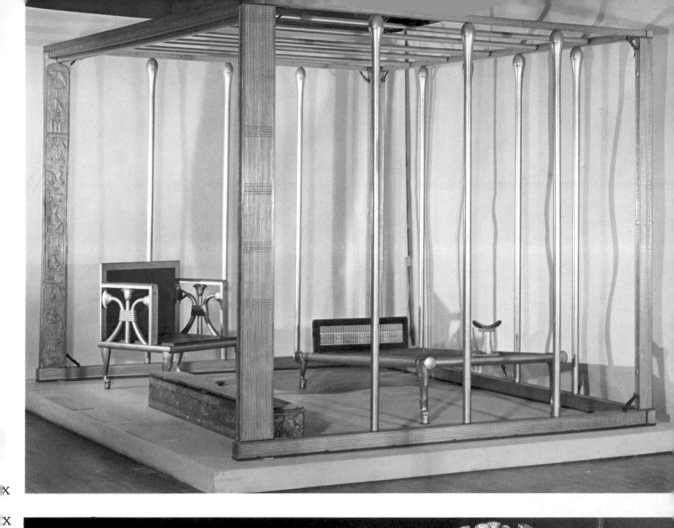

IX Tomb furniture of Hetepheres I, Great Queen of Snofru and mother of Khufu. It was found in a chamber at the bottom of a deep shaft close to Khufu's pyramid (*see also* plate 35).

X Wooden figures of servants from the tomb of Djehutynakht at el-Bersha.

XI The pyramids of Giza, seen from the south-east. From right to left: Khufu, Khafre and Menkaure. The three subsidiary pyramids of Menkaure can be seen in the foreground on the left.

XII The pyramid of Menkaure at Giza seen from the north, showing the granite casing at the bottom and the hole cut into the structure above by the Caliph Malek al Aziz Othman in AD 1215.

Plate 52

Far better preserved than any of these is the magnificent diorite statue of Khafre from the valley temple of his pyramid. Here the full mastery of the Old Kingdom sculptors is revealed for the first time. The artist has created an intensely human portrait, which at the same time is far removed from the everyday world. Out of his human face the king's eyes gaze into space and the incomprehensible realm of the divinity. His companions are not the mortals but the sun god who, in the shape of the Horus falcon, spreads his wings protectively around the king's head. The pharaoh has become the sacred link between man, whose form he bears, and the gods who rule the universe. The same enigmatic detachment is expressed in Khafre's other surviving portrait: the head of the Sphinx. Havoc, wrought for over 4000 years by man and the elements, has failed to obliterate the serene majesty of the features which the ancient Egyptian sculptor carved out of the living rock. The mastery in the expression of this face, which seems to look from our world into the next one, has haunted man for hundreds of generations.

Plate I

Khafre's portraits seem to stand between the ages of divine kingship and of the human beings on the throne who followed him. There is nothing divine or supernatural in the sensual face of Menkaure with its generous lips and slightly bulging eyes. It is again the uncanny skill of the sculptor who, in this representation, was to bring the pharaoh down to earth without sacrificing the family similarity with his father Khafre. This unmistakable likeness is retained in the portrait of Shepseskaf, in which the sensual countenance of Menkaure is almost degraded into vulgarity.

Plates 53 54

Plate 56

Neither is there any transcendental quality in the representations of the great queens. In spite of its mutilitated state, the head of Khufu's great wife, Queen Merytyetes, shows beauty and feminine warmth. The Boston Museum of Fine Arts has a charming double statue of the much-married queen, Hetepheres II, and her equally royal daughter, Meresankh III. The mother's arm lies protectingly over Meresankh's shoulder; they were both carriers of the dynastic inheritance and both spouses of Khafre. In Menkaure's sister-wife, Khamerernebti II, her brother's sensual expression is mildly accentuated through her feminine features. Passing on to the Fifth Dynasty, we search in vain in the face of Userkaf for traces of the uncompromising determination of Khufu and Djedefre, or for Khafre's divine mission. It is the face of a human executive with all his virtues and failings.

Plate 49

Plate 50

Plate 54

Plate 57

We have dealt earlier with the civil service in the pyramid age and we are fortunate that the consummate skill of the Fourth Dynasty sculptors, coupled with the demand for the closest possible likeness, has provided us with numerous portraits of high officials and their wives. Many of these are the strange 'reserve heads' found in their tombs. These may have served as substitutes if the mummy was destroyed, but we are in the dark as to their definite purpose. It is astonishing that on many of them the ears seem to have been broken off purposely. In one case they highlight the close connection with Africa, since the facial features of the wife of a high official leave no doubt that she was a Negress.

Plate 51

On the whole, these intelligent and determined faces would equally fit any modern meritocracy, and officials often liked to be represented at their work as 'scribes'. There are also many family groups, among them that of the dwarf Seneb. Dwarfs were much in demand as treasurers since they would be easily recognized and therefore less likely to attempt a quiet getaway with the valuables under their care. Even the earliest examples of portrait sculpture, such as that of Prince Rahotep and his wife, who lived at the time of Snofru, show the stamp of a sophisticated and astonishingly 'modern' society. He could be an army officer of today and the Lady Nofret would effortlessly pass muster in any elegant set of our own time. We even know what their servants and craftsmen looked like from the effigies which accompanied their masters in the life after death. Finally, Reisner's discovery of the tomb of Hetepheres has provided us with the furniture of Snofru's great queen which, in sheer elegance and the restrained use of gold, surpasses anything which the tomb of Tutankhamun discloses.

Plates 59, 63
Plate 60
Plate 62

Plate 61

Plates X, 4

Plate IX

What little has been left of Old Kingdom literature agrees with this picture of a cultured and dignified world. The advice of such men as Ptahotep, Kagemi and others reflects a sober wisdom which would have done credit to the philosophers of any later age. They praise the ideal of the 'silent man' who receives the order given by his superior without argument and who carries it out conscientiously and without giving himself airs. He must not boast of his learning but should always be ready to learn himself, if necessary from the poor and humble. He should be kind to petitioners and patiently hear out their case before making a decision. Greed and corruption are described as the worst malady, which is incurable and so contagious that any dealings with it are impossible.

Together with these stern precepts for the civil servant goes a good deal of more homely advice, such as not to bring a case against one's superior unless you are sure of its outcome. One should eat sparingly at a banquet, even if one has to master one's desire – which only takes a moment – because it is disgraceful to appear greedy. Finally, some good advice to those who visit their friends' houses not to approach the women: 'Men are made fools by their gleaming limbs and brief enjoyment soon turns into bitter regret.'

These brief glimpses of life in the Pyramid Age have been included to show the social and intellectual background against which we must regard the gigantic technological project. They reflect a sober and essentially practical society whose mind and reactions were eminently sensible and show little sign of devoting much effort to esoteric issues. Building pyramids, as we suggest, for political and economic reasons seems to fit a good deal better into the picture of this level-headed and sophisticated community than devoting prodigious effort in erecting several gigantic tombs to bury one pharaoh. The pyramids do not represent an aim in itself but the means to achieve an aim: the creation of a new form of society. These huge heaps of stone mark the place where man invented the state.

7 The Mexican Pyramids

On their first voyage to Mexico in 1518 the Spanish Conquistadors found pyramids and also discovered the use to which they were put. The doughty old soldier and chronicler of the conquest, Bernal Diaz de Castillo, accompanied this early expedition as a boy and he left us his account of this first visit to an offshore island:

Plate 64

> As soon as the boats were launched, the Captain, Juan de Grijalva, and many of us soldiers went off to visit the island for we saw smoke rising from it and we found two masonry houses, very well built, each house with steps leading up to some altars, and on these altars were idols with evil-looking bodies, and that very night five indians had been sacrificed before them. Their chests had been cut open and their arms and thighs had been cut off and the walls were covered with blood.
>
> At this we stood greatly amazed and gave the island the name of Isla de Sacrificios, and it is so marked on the charts.

Diaz's reference to 'houses' simply means that they were stone buildings and not the miserable palm thatch huts which the Spaniards had so far encountered. The mention of steps makes it clear that these buildings were small pyramids, as were found in Mexico by the hundreds later on.

When Columbus died in 1506, fourteen years after his first landfall in the Western Hemisphere, he was still certain that he had reached India. The islands of the Antilles which he and his captains had discovered were regarded as the outposts of the continent of Asia, and in his last voyage he was looking for a strait that would carry his ships to the 'India of the Portuguese'. The Portuguese, of course, knew better. They had refused Columbus' proposal in the first place because, unlike him, they had the correct circumference of the earth, established by Erathostenes in 250 BC, which they kept a closely guarded secret. The Portuguese research establishment, founded by Prince Henry the Navigator, had correctly decided that anyone sailing for India to the west would perish on the immense ocean. What they could not know was that America lay in the way of such a voyage.

The 'Indies' discovered by Columbus proved an embarrassment rather than a boon. Instead of treasures, the Spaniards found hunger and fever, and the natives, while relatively docile, preferred to die rather than work on plantations. However, there were persistent rumours of a rich and powerful country further to the west, which naturally they took to mean India. When in 1517 Hernandez de Cordova sailed from Cuba to the Bahamas in quest of slaves he was driven by heavy gales far from his course and finally touched land, which the Indians there called Yucatan. Unlike the timid and effete native of the Antilles, the inhabitants of the mainland proved warlike and treacherous. At the first landing, Cordova's men were lured a short way inland and promptly ambushed. From then on they found it difficult to go ashore anywhere and once even lost their casks which they had hoped to fill with fresh water at the mouth of a stream. However, on their ill-fated expedition to the village they had seen stone buildings and gold ornaments which convinced them that beyond lay a much higher civilization than they had encountered so far. This prompted the governor of Cuba, Diego Velasquez, to send Grijalva on the expedition to which Diaz's record, quoted above, refers.

Although Grijalva's men could not penetrate into the interior, they verified the existence of stone buildings, of an advanced culture and, most important, of gold. The next expedition, in the following year, was that of Hernán Cortes which conquered not only the Aztec capital but the whole of Montezuma's empire as well as the rest of Central America. He gained enormous treasures of gold and the Spaniards tortured innumerable Indians for generations to come, to reveal the location of their gold mines. They simply could not believe the truth – that Mexico had no mines. In fact all the gold for the ornaments and jewellery, duly melted down by the Spaniards, had been panned in the rivers of Central America and accumulated in Mexico over a long period of time, because gold does not rust away.

When at their first meeting Montezuma's envoys had asked the reason for the Spaniards' strange lust for gold, Cortes had replied with commendable frankness and cynicism that the white men suffered from a disease of the heart for which gold was the only remedy. At the same historical banquet the Aztecs, quite unintentionally, had their own back on their future conquerors. Most of the Spaniards were violently sick when they learned that the delicious roast they had eaten happened to be human flesh with a savoury sauce of human blood. They now realized why the arms and legs of the sacrificial corpses, mentioned by Diaz, had been cut off. They were required for the table. With the sacrifice of many thousands of victims each year, cannibalism became almost inevitable, and was practised quite generally. Purists like to state that it was 'ritual' and

32 A human sacrifice at the top of a Mexican pyramid. The victim is stretched over the sacrificial stone by four priests while a fifth opens the body with a stone knife. He then tears out the still palpitating heart and offers it to the sun. (Codex Florentino)

33 A priest, representing the god Xipe, is dressed in the skin of a flayed victim. (Codex Florentino)

part of religion, but the fattening of slaves in cages reported by the Conquistadors and the careful choice of succulent cuts, such as hands and thighs, make us suspect that the culinary aspects of cannibalism were not neglected.

Plate 70

Pyramids and human sacrifice at the top of them were discovered by the Conquistadors to be a standard feature of daily life throughout Mexico. Since human sacrifice came to an abrupt end with the Conquest, the actual number of sacrifices is not certain but native records show that at the dedication of the great temple of Tenochtitlan in 1487 twenty thousand victims were dispatched. When thirty years later the Spaniards entered the great square of Tenochtitlan, now Mexico City, they found a rack holding many thousands of skulls and similar depositories were discovered in all the other towns and even villages. The Aztecs were a warlike race and they had a multitude of thirsty gods, above all Huitzilopochtli, the humming bird who led them into battle.

His innumerable victims were led up the steps of the pyramid, each stretched with his back over the altar by four priests who had gripped

Fig. 32

his arms and legs. A fifth priest plunged a stone knife into his belly, ripping open the abdominal cavity, and deftly tore out the still pulsating heart from his chest to be offered on behalf of the god to the sun. Often the victims were first prodded into dancing around the altar, as the Spaniards saw their captured comrades doing on St John's night in June 1521. Victims in honour of Xipe Totec were crucified and flayed alive

Fig. 33

so that the priests could wear their skins. Tezcatlipoca, the smoking mirror, required his bound victims to be thrown onto glowing embers to be pulled out again in time to have their hearts torn out. Women, too, were sacrificed, being beheaded while dancing, and the tears of children taken for sacrifice were meant to signify rain which was needed.

There was a never-ending variety of ritual for which the pyramid had to provide the stage. It imposed certain and definite demands on the architect. First of all, the spectacle should be visible to a large audience

Plate 65

who should be able to watch the ritual in all its phases. At the beginning of the ceremony, the victim had to be identified with the god to whom he was offered. He was given the headdress characteristic of the god and his emblems. Then he took leave of mankind, being led up the steps of the pyramid, and this ascent into the sphere of divinity required a broad and impressive stairway. Much thought and architectural skill had been devoted by the Mexican builders to the various solutions of this problem, which we shall discuss presently in detail.

After the victim had reached the top of the pyramid, the central feature of the ritual, the sacrifice itself and the apotheosis of the dead man, had to be enacted. He was believed to join the god when his heart was offered up to the sun. It was therefore important that every detail of the victim's death throes should be observable to the crowd in the pyramid enclosure. It meant that the pyramid, while being sufficiently imposing, must not be too high. Finally, the corpse had to be disposed of, and this, too, should be done in a spectacular manner. For this purpose the body was rolled down the stairway which had to be steep enough to provide an uninterrupted passage to the ground. Finally, as a backcloth to the ritual there had to be a shrine at the top of the platform which was a sanctuary dedicated to the god and which served as an abode for the holy image. Some of the Aztec pyramids, such as that in the capital, Tenochtitlan, and another close by, at Tenayuca, carried at the top two sanctuaries, dedicated to different gods. At these twin structures only the pyramid itself was common to both cults but separate staircases led up side by side to the two sanctuaries.

Practically all the Aztec pyramids in the Valley of Mexico had a core of adobe bricks, which were faced with stone held together with mortar. This sets certain limits on the steepness of the stairs but, since the total height of the structure was modest, a fairly high angle of elevation could be maintained. Even the most important pyramids, such as the great temple of Tenochtitlan, rose to only about 30 m., not more than a fifth of the great pyramids of Giza. Since the staircase served as a stage for the initial phases of the sacrifice, the spectators' interest had to be focused on it and the impression of steepness was further enhanced by an accentuated elevation of the banisters near the top.

Fig. 35

Thanks to the use of different materials, the Mayas of Yucatan were able to construct steeper stairs, reaching higher. They built their pyramids throughout of stone, held together with a very strong lime mortar. When set, this type of structure was essentially monolithic and there was no danger of slip or plastic flow. In this way they could achieve angles of elevation of up to 75°, much steeper than anything attempted in Egypt, and about as steep as the remaining core of the Meidum pyramid. The great stairway of the 'Pyramid of the Magician' at Uxmal rises at an angle of almost 50° to a height of nearly 35 m. This is clearly at the very limit of practicability for a flight of steps; when I climbed it I certainly had to keep a good hold of the iron chain now provided for visitors to make a safe ascent. The steepness of these stairways, which was necessary for their sinister purpose, was brought home to me by a macabre incident at the pyramid of Kukulcan at Chichen Itza. Emerging from a tunnel at ground level, I came upon a group of Maya Indians in a hushed silence. At the bottom of the stairs was a large pool of blood. One of the Maya girls whom I had seen making the ascent a few minutes earlier had lost her footing and cracked open her skull.

Plate XV

Plate 68

At this pyramid another cunning device had been used by the architects to make the stairway appear even steeper than it is. This was achieved by making the banisters diverge slightly towards the top of the stairs. Standing, as the spectators were, directly in front of the pyramid, this architectural trick cannot be noticed and it is only from a fair distance that the diverging banisters can be perceived.

Plate 65

The great strength of their mortar allowed the Maya to create internal space in their stone buildings. Just as in Egypt, however, they did not discover the carrying properties of the barrel vault and also had to rely on the corbelled roof. The typical Maya arch is gradually narrowed towards the top, making ample use of the cantilever principle. Consequently, the ratio of internal space to the total size of their building is, in spite of the near-monolithic construction, fairly low. However, unlike the Aztec pyramids, those in Yucatan have mostly retained the crowning temple, often embellished by an elegant roof comb.

From what has been said so far it is clear that the Mexican pyramids differ in a number of essential features from those of Egypt. Whereas the

34 The Temple of the Inscriptions at Palenque is the only Mexican pyramid in which a tomb has been found up to now. From the sanctuary on top a stairway leads to the sarcophagus chamber at ground level

latter could not be ascended after completion, all the Mexican pyramids were provided with steps leading up to the stop of a truncated building. The basic idea of the Central American structures was simply to raise the sanctuary of the god high above the ground. The object was a stairway leading up to a temple. The purpose of the pyramids was therefore quite different in the two cases. Until fairly recently it was taken for granted that the Mexican pyramids never served as tombs. In 1951, however, an internal staircase was discovered in the 'Pyramid of the Inscriptions' at Palenque which led into an undisturbed tomb deep in the body of the structure. The staircase, which had been blocked with rubble, descends to a chamber in which the skeletons of four people, evidently sacrificial victims, were found. When a large stone slab at the far end of this chamber was removed it revealed a crypt whose floor was almost completely covered by the carved lid of a huge sarcophagus. It contained the skeleton of a man of magnificent stature whose face had been covered with a jade mask and who wore jade ornaments.

Fig. 34

Understandably this surprising discovery has led some archaeologists to suspect that all Amerindian pyramids might contain tombs; but the evidence for this is, so far, not very strong. No other tombs have as yet been found although tunnels have been driven through quite a number of the Mexican pyramids. The object of these particular excavations was not a search for tombs but an investigation of the internal structure of these monuments. Unlike their Egyptian counterparts many of the Mexican pyramids are composite buildings which have increased in size through successive accretions. Excavations have shown that the great pyramid of Tenayuca, for instance, passed through no less than six consecutive building phases, each being superimposed on the previous one. The universality of this practice also extended to the Maya buildings of Yucatan, and the pyramid of Kukulcan at Chichen Itza envelops an earlier one which was slightly smaller, with its temple just below the present sanctum. It is now accessible through an archaeological tunnel driven along the surface of the older structure, which has revealed the previous sanctum, containing the stone carving of a jaguar, painted red with large green spots of jade. The most famous instance of these accretions is in the 'Citadel' of Teotihuacan, where excavation of the central pyramid, a remarkably plain building, brought to light the highly ornate façade of an earlier phase. This is the famous temple of Quetzalcoatl, with beautifully carved panels embellished by the protruding heads of the plumed serpent and the water god Tlaloc.

Fig. 35

Plate 67

Often, as in the case of the temple of Quetzalcoatl, the underlying structure was partly demolished, and this leads to an explanation of the successive building changes at one and the same edifice. The object was not so much the enlargement of the structure as the alteration of its aspect. The peoples of Central America believed their world to be one of cyclic changes. They used a very complex calendar which featured, in addition to a year of 365 days, a period of 260 days which was made up of 13 'months', each of twenty days. It is not known how these two counts came about, and while one was certainly geared to the motion of the sun, the other seems to have been connected with the planet Venus and its year of 584 days. Here we cannot go into the somewhat intricate relation

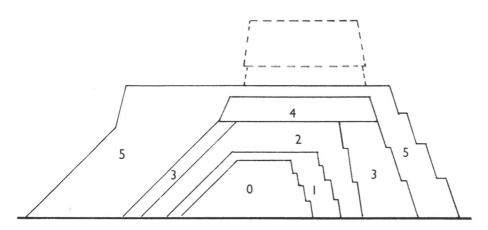

35 *Section of the pyramid at Tenayuca, showing successive enlargements. The original structure* (0) *was extended to mark astronomical time cycles of 52 years,* (1) *probably in AD 1299,* (2) *in 1351,* (3) *in 1403,* (4) *in 1455 and* (5) *in 1507, a few years before the Conquest by Cortes*

of these two counts, except to say that it led to a repetition of the same day-name in the same position of the cycle every 52 years. This period, and even more so the longer count of 104 years, were regarded as highly important spans of time after which a renewal of the world took place. The end of each period and the beginning of the next was believed to be of momentous significance and the approach of this moment a time of great danger. During the last five 'unlucky' days people fasted and destroyed their household belongings; on the final night children were kept awake to prevent them from turning into mice in their sleep.

Even more victims than usual were sacrificed while the Aztecs extinguished all fires throughout the land, awaiting the change of the era with dark foreboding. In the fateful night the priests ascended a mountain, on the top of which they determined by astronomical observations the moment of midnight. As soon as it had passed without the world's coming to an end, they kindled with a firedrill the first flame of the new epoch, suitably in the chest of a freshly sacrificed victim. Torches were lit from it and runners took the new fire to every part of the country.

These important turning points in the fate of their world were celebrated by replacing old things with new ones, and therefore the temples, too, had to be renewed. Whether rebuilding took place everywhere at 52-year intervals is not certain but it has been suggested that the successive phases of the pyramid at Tenayuca occurred in the years 1299, 1351, 1403, 1455 and 1507 AD. It has already been mentioned that cycles of 104 years were even more important; one has reason to believe that still longer periods were celebrated, which were significant enough to replace the customary style of architecture with an entirely new one.

Fig. 35

The concept of cyclic changes not only governed the life of the Aztec nation, but was also the basis of their mythical beliefs. In the past, they thought, there had been four worlds or 'suns', after the first of which men were eaten by jaguars, the second was destroyed by hurricanes, the third by fire, and the fourth by floods. Their own world was to be ended by earthquakes and its sun had continually to be fed with human blood to stave off this impending disaster. Thus, human sacrifice was forever needed to maintain the world. We are not certain as to the number slain annually when the Spaniards arrived in Mexico but some authorities have estimated it as high as 50,000 or more.

It seems inconceivable that year in year out these enormous numbers should have gone to a violent death without a popular revolt against this carnage. The reason for this extraordinary phenomenon was religious and based on the Aztec idea of life after death. Beyond this life was Mictlan, a cold cheerless place in the underworld. However, there also was a heaven, the abode of the gods to which some of the dead could be

36 A youth who for one year had represented the god Tezcatlipoca first broke his flutes on ascending the pyramid on which he was to be sacrificed. (Codex Florentino)

elevated, those who had fallen in battle or died on the sacrificial stone. Women, too, would go to heaven if they had died in childbirth, giving up their life to bear a future warrior. The parading of the victim up the steps of the pyramid was for him the prelude to a glorious and everlasting life which he entered when his heart was offered up to the sun. The sun was waiting for his blood. How strong the victim himself felt about his sublime destiny was shown by an instance that occurred during the Conquest. Every year a beautiful young prisoner was chosen to represent the god Tezcatlipoca. Throughout the year he was feasted like the god and during the last months four lovely girls became his companions. At the day of sacrifice he would bid them farewell, breaking one by one the flutes which he had played as he ascended the stairs of the pyramid. The current candidate remonstrated when Cortes forbade his sacrifice and thus cheated the youth out of the apotheosis awaiting him.

Fig. 36

The cult of blood and suffering was not confined to the instance of death. Self-torture and ceremonial bloodletting was a common form of penitence and of asking favours from the gods. For the priests it was a duty: the Spaniards described their frayed earlobes and the stench which

179

emanated from their long hair, matted with blood. Some of the most devout ones would pass a string with maguey thorns through their tongues. The Aztecs were a martial race and, as in other heroic societies, sadism and masochism went hand in hand with homosexuality. Diaz describes the first Aztec pyramid which the Spaniards encountered: 'There were clay idols made of pottery with faces of demons or women and other evil figures that showed Indians committing acts of sodomy with each other'. In his speeches Cortes admonished the Aztecs again and again to 'Give up their sacrifices, the eating of the flesh of their relations and the practice of sodomy'. In fact, the Spaniards, when picking up a prostitute, were often disgusted and horrified to find a man in women's clothes.

Plate XIII

In size the Aztec and Maya pyramids can be compared with the later Egyptian ones but they are far inferior to the huge monuments of the Egyptian Pyramid Age proper. However, there exist two immense pyramids only 50 km. from Mexico City, the ancient Tenochtitlan. When in the twelfth century the Aztecs entered the Valley of Mexico as an insignificant and despised tribe, these large pyramids were more than a thousand years old and even their origin was forgotten. Completely overgrown, they resembled natural hills rather than buildings and the real character of the site was only revealed by a broad ancient avenue, 4 km. long, which was as much overgrown as the hillocks flanking it.

Plate XIV

The Aztecs took these to be tombs and therefore called the avenue the 'Street of the Dead'. The two large pyramids they regarded as being sacred to the sun and the moon on the basis of a current legend but without any historical justification. The site itself they called Teotihuacan, 'The Place where Men became Gods', and this is the name it bears today because we do not know what the original inhabitants called it. Neither do we know what they called themselves, where they came from and what language they spoke.

Fig. 37

When the Conquistadors arrived in Mexico, the Aztecs had not as yet developed a script in our sense. The news of the white men's arrival was brought to Montezuma by his envoys in the form of a series of pictures, each telling an episode of the story. They were very much like strip cartoons, and even showed speech issuing from the persons' mouths. However, since they had no script, the speech scrolls of the Aztecs remained empty. A few of these pre–Columbian 'codices', as they are called, have been mercifully preserved but most of them were burnt by the pious Spanish friars who felt that these were works of the devil. Even if they had been preserved, it is doubtful whether the codices could have told us much about Mexican history. The Maya had developed writing earlier, and calendrical glyphs on some early stelae appear to record

37 The Mexican woman Marina, who became Cortes' mistress, acted as his interpreter. The scribe of the Codex Florentino illustrated her conversation with an Aztec by speech scrolls

dates corresponding to the beginning of the Christian era. Whether later glyphs – which we cannot decipher – represent a spoken language, we do not know. One may suspect that, like the Aztec codices, they are mainly inventories. It is too rarely realized that writing was not invented by the philosophers and poets but by the accountants.

The treatment which the codices suffered was shared by almost every item of Mexican religious art that was in existence at the Conquest. A few objects were sent by Cortes in 1519 to the Emperor Charles V and in the following year exhibited in Brussels. The great German painter, Albrecht Dürer, travelled from his native Nuremberg to see them and left us a description in his notes. He was full of admiration for this strange art, the power of which he recognized immediately. His appreciation was probably shared by only a few others since most of the objects have since been lost or destroyed. A small number of them, fortunately, found their way to the British Museum where they form some of its greatest treasures. Otherwise almost nothing was left undestroyed at the Conquest and the large collections in the magnificent Anthropological Museum at Mexico City are all archaeological finds, most of them of fairly recent date.

In the absence of a script or of a key to the Maya glyphs, the earth of Mexico has to provide all the information of America's prehistory. Aztec legends that were collected by the early Spanish historians are vague, even about the preceding two centuries when their bloodthirsty hummingbird led them into the Valley. The earliest civilization which their myths could recall was the legendary Tollan, the capital of a people called Toltecs.

XIII The Pyramid of the Moon, Teotihuacan, Mexico.

XIV The Street of the Dead at Teotihuacan, seen from the Pyramid of the Moon, with the Pyramid of the Sun to the left.

XV The great stairway of the 'Pyramid of the Magician' at Uxmal in Yucatan rises at an angle of almost 50° to a height of nearly 35 metres.

XIII

XIV

Archaeologists have since recognized the remains of Toltec art over a wide region of Mexico, from the Valley to Yucatan. Quite recently the site of ancient Tollan has been identified with the town of Tula in the province of Hidalgo. It seems to have flourished between AD 1100 and 1300. As for Teotihuacan, the Aztec legend had nothing to record and when the Spaniards asked the Mexicans who had built the pyramids and the Street of the Dead, they replied: 'the gods'.

Man probably appeared on the American continent during the last glacial period, perhaps 50,000 years or so ago. With so much of the water locked up in the huge ice sheets, the level of the oceans was lower than today and it may have been comparatively easy to cross the Bering Strait from Siberia to Alaska. That, as it seems, was the route taken by the hunting nomads who were, most likely, related to the Mongolian races of East Asia. Moving gradually south, some of the nomads became sedentary and developed agriculture, based on a grass from which they bred the maize plant, perhaps in the Gila valley of Arizona. As yet we know little about these early times but it seems that the first Amerindian civilization may have blossomed at the shore of the Gulf of Mexico. There a people whom we call 'Olmecs' established culture centres in which they left a peculiar type of sculpture, characterized by gigantic stone heads and a strange form of portraiture in which the upper lip was drawn up. These 'baby faced' figurines occur together with representations of the jaguar which evidently was regarded as a divine animal.

While it is quite possible that tomorrow's dig may turn up evidence for a precursor of the Olmec culture, we can do no better at present than to regard the early settlements on the Gulf as the cradle of Amerindian civilization. One of the most important sites near a village called La Venta evidently served as a cult centre for the agricultural population of the neighbourhood. Just like the original followers of Horus in Egypt, the Olmecs of La Venta exhibited a number of accomplishments about the origins of which we know nothing. Two features, in particular, stand out; they built cult mounds and they had sufficient astronomical knowledge to establish a calendar. Both these achievements were passed on to the Mayas of Yucatan and to the Valley of Mexico.

So far we have said nothing about the time when this early civilization came into being. In the absence of any historical records archaeologists have had to rely on the artefacts that were dug up, particularly the little clay figurines which are so typical of Central America. Classifying their styles and correlating their location had for many decades been the only guide by which archaeologists, men like Caso, Linné, Noguera and Vaillant, tried to establish a sequence of dates. It was an undertaking of great complexity, full of uncertainties and pitfalls. Worst of all, it did not lead to any form of exact dating and often the experts' opinions on one and the same site differed by quite a few centuries.

All this was suddenly changed by nuclear physics. In 1949 Professor W. F. Libby of the University of Chicago developed a radioactive test which permitted the age of organic deposits, such as wood or bone, to be determined with remarkable accuracy, and for which he received the Nobel Prize in 1960. The method is based on the radioactive decay of carbon nuclei with the atomic weight 14,(^{14}C). Almost all the carbon existing in the earth's atmosphere as carbon dioxide has nuclei with weight 12,(^{12}C), which are inactive, and only one part in a million million is made up of the radioactive ^{14}C. The origin of the ^{14}C is due to neutron bombardment of atmospheric nitrogen ($^{14}N + n \rightarrow {}^{14}C$), the neutrons coming from the cosmic radiation impinging at a steady rate on our planet. The newly created ^{14}C nuclei are unstable and in due course revert to ordinary nitrogen by emitting a beta ray ($^{14}C \rightarrow {}^{14}N + \beta$). In this way the concentration of radioactive ^{14}C in atmospheric carbon dioxide is kept constant, being continually created from atmospheric nitrogen and continually destroyed by its own radioactive decay.

All living plants and animals take up carbon from the atmosphere to build it into their tissues, including the very small fraction of ^{14}C. The radioactive decay of ^{14}C is fairly slow and, in any given sample, half of the ^{14}C nuclei will have reverted into nitrogen in 5,500 years. While in the atmosphere this loss is made good constantly by cosmic ray bombardment, the same is, of course, not true for plant or animal tissue that has been buried in the earth. In this the ^{14}C content will decay without being restocked from the atmosphere. In fact, the fraction of ^{14}C in buried samples will diminish by about one per cent every eighty years. Thus it is possible to determine the age of these samples by measuring the ^{14}C proportion in their carbon content.

While the physical basis of carbon-dating is straightforward, its practical application requires very sensitive instruments and is open to errors which have to be avoided. The amount of beta radiation revealing the ^{14}C content is very small indeed and anything that has happened to the sample in the course of centuries, such as waterlogging or prolonged exposure of small samples to the atmosphere, may falsify the results. It is therefore advisable to carry out tests from different samples at the same site whenever possible. Nevertheless, already in its first applications, carbon-dating proved its worth by giving dates from material in the Zoser and Snofru pyramids which closely agreed with the historically accepted ones. The method is therefore immensely valuable for determining the age of pre-Columbian samples for which we have no independent dating whatever.

It was carbon-dating that provided the surprise of the great age of the Gulf civilization. Samples from the Olmec site at La Venta suggest a flowering of that culture between 800 and 400 BC, many centuries earlier than had previously been suspected. Similar tests have also provided a guide to the mysterious city of Teotihuacan and it appears that the two great pyramids were constructed just before the beginning of the Christian era. Combining the archaeological evidence with carbon-dating, we can begin to reconstruct this early growth of Amerindian civilization. It seems fairly certain now that the origin of the Maya glyphs and their knowledge of the calendar came from the Olmecs at the Gulf but, while the Maya built steeper and higher pyramids than the cult mound of La Venta, they never passed through the phase of gigantic monuments such as those erected at Teotihuacan. These, the largest structures ever erected in America, provide a close similarity with the Pyramid Age of Egypt.

The forerunner of Teotihuacan in the Valley of Mexico was Cuicuilco, just south of the present university campus of Mexico City. The cult mound is a circular and rather flat step pyramid, with a base diameter of 145 m. but only 20 m. high. Nowadays the flat appearance is further enhanced by the fact that the building was engulfed to a height of nearly 10 m. by lava when the volcano Xitle erupted about 2000 years ago. This agrees with the type of figurine found there and with the radiocarbon tests which date Cuicuilco at about 400 BC. The mound itself, totalling in its final stage about 7000 m.^{3}, was built in two phases: the first had two steps, to which a further two were later added. It was evidently abandoned well before the eruption took place.

The material chiefly employed in the construction of this 'pyramid' was clay, strengthened in parts with large river boulders. The builders appear to have been aware of the danger of plastic flow to which a clay

Plate 66

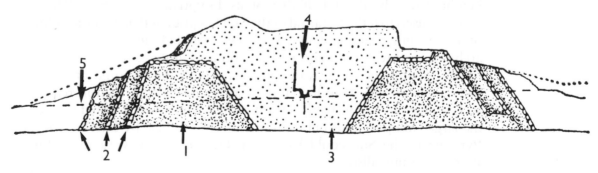

38 Section through the circular mound at Cuicuilco. It was constructed as a ringwall of earth and stone (1) with stone covering (2). The centre was filled with earth (3) in the middle of which altars (4) of successive building stages were discovered. The mound was engulfed by lava (5) from an eruption of the volcano Xitle (after Vaillant)

Fig. 38

structure is prone when exposed to rain. Although the mound was extremely flat, it was clearly considered necessary to strengthen the circumference against slip. The clay nucleus is therefore surrounded by a ring-shaped dyke made up of a mixture of clay and stones whose walls were formed by large stones embedded side by side in clay. It appears that mortar was not known, and added strength was obtained by providing the dyke with a series of outer walls, not unlike the buttress walls employed by Imhotep in the construction of the Step Pyramid of Saqqara. Trying to reconstruct the building process, one would suspect that the outer dyke was erected first and that the clay filling was subsequently tipped into the central cavity.

The main reason for assuming this type of construction is the deployment of labour in the most efficient manner. If, as seems likely, a large enough labour force was available, the fastest method of erecting the pyramid was to employ the workers at the periphery of the structure. This would allow the builders to use the maximum number of men simultaneously without their getting into each other's way.

Steps led up to the platform from both east and west, and the remnants of altars were found both at the height of the fourth and at that of the second, buried, platform. The altars were probably surmounted by roofed buildings which have long since disappeared. The Cuicuilco cult mound is the exact opposite of the Aztec pyramids at the time of the Conquest. We do not know what kind of ritual was enacted at the altars but it is obvious that the flat and low platform cannot have provided a good 'stage' for a spectacle, such as was the purpose of the Aztec pyramids.

Plate XIV

Fig. 39

All evidence indicates that Teotihuacan is somewhat later than Cuicuilco, but not very much later. It appears that the great Pyramid of the Sun was the earliest edifice of note at this site. The area covered by it is almost exactly the same as that of the Khufu pyramid but its original height was only about half that of its Egyptian counterpart. This, of course, means that the Pyramid of the Sun has just less than half the volume of the Khufu pyramid and rather less than half its weight. Khufu's architects had to quarry and pile up about $6\frac{1}{2}$ million tons of limestone for his monument whereas the men who built the Pyramid of the Sun had only to provide $2\frac{1}{2}$ million tons of stone and earth. The effort required at Teotihuacan was probably a third of that which was devoted to one of the large Giza pyramids but even so a recent estimate by Stierlin that the Pyramid of the Sun could have been built by 3000 workers in thirty years seems unrealistic.

However, before attempting to correct this estimate, we must describe the construction of the two large pyramids at Teotihuacan. Neither of them seems to have any internal chambers or corridors; our knowledge

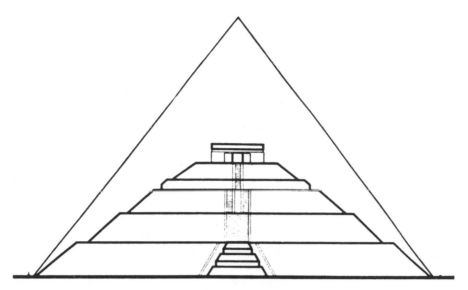

39 Scale comparison of the Khufu Pyramid at Giza (approximately 146 metres high) and the Pyramid of the Sun at Teotihuacan

is entirely based on surface examination and on the archaeological tunnels which have been driven into them. The first archaeological work on the Pyramid of the Sun was carried out by Leopoldo Batres at the beginning of this century and was inspired by President Porfirio Diaz. The occasion was the centenary of Mexico's liberation from Spanish colonial status and its foundation as a sovereign state in 1810. Batres set to work with great energy and a large labour force. He cleared the pyramid of the vegetation covering it and then tried to lay bare its real surface. In his enthusiasm he unfortunately went too far, removing what had been left of the original outer layer of stone, mortar and plaster from the entire north, east and south faces. The result was disastrous. The underlying adobe surface started to dissolve in heavy rains and began to exhibit plastic flow which threatened to destroy the whole edifice. It was saved only by the very high viscosity of the dissolving clay which rendered the disintegration slow enough to be arrested by hurried remedial measures.

The three exposed faces of the monument were given a new skin of stones and cement, so that today we see the original surface only on the frontal western side which Batres had left largely untouched. The result of his precipitate action is that the pyramid is now somewhat smaller than originally and that all its original surface features have disappeared. However, by peeling off about 7 m. of the outer layer he laid free a number of stone walls which stand out from the building like fins and which had the purpose of holding the original surface in place.

Two tunnels have been driven through the Pyramid of the Sun. The first, dug by Gamio in 1917, enters the monument in the middle of the east face and goes through to its centre. The second tunnel constructed in 1933 by Eduardo Noguera enters at the centre of the western face and meets the Gamio tunnel. Both tunnels are roughly horizontal and run close to the base of the pyramid. These investigations yielded a number of very important results. First and foremost, no sign of an earlier pyramid was found on which a later structure was superimposed. This means that the Pyramid of the Sun was erected in one operation to its present size. Secondly, there are no internal strengthening features and the only means of holding the great mound together is an outer skin of between 15 and 20 m. thickness made up of adobe and stones. The possibility cannot be excluded that, higher up in the edifice, fin walls of stone were introduced, of which the visible fins laid bare by Batres are part. Such fin walls to hold the loose fill were certainly used in the slightly later Pyramid of the Moon; however, there is no indication at ground level of their existence in the older pyramid. The fill visible in the tunnel walls consists of clay, stones, gravel and various types of soil containing figurines and potsherds.

The fact that the levels of fill slope towards the centre has been taken as an indication that a tomb may be concealed under the monument. While we do not wish to dispute the suggestion, this inward dip may simply be a result of the method of construction. When discussing the mound at Cuicuilco we mentioned the likelihood that it had started as a ring-shaped dyke into the centre of which the fill had been tipped. In its basic structure the Pyramid of the Sun much resembles Cuicuilco and it is conceivable that for the same technological reasons – to bring the maximum working force to the site – a similar type of construction was chosen at Teotihuacan.

A still larger pyramid, exceeding even Khufu's monument in bulk, existed at Cholula but it was largely destroyed by the Spaniards, who built a church on its ruins. Although the core of the Cholula pyramid was built at roughly the same time as Teotihuacan, it was then much smaller than the pyramids at that site. However, whereas the civilization of the Teotihuacanos vanished long before AD 1000, Cholula remained an active religious centre down to the time of the Conquest. Throughout its history of one and a half millennia, the original pyramid was enlarged at least four times and eventually, with a volume of 3 million m.^{3}, became the largest building ever erected on earth. Its composite structure has been extensively investigated by tunnels totalling 6 km. in length. The buried face of the Teotihuacano period shows that the outside of the pyramids of that time was covered with religious paintings including the 'butterfly god', who seems to have been worshipped extensively in Teotihuacan.

Fig. 40

40 Representations of the butterfly god of Teotihuacan on ceramics. The top figure shows him associated with the rain god Tlaloc (after Séjourné)

However impressive the final form of the Cholula pyramid was, it recedes against the magnificent achievement of the Pyramids of the Sun and the Moon which were erected in a short span of time, in possibly less than half a century. It turns out that in this, and many other respects, they are the representatives of an Amerindian pyramid age which closely approximates the Fourth Dynasty in Egypt. The parallel becomes even closer when we regard the amount of labour involved at Teotihuacan against the cultural and economic background of the Valley of Mexico 2000 years ago.

The total amount of material to be quarried, carried to the site, lifted up to an average height of 20 m., distributed and rammed in, was roughly $3\frac{1}{2}$ million tons. Most of the pyramid fill is excavated subsoil, but an appreciable amount of quarried stone and prepared adobe was also required. Some of this had to be obtained from a distance of at least several kilometres. The implements available were wooden and stone tools. There is no record of sledges being used for transport, beasts of burden did not exist, and the wheel had not been invented at the time of the Conquest, 1500 years later. All loads had to be carried, and in addition to the workers actually engaged in the building process others were needed to supply the whole force with food and water. Although the population was certainly accustomed for generations to the local conditions, it has to be remembered that the diminished amount of oxygen at an altitude of 6000 feet will have had an effect on the efficiency of heavy labour.

Taking all these factors into account we might assume an average of 75 kg. per man to be placed per day. This estimate, of course, covers all the varied activities required by the project. We assume further that the workers were, as in Egypt, agricultural labourers and that, in order to maintain food production, they could spare, at best, a hundred days per annum on pyramid construction. For a building period of thirty years this leads to a labour force of about 15,000 men.

It has to be emphasized that, just as in our estimate of work in Egypt, the number cannot be expected to be correct except within an order of magnitude. However, it is quite clear that the project could not have been undertaken as a secondary activity. In other words, a large proportion of the population must have been involved in it for a very considerable time. Again, as in Egypt, the very large pyramids occur early in the development of civilization.

We are further aided in our assessment of the conditions under which the pyramids were built by the figurines that were found embedded in the building material in large numbers. These artefacts are helpful in determining the period at which the work was done and they agree with the available carbon dates. The figurines in the Pyramid of the Sun all belong to the so-called Tzacually period which came to an end at about 100 BC. Even more important is the fact that different villages used slightly different styles for their figurines and pottery and the distribution of styles found in the pyramid material indicates that the builders came from a fairly widespread area in the Valley.

Summarizing these findings, we arrive at the picture of an agricultural village population providing labour for a large central project. Unlike Cuicuilco, Teotihuacan cannot have been merely a cult and pilgrimage centre. This becomes apparent when we compare the technological efforts involved in the two projects. At Cuicuilco about 20,000 tons of material were invested against $3\frac{1}{2}$ million in the earliest phase at Teotihuacan. While the first could be achieved by a fairly limited number of tribesmen, the second required a well-organized population. And for this a great deal of supporting evidence has been assembled in the last few years.

Until recently archaeologists have tended to look upon Teotihuacan merely as a magnificent ceremonial centre, permanently inhabited only by a priestly society and its attendants with a small supporting population. Its ceremonial character is certainly emphasized by the grandeur not only of its pyramids but, even more, by its general layout. The central feature, *Plate XIV* the Street of the Dead, is 45 m. wide and 4 km. long. It is flanked on both sides by smaller pyramids which had been mistaken by the Aztecs for tombs. At its northern end stands the Pyramid of the Moon overlooking a plaza framed by a number of lesser pyramids. At its western side the palace of the Quetzal butterfly has been recently excavated. The Pyramid of the Sun and its large surrounding court stand a little to the east of the central avenue, and east of its southern end lies another impressive court with the temple of Quetzalcoatl.

Plate 67

The last two decades have seen an immense amount of archaeological work at Teotihuacan. I first visited the city in 1951 and hardly recognized it when I saw it again fifteen years later. The Street of the Dead had been cleared in all its length and the Mexican National Institute of Anthropology and History, as well as a number of American archaeologists, had carried out a huge amount of excavation throughout the Teotihuacan area. A survey of all these results revealed the astonishing fact that, far from just being a ceremonial centre, Teotihuacan had been an immense city, housing at the height of its development about 150,000 to 200,000 people. The urban area covered no less than 20 km.² of closely-built housing accommodation, workshops; markets and temples. It was a well-planned city, laid out, as the Street of the Dead and its plazas show, on a grandiose scale, teeming with life as early as 2000 years ago – the first and the most populous urban centre on the American continent.

We have said already that we do not know who the Teotihuacanos were. They left no legends, no script and no discernible heritage. They came in the last few centuries B C; they built a huge city and their influence seems to have spread far beyond the Valley of Mexico into Yucatan. When they disappeared at about AD 600 nothing of the flourishing civilization was left except the ruins of their buildings. The study and excavation of these provides us with the only information which we have of this vanished world. Here the work has only begun and it is a foregone conclusion that in a few decades we will know much more about the Teotihuacanos than today.

The age of Teotihuacan must have been a peaceful one. There are no signs of fortifications or of a rebuilding of urban districts after destruction by an enemy. Rebuilding was confined to the sacred precincts, and for this we have ample evidence. The reconstruction of the temple of Quetzalcoatl has already been mentioned; it seems that remodelling took place at many other buildings, including the large platforms in front of the Pyramids of the Sun and the Moon. Possibly a religious reformation or a highly important calendrical change may have taken place at about AD 300 which resulted in a new and very severe style of architecture. All the temple façades were remodelled by the introduction of large, un-sculptured panels which, by a cunning cantilever construction, surmounted inclined, rising planes. The effect, as we see it today, is most impressive in its monumental simplicity and the uncompromising juxtaposition of bright light and deep shade.

The divinities worshipped at Teotihuacan seem to have been the gods of fire, water and wind. The last was later represented by a feathered serpent, Quetzalcoatl, and Toltec legend identified him with an early cult hero, a god of learning who forbade human sacrifice. While human sacrifice was probably practised at Teotihuacan, it does not seem to have been prominent and the evidence for it is thin. Four skeletons of children buried in a sitting position and facing outwards were found under the corners of the temple of Quetzalcoatl, and Laurette Séjourné discovered

Plate 70

a large bowl with the bones of a set of upper thighs which she regarded as evidence of cannibalism. It seems unlikely, however, that the Aztec ritual of mass sacrifice existed, since the oldest pyramid, that of the Sun, is far too high to serve as a suitable stage. Human figures at the top appear diminutive when viewed from the ground and the disposal of the victim's body would have been a slow and laborious process.

While we do not know why and how the Teotihuacanos vanished from the scene there are indications that the civilizations of Central America passed through a crisis in the last centuries of our first millennium. Unlike Egypt in its desert-bound valley, Central America was wide open to migrating nomadic tribes from the north. It seems that waves of invaders pushed their way southward; the Toltecs were evidently one of the first. Toltec civilization has all the trappings of a warlike society, to some extent tempered by contact with the higher culture which it had encountered. Whether the Toltecs themselves destroyed Teotihuacan we do not know, but it is certain that Toltec influence penetrated as far as Yucatan where it impressed its warlike glory of human sacrifice on a peaceful agricultural society. The Toltecs, in turn, were superseded by the savage Chichimec tribes, one of which were the Aztecs.

The magnificent city of Teotihuacan arose out of an agricultural village population, and at the very beginning of its history stands the immense Pyramid of the Sun. The parallel with the Egyptian pyramid age is truly compelling. Here, in Central America, and quite independent of Middle Eastern civilization, villagers had been brought together to erect an immense pyramid, and in doing so laid the foundation of a highly organized community. If anything, the Amerindian pattern of development is even more clear-cut than that on the Nile. Man, after developing agriculture, lived in villages – small units where everybody knew everybody else and everybody else's problems. As the population density increased, demarcation disputes between villages and tribes became unavoidable. The only way out of this dilemma was a central administration, strong and intelligent enough to keep peace. When we look for the way in which it was brought into being, we discover a strange thing: at the beginning was the great pyramid. It seems that this large-scale co-operative effort was the manner in which the new form of human society, the centralized state, had to be created.

Once a few large pyramids had been built, the organization and welding together of the village population into a new, more diversified, pattern had become an established fact. No further pyramid-building on a gigantic scale was required. Human labour could now be channelled into a multitude of other activities, all of them planned by the central government. The city of Teotihuacan is a memorial to this first large-scale organization of man on the American continent. Just as the Old Kingdom administrators thought that their pattern of society was so successful that it deserved to be eternal, so the leaders at Teotihuacan must have believed that nothing would change their blessed world. Neither conceived the idea that their superior pattern of life required defence. Both were wrong, but in the end, the new organization of man, the state which the pyramid had created, survived all vicissitudes.

8 The Meaning of a Pyramid

We have reached the end of our detective story of exploration into the distant past, and the time has come to take stock. First of all, let us restate the problem that we have solved. The riddle of the pyramids arises out of a discrepancy which many people have found difficult to accept. It is the disparity between the effort of heaping up 25 million tons of quarried limestone and the sole object of burying under them three pharaohs. However much the Egyptians were interested in the afterlife, eight million tons of rock, all nicely shaped and smoothed, per pharaoh must seem excessive. It is therefore not surprising that various alternative uses for the pyramids have been proposed. All of these, however, turn out to be a good deal less acceptable than the straightforward tomb theory. Moreover, we have Herodotus' statement that the pyramids were tombs, and even if we have doubts whether it was the kings' bodies or their souls which were buried in them, the funerary function of the pyramids is firmly established.

My own solution came as a surprise – at least to me. The object of the whole exercise was not the use to which the final product was to be put but its manufacture. Pharaohs could be buried and were, in fact, buried much more cheaply. What mattered was not the pyramid – it was *building* the pyramid.

There are a number of highly encouraging features in this solution. In the first place it does not contradict the well-established fact that the pyramids were funerary monuments. Secondly, it provides a rational explanation for the colossal labour effort, since employment of labour on an immense scale was the main political and economic object. Thirdly, and this is particularly gratifying, I did not set out to prove my point. My interest was confined to a technological disaster, and the solution of the main problem arrived quite unsolicited. Finally, the solution could be tested on a completely isolated system – the Mexican pyramids – and the test turned out to be successful beyond expectation.

Before proposing a new theory, a scientist usually surveys his material critically, searching for weak points or inconsistencies. There may be some, but if so, I have not been able to detect them. On the other hand, the consistent nature of the four points enumerated in the preceding paragraph encourages me to think that my conclusions would have to contain quite a number of errors before the theory could be proved invalid.

So let us assume for the present that the solution proposed in this book is correct and let us see where we go from there – apart from future corroborative evidence, with which even the best established theory can always do. It would indeed be a poor and sterile theory unless it opens more questions than it has answered.

The first question suggests itself immediately. If man 5000 years ago looked for a great, unifying common task, why did he choose a pyramid instead of something useful, such as an irrigation scheme? Here the answer is simple. Irrigation projects had been in existence in Egypt long before the pyramids but they were always local efforts, giving benefit to a few villages. Even a more ambitious scheme, such as the Bar Yusuf connecting the Nile with Lake Moeris in the Fayum, would hardly have brought the people together in one locality, and its execution demanded a level of hydrological engineering which, at the beginning of the Fourth Dynasty, was well beyond their ability. The same argument also applies to the more basic and straightforward project of damming up the Nile at the apex of the Delta. It is worth remembering that when the French eventually undertook it at Kaliub in about 1860, the dam proved a dismal failure because they had underestimated the seepage of water under its foundations.

No, the construction of an impressive man-made mountain was not a matter of choice. It was the only means of doing something spectacular with the large labour force that they wanted to gather, and a mountain of $50°$ elevation was, as we have seen, the best they could manage. In Chapter 6 we have traced its development through the escalation of Zoser's monument, which resulted in the Step Pyramid. The building of a distinctive mark in the landscape by making a large heap is still with us in the desire of children making a sand castle. Moreover, this primitive urge is testified to in the Bible (*Genesis*, XI, 4): 'Let us build us a city and a tower whose top may reach unto heaven; and let us make a name'. The Egyptians of the Fourth Dynasty certainly made their name by building the pyramids.

The second question is equally obvious. Why was the building of immense pyramids discontinued? The answer has, to some extent, already been given earlier in this book. Once, through the process of building pyramids the formation of a centralized state had been achieved, there was little point in continuing this activity. Building pyramids in Egypt

197

to bury kings, and in Mexico to sacrifice humans, continued, but these later pyramids were on a scale so much reduced that the primary object of concentrating a large labour force clearly did not apply. In both orbits, pyramid-building had achieved its aim and there was no point in prolonging it. Once the object of creating the centralized state had been attained, independently in the two independent hemispheres, it had found its place in the development of society, and it had not to be invented again. It is interesting to note that the only project of commensurable size, the Great Wall of China, followed the pyramids by 2000 years and that its purpose was not in building it but in the use of the final product – to save the state from barbarian incursions.

Finally, we must ask the question whether pyramid building is likely ever to occur again. We have seen that it was the means by which human society was transformed from a rural village economy to an entirely new form of community life, the state. The world of village and tribe had reached a condition in which no further progress could be made, except through a drastic change, such as took place in Egypt 5000 years ago. Without this change it would have remained stationary, as it has in many parts of Africa almost to this day. The state as created by the Fourth Dynasty was the nucleus from which, through an infinite variety of expansions, mankind has progressed to its present form. However, the framework, the national state, has been retained essentially unchanged. The existence of national states soon gave rise to organized wars between them, a pattern that has not been changed in its basic features for five millennia. States have come and gone, nations have risen and fallen, but the pattern of their life and strife has been retained in that uneasy equilibrium which we call 'the balance of power'. There have been fluctuations, periods in which national wars were almost abolished as, for instance, under the Pax Romana, the Holy Roman Empire of the German nation, and even in the hope of a Pax Britannica. However, all these had to fail because the globe was too large, and from somewhere an enemy would arise to force mankind back into the old pattern of national war.

In the lifetime of many of us two of these wars have engulfed the whole world, involving not only the fighting forces but also resulting, in one way or another, in the slaughter of many millions of civilians. Since then, however, two important things have happened. The doomsday machine has been invented and the world has shrunk. The nuclear arsenals have become so extensive that not only can the attacking power win by rapid devastation, but the losing one could, by the judicious addition of long-lived radio-isotopes, arrange for the suicide of vanquished and victor alike. Under these circumstances even the politicians have recognized that mankind can afford only one more world war and that we had better not have it. In fact, we have arrived at the stage where the time-honoured system of asserting the sovereignty of national states by war has ceased to function. With it, one suspects, the justification for the national state as an essential form of human society will also fade away.

The world has become much too small for the different shades of men and their individual languages to play separate games. They certainly would find ways of irritating each other. The only thing left to us is the creation of a new pattern of life which takes in all members of the species *homo sapiens*. In other words, there is no alternative to a very drastic change that is acceptable to everybody. And that means that we have to get together, to work together and to get better acquainted with each other. Together we must build a new pyramid.

Unfortunately, it is as yet by no means clear what form and character this new pyramid will have. Its object, on the other hand, is well-defined. It has to be a unifying common task of such magnitude that its impact will be felt throughout the world. Among the various suggestions which have been offered, uplifting the poor and stopping pollution take first place, and they are worthy causes that are in people's minds. However, while I would consider both as priority programmes, I am not so sure that they are likely to provide what is wanted. A little while ago I accompanied a group of enthusiastic young people to the shores of a huge crater lake in the West African jungle. There are no roads to it, only a track which becomes impassable in the rainy season. Along the shores of the lake live 10,000 people without any medical care in what still is the white, and also the black, man's grave. The infant mortality is very, very high.

Against severe odds the young missionaries are setting up a small hospital at the lake and since its fetish does not permit the presence of metal, they intend to visit the villages by the shore in a glass-fibre boat. My forecast is that, if they are successful, the population will have doubled in five years, with still 10,000 needing medical care and 20,000 needing food. Since the worst pollution on our earth is the uncontrolled proliferation of the human species, the well-meaning enthusiasts will have innocently, but handsomely, contributed to it.

I have purposely chosen this rather extreme example to show that most worthwhile common tasks tend to be fraught with difficulties. The trouble with all such programmes is that they are designed to achieve a particular end effect. The great strength and beauty of the pyramid projects lay in the complete uselessness of the final product. Their importance was provided by carrying them out and not by achieving a stated aim. The Egyptian and Mexican pyramids were designed for entirely different uses but the main purpose, that is, engaging a large number of people in a common task, was the same for both. If we want our new pyramid to succeed, we have to make sure that the final edifice is as useless as possible. This will allow for any amount of error and faulty direction in the project since, by definition, a useless final product cannot be made more useless by mistakes.

When an article of mine on the pyramids was published in the *Neue Zürcher Zeitung* I was amused to learn that my colleagues at CERN, the European Nuclear Research Centre, got the idea that it was really less concerned with the pyramids than with them. Their suspicion was, of course, not completely unfounded except that they had taken themselves too seriously by at least three orders of magnitude. The miserable 50 million pounds which they annually spend on trying to find a particle, which is still more fundamental than the fundamental ones, amount, at present standards, to a ridiculously small pyramid.

There is only one project in the world today which, as far as one can see, offers the possibility of being large enough and useless enough to qualify eventually for the new pyramid. And that is the exploration of outer space. When for the first time man stepped on to the moon, the whole world sat glued to their television sets, each viewer identifying himself with the astronauts. It stirred their imagination more than any other event in our time. For a moment the pride in human achievement silenced even the clamour for three instead of two Sundays a week and the rallying call for saving from extinction the Puerto Rican parrot.

In the end, the results of space exploration are likely to be as ephemeral as the pharaoh accompanying the sun. The effort in money or, what is the same, in labour will be gigantic. No other incentive will be provided than the satisfaction of man to make a name for himself by building a tower that reaches unto planetary space. Five thousand years ago the Egyptians, for an equally vague reason, accepted a monstrous sacrifice of sweat and toil which led man into a new form of society. Perhaps we should build the space pyramid, and the effort in doing so together may be the necessary sacrifice which we must bring to gain a new and peaceful world community.

Astronomy, Prophecy and Reality

The foremost duty of a scientist is to stick to the facts. This imperative regard for truth is not, like the medical Hippocratic oath, based on ethics but solely on self-preservation. The German proverb that 'lies have short legs' is doubly valid in science, because you are bound to be found out sooner or later, and usually sooner. While this usually does not harm a politician, one's fellow scientists tend to have a longer memory than the electorate and permit little things like that to interfere with your future career. This is a useful deterrent against what is professionally known as 'fudging' the data. However, science on an inspired level requires more than making and collecting observations; it also involves the drawing of conclusions, and possibly the formulation of a theory. At this stage imagination is needed and this involves a much more difficult task than not lying to others – you must also try not to lie to yourself.

Usually scientists are willing to give any theory, however, doubtful, a try, provided it shows imagination and it offers new ideas. When the late Wolfgang Pauli was asked to assess a somewhat unimaginative research paper, he sadly shook his head and said: 'It isn't even wrong.' However, scientists also know that new ideas are worthless, unless they can be checked and supported by confirmatory evidence. For instance, the notion that the moon is made of green cheese had been made unlikely by a great deal of solid research – even before astronauts went there and established that it is made of rock. It is much the same with the great number of pyramid theories which have been put forward throughout the ages.

Let us take as an example the recently publicized idea that the pyramids owe their existence, in some unspecified manner, to a visit from outer space 40,000 years ago. Scientifically such a hypothetical visit cannot be disproved but, on the other hand, there exists no evidence whatever that it did take place. Thus, the idea has not the status of a theory but that of other works of science fiction, being probably equally entertaining and stimulating to the imagination of its readers. A scientific theory has to be judged by its credibility, which depends on the supporting evidence. Its value increases with the volume of such evidence but if irrefutable proof of its impossibility is forthcoming, it has to be rejected. A 'theory' for which no evidence at all can be found, has zero credibility.

Unfortunately, there are very few theories with either zero or 100 per cent credibility and in order to decide on their merit, the evidence has to be weighed. Here we have to class that category of speculation to which belongs the use of pyramids as astronomical observatories or metric standards. In fact, science in all its branches contains rather larger twilight areas of shaky facts and doubtful theories than the textbooks care to admit.

My interest in the pyramids of Egypt was kindled by a book which I read as a schoolboy in Berlin. It was written by a German engineer, Max Eyth, who in the 1860s spent many years in Egypt, trying to sell steam ploughs to the Khedive. The oriental approach to his efforts seems to have left Eyth with enough time on his hands to write novels suitable for boys and in this he was even more successful than in his mercantile ventures. The novel was entitled *The Battle for the Cheops Pyramid* and had as its theme the struggle of two brothers, one wanting to use the stones of the pyramids to build a dam across the Nile, while the other wished to see the Khufu pyramid restored as a sacred object.

There is a grain of truth in this story. There was indeed a serious suggestion to build the barrage at Kaliub, north of Cairo, with stones from the pyramids, but the proposal was dropped because it was found to be impracticable. The man who regarded the Khufu pyramid as sacred was Piazzi Smyth, Astronomer Royal for Scotland, who at that time spent four months at Giza, trying to substantiate his theory of the monument by accurate measurements. Eyth, being an engineer, became fascinated by the strange mathematical relationships which, according to Piazzi Smyth, were embodied in the pyramid, and he devoted a whole chapter in his novel to them. The most astonishing fact was the accuracy with which the ratio of height to circumference of the base expresses the squaring of the circle.

We have mentioned this fact in Chapter III of this book and the rather trivial explanation provided by the use of a rolling drum for the measurement of length. However, Piazzi Smyth did not know this and neither did I when I read Eyth's book. There were many other intriguing mysteries into which I began to probe with the enthusiasm of a schoolboy, hot on the trail of discovery. However, I soon discovered that either Eyth had got mixed up in his report or the Astronomer Royal for Scotland had overshot his mark. If not, I would have to accept that a mysterious relation existed between the diameter of the earth and its distance from the sun. For a time I lost interest, but when I entered Berlin University I enjoyed the privilege of using the Prussian State Library and asked for Piazzi Smyth's original work, only to learn that it did not appear in the catalogue. Imagine my delight when I came to Oxford in 1933 to discover three copies of *Our Inheritance in the Great Pyramid* on Blackwell's shelves. I immediately bought one of them and found it most instructive reading.

To my astonishment I also discovered the existence in the English-speaking world of a huge literature on the Great Pyramid, written by adherents and followers of Piazzi Smyth. It was entirely devoted to prophecies based on a peculiar mixture of mathematics and of quotations from Holy Writ: in fact, a formula invented by the Astronomer Royal for Scotland. There is not really much point in discussing this particular literature which is incredibly voluminous, repetitive, dull and uninspired; not a patch on the master. The prophecies are all based on measurements, in forever varying units, along the pyramid passages. As an example I have taken a book, chosen at random (Basil Steward, *The Great Pyramid*), first published in 1925, and from it the least involved of its diagrams. Since I refused to buy an earlier work which explains this, I do not know what actually happened at the step marking 25 January 1844. However, as can be seen, war broke out – for the British – on 5 August 1914, and mankind entered a low and humiliating passage until 11 November 1918, when everybody emerged into the lofty antechamber. In the 3rd edition, published in 1931, the author announced triumphantly that he had correctly predicted the coming of the next dark age on 29 May 1928, and, had they but listened to the prophecy, God's chosen people could have foreseen the crash of the market on Wall Street. From now on we are in

Fig. 41

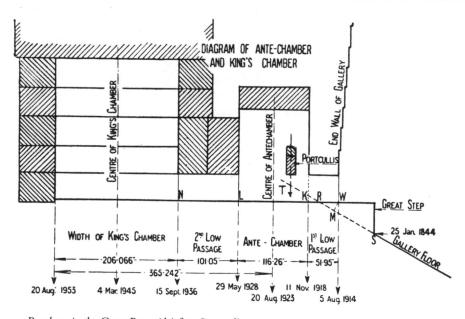

41 Prophecy in the Great Pyramid (after Steward)

the future as far as the 1931 edition is concerned, and we see that the kingdom of Heaven started most suitably with the formation of the Axis Pact by Hitler and Mussolini in September 1936. With an uncanny near-miss of only one month the centre of the blessed age is marked by the explosion of the first nuclear 'device' on Alamogordo Flats. And here we sit, never realizing that the world came to an end on 20 August 1953!

This trite nonsense is a far cry from the master's spirited and entertaining writing. Piazzi Smyth may have been wrong – as we shall presently see, he certainly was – but his imagination and the racy style of his prose are unique. Born in 1819 at Naples, the son of Admiral W. H. Smyth, F.R.S., young Charles Piazzi was to become Astronomer Royal for Scotland and professor at Edinburgh at the age of only 26. At 38 he was elected into the Royal Society, but seventeen years later, possibly uniquely, he resigned his Fellowship over a disagreement concerning the Society's unwillingness to publish a paper which he had submitted. Needless to say, it dealt with Piazzi Smyth's theory of the Great Pyramid. One intriguing question remains: when, why, and how did this brilliant scholar, the Astronomer Royal for Scotland, run off the rails?

He had entered astronomy as a tall, serious lad of sixteen at the new Cape Observatory. Sir John Herschel's diary records for Sunday, 22 October 1835: 'Occupied in reading a Monstrous budget of European letters. While so engaged with M. in the Bulbgarden, Maclean brought over young C. P. Smyth, Captain S's. son, his new assistant with whom held a long entretien and who passed rest of day here'. In fact, young Charles Piazzi became Chief Assistant at the Cape and made good where several of his predecessors had failed. His enthusiasm for work at the observatory as well as in the geodetic observations, in what was then a wilderness, much impressed Herschel. Smyth, in turn, became an ardent admirer of the great astronomer and participated with much success in Herschel's spectroscopic researches, leading to the first photographic recording of the spectral lines. Young Smyth certainly was an astronomer of exceptional talent as well as a hard conscientious worker. There can be little doubt that Herschel's recommendation helped him to secure the Astronomership Royal for Scotland at such an early age and also in his election into the Royal Society. All this happened before the fateful year 1860.

Interest in the pyramids became widespread, first through the work of the French scientists accompanying Napoleon's campaign and then, to an even greater extent, by the exploration of Vyse and Perring, published in 1840. Two items of astronomical significance immediately attracted Herschel's attention. The first was the remarkably accurate alignment of the four sides of the pyramids to the cardinal directions and the second was the polar passage. Using Vyse's data for the Khufu pyramid, Herschel suggested that it might be possible to determine astronomically the age of the building. In addition to the earth's rotation in 24 hours, its axis carries out a slow conical motion, such as we see in a spinning top. This precession, as it is called, has a period of about 26,000 years. An observer looking along the entrance passage would therefore see a very slowly changing portion of the night sky since his 'telescope' moves gradually with the earth's axis. After 26,000 years the passage would point again in the same direction. It occurred to Herschel that the Egyptian architects had most likely aligned the passage to a bright star and he therefore looked for a bright star which would have stood at the celestial pole about 4000 years ago. He found it in α Draconis and from the precession he calculated that it must have shone down the pyramid passage at about 2800 BC. This, indeed, fits in with modern archaeological evidence for the age of the monument.

However, Herschel was careful to point out that he did not think the pyramid had served as an observatory. This is supported by recent investigation of the only undisturbed pyramid passage, which was discovered in the Bent Pyramid in 1948. On opening this upper passage, it was found to have been filled throughout its length with closely fitting stone plugs which made it extremely difficult to clear. The same was, no doubt, the case for all pyramid passages and some of the plug blocks in the Khufu pyramid's upper passage are still *in situ*. Thus, the polar entrance passage cannot have been used for observation because it was blocked. It evidently served some magical purpose for the spirit of the pharaoh who, of course, would have found no difficulty in seeing or moving through the plug blocks. Whatever purpose the alignment of the pyramid sides and passages was meant to serve, no useful astronomical meaning can be discerned.

Among his many activities Herschel served for many years on the Standards Commission. There had been various attempts to introduce in Britain decimal and metric units of measurement and Herschel was very much against this. He and his friends succeeded in watering down the findings of a Parliamentary Committee in 1855 to a mere statement that decimal and metric standards would be more convenient. Finally, in 1869, he resigned in protest from the Standards Commission because it favoured a Bill for the introduction of the metric system. In the end he won and Britain had to wait for another century before decimal coinage, the centimetre and the centigrade gained entry. It was this long drawn-out battle of the standards which gave rise to the pyramid prophecies.

It will probably never be known how much, if at all, Herschel supported his pupil's ill-advised campaign of the inch against the centimetre. There can be no doubt that once he got it going, Piazzi Smyth's innate eccentricity, his Scottish puritanism and his wish to find a connection between Britain and the Bible, completely took over. Being aware of Herschel's opposition to metrication and of his work on the Khufu pyramid, Piazzi Smyth set out on a campaign in which scientific and theological arguments are inextricably mixed. One feels that he must have believed in his logic but one would be happier if his method had been less clever. The argument itself is deadly in its simplicity: the great pyramid was built in inches. The profound mathematical truths contained in it show that its construction was inspired directly by God. Hence the inch is a God-given measure and as such necessarily superior to the centimetre which was inspired 'by the wildest, most blood-thirsty and most atheistic revolution of a whole nation, that the world has ever seen'. It is difficult to argue with him.

Curiously enough, the argument was not even of Piazzi Smyth's making. He took it over from a Mr John Taylor who, in 1859, and in his seventy-ninth year, published a book entitled *The Great Pyramid, Why Was It Built and Who Built It?* Taylor was neither an Egyptologist nor an astronomer but a retired publisher. However, he seems to have been the first person who, using the angle of a casing stone given by Vyse and Perring, found that the relation of height to circumference was astonishingly near to $1/2\pi$. He rightly pointed out that the Egyptians of that age could not have known this irrational number and concluded that the builders must have had divine guidance, also employing British measures. The close connection of Britain with early Hebrew history was just then fashionable, since one Richard Brothers had claimed the British to be the descendants of the lost tribes of Israel. The fact that this 'Nephew of the Almighty' was arrested for prophesying the death of the king and confined to a lunatic asylum did not prevent the ranks of his adherents from swelling.

With the number π defining the *shape* of the pyramid, its *size* had to be found of equal import. Sure enough, it turned out that the unit of length used in the edifice, the 'pyramid inch', is the five-hundred-millionth part of the earth's polar axis. The five is significant because the pyramid has five faces. Most important of all, the pyramid inch is only by one part in a thousand longer than the British inch. This seemed a permissible error when considering that the lost tribes had to carry around the standard measure since the time of King Sargon of Babylon, and under trying conditions. The fact that the inch, British or pyramid, was represented by the earth's axis, a straight line, was one in the eye for the French metre based on the curved earth's quadrant. It seems to have pleased Herschel, although we do not know how much he liked to identify his views with those of Mr Taylor. As far as Piazzi Smyth is concerned, it now becomes the 'Taylor–Herschel pyramid analogy'.

John Taylor's pyramid theory, based as it was on Brothers' British Israelite hypothesis, would clearly have gone the way of so many crank ideas but for Sir John Herschel's antagonism to metrication and Piazzi Smyth's ardent support. The standing of the Astronomer Royal for Scotland, backed by the name of the eminent Herschel, lifted the whole thing on to the level of potential scientific respectability. All that now remained was to find the pyramid inch *in situ*, and this is where the real trouble started.

In the winter 1864/65 Piazzi Smyth and his wife went to Egypt in search of the inch. In the antechamber of the Khufu pyramid he found, on a vertical granite slab, a semi–circular mason's boss which had clearly been left for lifting the slab into position. It was extremely rough but Piazzi Smyth decided that it was one pyramid inch high and five pyramid inches wide. He was honest enough to give a picture of it in his book which certainly does not give the impression of being the eternal standard handed down by God. Credibility was not improved when years later one of his adherents was found filing the boss down to the theoretical value. Piazzi Smyth then measured the circumference of the building and divided it by 365.242 – the number of days in a year – and then by 100 which again gave him the pyramid inch.

From now on there was no end to measurement and computation through which the great pyramid reveals the density of our planet, the number of men living on earth (in 1870) and many other wondrous data. We cannot enumerate and explain them all since this required, as Piazzi Smyth has shown, 616 pages. As his account proceeds, mathematics merges more and more with religious significance, leading to prophecies derived from the length of the passages measured in pyramid inches. Smyth clearly expected something really drastic to happen in 1881. Whatever it was, he survived it well, dying of natural causes in 1900 at the age of 81. However, unlike his trigger-happy modern disciples, quoted above, Piazzi Smyth's figures do not seem to foretell an immediate doom. Having taken the liberty of using the Astronomer Royal's own data for my computations, I give myself at least another five hundred years to prepare for it.

Nothing, perhaps, will convince us better of the prophet's sincerity than the crusading spirit expressed in his writing. He realized, of course, that one extremely weak point of his theory was the existence of other pyramids, none of them containing any divine revelations. He got around this difficulty by declaring the Khufu pyramid the most ancient and the others as 'imitation pyramids'. Naturally, Egyptologists did not agree with this and, incidentally, not with his other theories either. However, Smyth found ample grounds for dismissing them wholesale on the third page of his introduction as 'too earnest cultivators of the mystical mythology of the land of Ham, and never so happy as when erecting in the museums of this Christian country and at the public expense, some of the grossly animal-headed idol gods'. The companion of the pyramids, the great Sphinx, he rejects because 'that monster, an idol in itself, with symptoms typifying the lowest mental organization, positively reeks with anti-Great Pyramid idolatry throughout its substance'.

Even worse than the Egyptologists were the tourists profaning the King's chamber by 'lurid lighted revelry', smoking and surrounded by 'demon-like Arabs of every degree – black, brown and grey – howling all of them for baksheesh'. He calls for 'a strict prohibition issued in Scottish Covenanter phrase against promiscuous dancing by all travellers, whether educated or ignorant; and also against that vice of the savage, learned so readily by civilised Anglo-Saxon men from the mongrel American Indian, viz., smoking burning tobacco over Cheops' totally mistaken gravestone'. All this fits in with Eyth's pen-portrait of Piazzi Smyth, thinly disguised in his novel as the Rev. Joseph Thinker. There is an almost protective warmth in the German engineer's description of the tall, thin eccentric in his black suit. Piazzi Smyth was infuriated that tourists gave baksheesh to their Arab guides in order to deface the sacred monument through having their initials carved on the stones at the top. It amused Eyth, because Smyth did not realize that the pyramid itself remained unharmed. In order to make their work easier and to find enough space for new initials, the fellahin periodically covered the surface of the stones with soft fresh lime.

The scientific refutation of Piazzi Smyth's theory came from an unexpected quarter and was almost as ludicrous in its final consequence as the prophecies themselves. One of Smyth's staunchest supporters was a chemical engineer with some experience in railway construction. He maintained that the theory should be supported by still more accurate geometric measurements at Giza. He set to work on devising methods and suitable instruments, which proved a long drawn-out task. As the engineer's son grew up, he took part in his father's preparations, and they decided that they would both go to Egypt. Finally, the work had become so protracted that the engineer himself became too old for the undertaking and in 1880 the son went out by himself. He carried out a brilliant and extremely accurate triangulation of the Giza site which showed, beyond a shadow of doubt, that Piazzi Smyth's measurements had been wrong and that there was nothing to support his theories. Incidentally, the young man's name was Matthew Flinders Petrie and he became the greatest Egyptologist of his time.

As was to be expected, Piazzi Smyth was not seriously worried by Petrie's results. He simply found necessary corrections which not only put things right, but brought still more revelations. An ever-increasing number of followers gladdened his heart and vindicated his grand crusade for the inch. After his death the pyramid prophecies went on unabated and are still to be found today, more than a century after the Taylor-Herschel pyramid analogy.

Unlike the Babylonians, the ancient Egyptians were poor mathematicians and astronomers. Their methods of computation were cumbersome and tedious. Altogether they were always guided by the practical needs and nowhere developed theory. Astronomy consists of the observation of the heavenly bodies whose regular motion provides a valuable measure of time. These allow a reckoning not only of the hours of the day and night but also of the seasons of the year. The motion of the stars tells the farmer when to sow and to reap and, in Egypt, when to expect the annual rising of the Nile. Egyptian astronomy was certainly good enough to permit the establishment of an accurate calendar that took account of an extra day every four years.

At all times the motion of the heavenly bodies has also been used to forecast the future of man; it is well to remember that when Kepler established his planetary laws, which led to Newton's theory of universal gravitation, he was actually paid for casting horoscopes for the King of Bohemia. For the Chaldeans astrology played a most important part in their life. The practical Egyptians, however, seem to have paid far more attention to the correct prediction of the inundations than to the less well-established influence of the stars on their personal fortunes. The astronomical influence on pyramid design is confined to accurate alignment along the cardinal directions and to the polar passages. These two features, evidently serving magical purposes, are not independent of each other. The symmetry of the pyramid structure, with a corridor pointing to the pole star, also required that its sides should be directed to true north. The simple way in which this had been achieved has been discussed in detail by Edwards in his well-known book on the Egyptian pyramids. In fact, it was only with the introduction of polar passages that pyramids became accurately aligned.

The Mexican pyramids, too, show features of astronomical significance. The Pyramid of the Sun at Teotihuacan, whose position determines the layout of the Street of the Dead and the whole sacred complex, faces 17° north of true west. This means that, on the day when the sun passes through the zenith, it will set exactly in the main axis of the pyramid. Thus, the building incorporates in its design the record of its own geographic position. In view of the highly developed Central American calendar it seems safe to assume that these early pyramids in the Valley of Mexico were observatories which served in the determination of the relevant data. In this function they certainly differed from the Egyptian pyramids, and this makes it less likely that the two sets of monuments had a common origin.

Whether or not the civilization of the Americas had its roots in the Old World has been a much debated question for centuries and the pyramids have played a large part in this controversy. The Conquistadors themselves often believed that the strange but highly developed culture which they encountered had come, in some mysterious way, from European antiquity. Whereas the Portuguese seafarers of the early sixteenth century were children of the Renaissance, the Spaniards had remained intellectually in the Christian world of the Middle Ages. The Bible was their guide in every aspect of life, and they tried to derive Amerindian civilization from the *Book of Genesis*. The early Spanish chroniclers, Bernardino de Sahagun and Juan de Torquemada, go to some length in establishing a biblical or, at least, a European origin which they tried to prove by customs, symbols and similarity in certain words. Since their time, innumerable explanations of this kind have been proposed, drawing attention to the sign of the cross, the star of David and the similarity between the name Mexico and the word Messiah.

This last contention came from the champion of the Hebrew heritage of Mexico, Lord Kingsborough. He was a dedicated eccentric like Piazzi Smyth who, however, unlike the Astronomer Royal for Scotland, came to a sad end. Edward King was the eldest son of the third Earl of Kingston. When in 1799 his father succeeded to the title, Edward King was known, by courtesy, as Viscount Kingsborough. In 1814 he went up to Oxford to study classics but did not graduate. Instead, he became engrossed in the Mexican codices of the Bodleian Library. He decided that the material contained in them should be made known to the world of learning and commissioned Augustin Agio to copy them for publication. He embodied in his work Sahagun's unpublished manuscript and those of other early authors on Mexico. Perhaps Kingsborough's resolve was due to a remark made many years earlier by Alexander von Humboldt: 'It were to be wished that some government would publish, at its own expense, the remains of the American civilization'.

The last of Kingsborough's nine volumes, in imperial folio, is devoted to his compendious notes, comparing the Mexican finds with Hebrew customs, language and quotations from Scripture. This was in 1830, the heyday of Brothers' theory of the lost tribes of Israel. In his great work on the Conquest of Mexico William H. Prescott, who was Kingsborough's contemporary, notes, however, that 'His theory, whatever its merits, will scarcely become popular'. On the other hand he admits 'that by this munificent undertaking which no government, probably, would have and few individuals could have executed, he has entitled himself to the lasting gratitude of every friend of science.' After praising the 'mechanical execution of the book', Prescott remarks: 'Yet the purchaser would have been saved some superfluous expense, and the reader much inconvenience, if the letter-press had been in volumes of an ordinary size'. I fully sympathized with Prescott when the nine volumes, getting on for two hundredweight, were wheeled in laboriously for my use.

This extravagance in publication proved Kingsborough's undoing. The production of the book had cost Kingsborough in 1831 no less than £32,000, a bill which he could not pay. A paper manufacturer brought a suit against him, Kingsborough was arrested and died in 1837 in the Sheriff's prison at Dublin, forty-two years old.

In addition to those who claim a biblical descent for Amerindian civilization a host of theories has been proposed according to which voyagers from across the Atlantic had come, at one time or another, to America to leave their mark on the cultural pattern of the New World. Most of these fall back on the legend of the white god Quetzalcoatl who had prophesied at his disappearance from the world of men that he would return from the east. This is not the place to discuss the credibility of these suggestions, neither can we offer an opinion on whether the legend of the plumed serpent refers to the Vikings or to Egyptians in reed boats. If the latter were the case it must seem curious that the Egyptians should have instructed the Indians in the building of large pyramids, an occupation which they themselves had given up 2000 years earlier.

Select Bibliography

Many of the works cited, particularly Edwards and Vaillant, contain extensive bibliographies. In the present select bibliography reference to articles and journals have only been made where these are of special importance to the subject of this book.

A. Egyptian Pyramids

ALDRED, C. *Egypt to the End of the Old Kingdom.* London, 1965.

ALVAREZ, L. W. *et al.* Search for Hidden Chambers in the Pyramids. *Science* 167 (1970), 832–39.

BADAWY, A. *A History of Egyptian Architecture.* Cairo, 1954.

BAEDEKER, K. *Ägypten.* Berlin, 1876. G. Ebers, 459.

BELZONI, G. *Narrative of Operations . . .* London, 1820.

BORCHARDT, L. *Das Grabdenkmal des Königs Ne-user-Re.* Leipzig, 1907.

— *Das Grabdenkmal des Königs Nefer-ir-ka-Re.* Leipzig, 1909.

— *Das Grabdenkmal des Königs Sahure.* 2 vols. Leipzig, 1910–13.

— *Einiges zur dritten Bauperiode der grossen Pyramide bei Gise.* Berlin, 1922.

— *Die Entstehung der Pyramide an der Baugeschichte der Pyramide bei Mejdum nachgewiesen.* Berlin, 1928.

BREASTED, J. H. *History of Egypt.* Chicago, 1919.

BROWNE, W. G. *Travels in Africa, Egypt and Syria.* London, 1793.

ČERNÝ, J. *Ancient Egyptian Religion.* London, 1952.

CLARKE, S. and ENGELBACH, R. *Ancient Egyptian Masonry.* Oxford, 1930.

DENON, V. *Voyages dans la Basse et la Haute Egypte.* Paris, 1803.

DUNHAM, D. *The Royal Cemeteries of Kush.* 4 vols. Boston, Mass., 1950 57.

— Building an Egyptian Pyramid, *Archaeology.* 9 (1956), 159–65.

EDWARDS, I. E. S. *The Pyramids of Egypt.* Rev. ed. Harmondsworth, 1961; and London, 1972.

EMERY, W. B. *The Tomb of Hor-Aha.* Cairo, 1939.

— *Great Tombs of the First Dynasty.* 3 vols. Cairo and London, 1949–58.

— *Archaic Egypt.* Harmondsworth, 1961, repr. 1972.

ERMAN, A. *The Literature of the Ancient Egyptians.* London, 1927.

FAKHRY, A. *The Bent Pyramid.* Cairo, 1959.

— *The Pyramids.* Chicago, 1969.

FIRTH, C. M., QUIBELL, J. E. and LAUER, J.-P. *The Step Pyramid.* 2 vols. Cairo, 1935–36.

FRANKFORT, H. *Kingship and the Gods.* Chicago, 1948.

GARDINER, A. *Egypt of the Pharaohs.* Oxford, 1966, repr. 1972.

GONEIM, M. Z. *The Buried Pyramid.* London, 1956.

— *Horus Sekhemkhet.* Cairo, 1957.

GRINSELL, L. *Egyptian Pyramids.* Gloucester, 1947.

HAYES, W. C. *The Scepter of Egypt.* 2 vols. New York and Cambridge, Mass., 1953–59.

HELCK, W. *Untersuchungen zu den Beamtentiteln des ägyptischen alten Reiches.* Glückstadt, 1954.

HÖLSCHER, U. *Das Grabdenkmal des Königs Chephren.* Leipzig, 1912.

HURRY, J. B. *Imhotep.* Oxford, 1926.

JÉQUIER, G. *Le Mastabat Faraoun.* Cairo, 1928.

JUNKER, H. *Giza, Grabungen auf dem Friedhof des Alten Reiches bei den Pyramiden von Giza.* 12 vols. Vienna, 1929–55.

— *Pyramidenzeit.* Zurich, 1949.

KEES, H. *Totenglauben und Jenseits-Vorstellungen der alten Ägypter.* Berlin, 1956.

KOZINSKI, W. *The Investment Process Organization of the Cheops Pyramid.* Warsaw, 1969.

LAUER, J.-P. *La Pyramide à degrés.* 3 vols. Cairo, 1936–39.

— *Le Problème des Pyramides d'Egypte.* Paris, 1948.

— *Observations sur les Pyramides.* Cairo, 1955.

— *Histoire Monumentale des Pyramides d'Egypte.* Cairo, 1962.

LUCAS, A. *Ancient Egyptian Materials and Industries.* 3rd ed. London, 1948; 4th ed. London, 1962.

LEPSIUS, R. *Über den Bau der Pyramiden.* Cairo, 1843.

— *Denkmäler aus Ägypten.* Berlin, 1849.

MARAGIOGLIO, V. and RINALDI, R. *L'Architettura delle Piramidi Menfite.* Vol. 3. Berlin, 1964.

MASPERO, G. Opening of the Meidum Pyramid. *Archéologie,* 1887, 117.

MENDELSSOHN, K. Science at the Pyramids. *Science Journal* 4 (1968), 48.

— A Scientist looks at the Pyramids, *American Scientist* 59 (1971), 210.

— A Building Disaster at the Meidum Pyramid. *Journal of Egyptian Archaeology* 59 (1973).

MURRAY, M. A. *Index of Names and Titles of the Old Kingdom.* London, 1908.

NORDEN, F. L. *Travels in Egypt and Nubia.* 2 vols. London, 1757.

PETRIE, W. M. F. *The Pyramids and Temples of Gizeh.* London, 1883.

— *Medum.* London, 1892.

— MACKAY, E. and WAINWRIGHT, G. A. *Meydum and Memphis* III. London, 1910.

— WAINWRIGHT, G. A. and MACKAY, E. *The Labyrinth, Gerzeh and Mazguneh.* London, 1912.

— *Egyptian Architecture.* London, 1938.

POCOCKE, R. *A Description of the East.* London, 1743.

REISNER, G. A. *Mycerinus.* Cambridge, Mass., 1931.

— *The Development of the Egyptian Tomb down to the Accession of Cheops.* Cambridge, Mass., 1935.

— *A History of the Giza Necropolis* I. Cambridge, Mass., 1942.

— and SMITH, W. S. *A History of the Giza Necropolis* II. Cambridge, Mass., 1955.

RICKE, H. *Bemerkungen zur ägyptischen Bauforschung des Alten Reiches.* 2 vols., Zurich and Cairo, 1944–50.

ROBERT, A. *Annales du Service des Antiquités de l'Egypte*, 3 (1899), 77.

ROWE, A. Excavations of the Eckley B. Cox Jr. Expedition at Meydum, Egypt, 1929–30. *Museum Journal*, Pennsylvania, March, 1931.

SETHE, K. *Urgeschichte und älteste Religion der Ägypter*, Leipzig, 1930.

SMITH, W. S. *The Art and Architecture of Ancient Egypt*. Harmondsworth, 1958.

SMYTH, C. P. *Our Inheritance in the Great Pyramid*. London, 1877.

VANDIER, J. *Manuel d'archéologie égyptienne*. Vols. 1, 2. Paris, 1952–55.

VYSE, H. and PERRING, J. S. *Operations carried out at the Pyramids of Gizeh*. 3 vols. London, 1840–42.

B. Mexican Pyramids

DIAZ DEL CASTILLO, BERNAL. *True History of the Conquest of New Spain* (trans. A. P. Maudslay). 5 vols. London, 1908–16.

DISSELHOFF, H. D. and LINNÉ, S. *Ancient America*. Baden, 1961.

GAMIO, M. *La población del valle de Teotihuacán*. 3 vols. Mexico, 1922.

HAGEN, V. W. VON. *The Ancient Sun Kingdoms of the Americas*. London and New York, 1961.

HEIZER, R. F. and BENNYHOFF, J. A. Archaeological Investigation of Cuicuilco. *Science* 127 (1958), 332–33.

KINGSBOROUGH, LORD EDWARD. *Antiquities of Mexico*. London, 1831–48.

KUBLER, G. *The Art and Architecture of Ancient America*. Harmondsworth, 1962.

LEHMANN, W. *Aus den Pyramidenstädten in Alt-Mexiko*. Berlin, 1933.

LINNÉ, S. *Archaeological Researches at Teotihuacan*. Stockholm, 1934.

— Radiocarbon Dates in Teotihuacan. *Ethnos* 21 (1956), 180–93.

MARQUINA, I. *et al. La pirámide de Tenayuca*. Mexico, 1935.

— *Arquitectura prehispanica*. Mexico, 1964.

MILLON, R. F. The Beginnings of Teotihuacan. *American Antiquity* 26 (1960), 1–10.

— Teotihuacan: Completion of Map of Giant Ancient City in the Valley of Mexico. *Science* 170 (1970), 1077–82.

— and DREWITT, B. Early Structures within the Pyramid of the Sun at Teotihuacan. *American Antiquity* 26 (1961).

NOGUERA, E. Antecedentes y Relaciones de la Cultura Teotihuacana. *El México Antiquo* 3 (1935), 1–81.

PETERSON, F. A. *Ancient Mexico*. London, 1959.

PRESCOTT, W. H. *History of the Conquest of Mexico*. 3 vols. New York, 1843.

SÉJOURNÉ, LAURETTE. *Burning Water*. London, 1956.

SELER, E. Die Teotihuacan-Kultur des Hochlands von Mexiko. *Gesammelte Abhandlungen zur Amerikanischen Sprach-und Alterthums Kunde* 5 (1915), 405–585.

SOUSTELLE, J. *La Vie quotidienne des Azteques*. Paris, 1955.

SPINDEN, H. J. *Ancient Civilizations of Mexico and Central America*. New York, 1946.

STIERLIN, M. *Ancient Mexican Architecture*. London, 1968.

VAILLANT, G. C. *The Aztecs of Mexico*. New York, 1944, 1962.

List of Illustrations

All illustrations not otherwise acknowledged are by the author or from his photo collection.

Colour Plates

Monochrome Plates

Figures

Index

Numbers in italics refer to illustrations